Raspberry Pi IoT In C Using Linux Drivers

Second Edition

Harry Fairhead

I/O Press
I Programmer Library

Harry Fairhead,

Raspberry Pi IoT In C Using Linux Drivers, 2nd Edition

ISBN: 9781871962857 (Paperback)

ISBN: 9781871962161 (Hardback)

First Printing, January 2024
Revision 0

Published by IO Press   www.iopress.info
in association with I Programmer   www.i-programmer.info
and with I o T Programmer   www.iot-programmer.com

For updates, errata, links to resources and the source code for the programs in this book visit its dedicated page on the IO Press website: www.iopress.info.

Preface

The Raspberry Pi and similar Linux-based, low-cost devices are an obvious choice for IoT and physical computing applications. The big problem is adding and using external devices such as sensors and motors. You can argue that writing code in an efficient language such as C to directly access the hardware is a simple and direct approach to the problem and I am a fan of this technique. This said, for many applications the devices in question are so standard, or so complicated, that the use of a Linux driver is an even bigger simplification.

An appropriate Linux driver can provide access to a possibly complex device without you having to learn exactly how that device works – but wait you have potentially just swapped one learning task for another. Linux device drivers are under-documented. When they are documented at all, it is often from the point of view of the kernel programmer and driver creator. There is typically little help for the non-Linux expert and it is often equally puzzling for the Linux expert. So, instead of having to deal with the complexities and ambiguities of a device, you have to deal with the complexities and ambiguities of a driver. This book is my attempt to put this right and allow Linux drivers to be an easy and powerful way to use devices.

Of course, no book can cover every driver in detail. What this book does is to explain the typical ways that you use a typical driver. It outlines the questions you need to ask to get things working and the ways you might find answers. Once you have seen a small selection of drivers of different types in action then encountering a new one is no longer such a strange and baffling experience.

This second edition was prompted by the advent of the Pi 5, welcomed as the fastest member of the Raspberry Pi family. What came as a shock as we started work with it is that, from the point of view of IoT it is incompatible with the rest of the family, This is due to the use of a custom chip, the RP1, which is a similar to the microcontroller at the heart of the Raspberry Pi Pico family. Luckily, although the Pi 5 cannot work with the standard IoT libraries it does behave in the same way under Linux drivers and so this new version does include the Pi 5.

Coverage also includes the Pi Zero 2W which has a quad-core chip making it more capable than both the original Pi Zero and the WiFi enabled Pi ZeroW.

All of the programs in this book are in C and you might ask why if we are programming in C don't we adopt a lower-level approach? The answer is that, if you can make them work, Linux drivers offer a potentially machine-independent way to interface to devices that you can implement quickly. Drivers are also not subject to the limitations of user space programs and so often do more and do it more reliably. If you do want to work at a lower level you probably need *Raspberry Pi IoT in C, 3rd Edition,* ISBN:9781871962840. You might even decide that it is worth the time to create a driver. This book doesn't tell you how to create drivers, it is dedicated to how you consume them, but many of the ideas in user space translate to kernel side code.

This book isn't an introduction to the Raspberry Pi or to Linux and it is assumed that either you are already familiar with them or can get up to speed with the many existing introductory resources. This edition has been updated to the latest versions of Pi OS, Bookworm for the Pi 4 and 5 and Bullseye for the others.

After a quick tour of the Raspberry Pi ecosystem, we introduce Visual Studio Code and how it can be used to develop remotely. The first IoT program anyone writes is "blinky" to flash an LED and this book is no exception, but it might not be quite what you expect. Instead of using a GPIO (General Purpose Input Output) line we use the Linux LED driver to flash an LED on the board – no hardware and no fuss. The GPIO isn't left out, however, as the next three chapters focus on its use via the new GPIO character driver, which replaces the old and very common sysfs GPIO driver. This is the way to do modern GPIO.

A key component in any look at Linux and its relationship to hardware is the relatively new Device Tree, DT. Most accounts of the device tree are aimed at device driver writers. My account is aimed at device driver users and to this end we look at the DHT22 temperature and humidity driver. After a brief detour into some basic electronics, we look at Pulse Width Modulation which is supported via a driver rather than needing to be implemented using the GPIO bus. From here we tackle the two standard buses, I2C and SPI, in a set of chapters that take us through the basics and then the two attempts to impose a higher organization, the hardware monitoring system, hwmon, and Industrial I/O, IIO. The penultimate chapter is a look at the third standard bus, although generally not supported in hardware, the 1-Wire bus.

Up to this point we have been mainly using device overlays provided for us, but the final chapter takes things to the next level, showing you how to create your own custom overlays by writing fragments of the device tree. Most of the documentation covers this from the point of view of the Linux driver writer, but here you will find an introduction to writing short custom overlays for drivers that already exist. It's not everything you need to know about the device tree, but it is usually enough.

Thanks as ever to my painstaking editors, Kay Ewbank and Sue Gee, for dealing with the many errors of my initial draft, hopefully few remain.

Harry Fairhead
January 2024

Table of Contents

Chapter 4
The GPIO Character Driver   **49**

Chapter 5
GPIO Using I/O Control   **69**

Chapter 6
GPIO Events   **79**

Chapter 1

Choosing A Pi For IoT

The Raspberry Pi has had a dramatic impact on the world of computing, and in particular the IoT - Internet of Things which often requires multiple devices. The term IoT has become very popular and now tends to be used in place of terms such as embedded processing, and physical computing. The ideas, however, are related and in the rest of this book the term IoT will be used to mean a system being used to interface with the real world, usually via custom electronics, even if the Internet isn't explicitly involved.

As this book is about using the Pi to connect to the outside world, it is the Pi as a microcontroller or embedded IoT device that interests us the most.

The Raspberry Pi Or A Microcontroller?

Compared to the Pi, the Arduino and any similar microcontroller is a very low-powered computer. The basic Arduino isn't capable of running Linux, which is a full operating system. It simply runs the one program you have written for it. However, the Arduino and similar devices have a big advantage – they have dedicated, usually analog, I/O lines. The Pi doesn't have the same variety of I/O lines, but it has enough for many jobs and it can be easily expanded with the use of standard expansion boards called HATs (Hardware Attached on Top) because of the way they plug in. Some HATs are so commonly used that they are considered more or less standard and have their own Linux drivers.

To make the difference plain, you can use a Pi for almost any job that a desktop computer can do, including any server role. An Arduino, on the other hand, isn't up to this sort of work. Sometimes the fact that the Pi is a full computer makes it even more suitable for low-level jobs. For example, you want a new door bell? Why not use a Pi and have it say hello using a voice synthesizer.

In short, the Pi gives you more computing power for less money.

Everything isn't perfect with the Pi and the IoT. In particular, the use of Linux means that you can no longer pretend your program is the only program running. Linux is a multitasking operating system and it can suspend any program at any time to give another program a chance to run. If you are familiar with microcontroller programming then it will come as something of a shock that you do not have complete control of the machine. What is more, Linux isn't the easiest operating system to get to grips with if you are a beginner.

All of these problems and more can be overcome with a little work and it is worthwhile. The Pi is a fast and capable IoT computer and would still be a good choice even if it cost a lot more. We are entering a new era of embedded computing when the device that runs your washing machine is as powerful as your desktop computer.

Which Raspberry Pi?

The Raspberry Pi family has grown over the years and it can be difficult to keep track of the differences between the models. As far as the IoT goes, while you can use an early Pi 1 or Pi 2 model A or B to do any of the tasks described in this book, it is much better not to. The modern range of devices is so much better suited to the task because they are more powerful and if you are starting a new project it is better to use one of the current models. This said, the very latest Pi 5 is more expensive than the Pi 4 which is in turn more expensive than the Pi 3 and they are all currently available. Cost rather than computing power can be an issue in an IoT project and so you cannot completely write off earlier models. The later models are also available with different amounts of memory and this is not something you can upgrade without a soldering iron and plenty of skill – and not recommended even then.

All this makes choosing a Pi difficult. My best advice is to use the fastest and most powerful Pi you can for development and when you have something working see what computing power is actually needed before deploying the finished program.

Pi Zero Range

The smallest in the Raspberry Pi family, and the cheapest at $10, is the Pi Zero which is about half as fast as a Pi 3, ten times slower than the Pi 4 and twenty times slower than the Pi 5. Even though it isn't as powerful, it is often sufficient for IoT tasks and wins on price and power use. The Pi Zero only has a single USB connector and no networking. The Pi Zero W, more expensive at $15, has onboard WiFi and if you want a connected device it is the obvious choice.

Both the Pi Zero and the Pi Zero W have a single-core CPU, which means your program will be interrupted by the operating system to keep the device working. In many applications this doesn't matter, but if it does then the latest in the family, the Pi Zero 2W has a quad-core CPU, costs the same as the Pi Zero W and otherwise has the same specification. It is based on the same CPU as the Pi 3 and has a very similar overall architecture.

Pi Zero – small and low cost   Pi Zero W – with WiFi   Pi Zero 2W - four cores

Pi Zero	Pi Zero W	Pi Zero 2W
No WiFi	802.11 b/g/n wireless LAN	802.11 b/g/n wireless LAN
No Bluetooth	Bluetooth 4.1	Bluetooth 4.2
No Bluetooth	Bluetooth Low Energy (BLE)	Bluetooth Low Energy (BLE)
1GHz, single-core CPU	1GHz, single-core CPU	1GHz, quad-core CPU
512MB RAM	512MB RAM	512MB RAM
No Ethernet	No Ethernet	No Ethernet
Micro USB	Micro USB	Micro USB

Going Beyond The Pi Zeros

The original Raspberry Pis were available as an A or a B sub-type. The As lacked multiple USB connectors and a wired network connection and so were slightly cheaper. Since the Pi 4 there has only been the B version.

Another confusing factor is that when the Pi 3 was upgraded to have a quad-core processor, making it slightly faster, and doubling its memory, the two models were the Pi 3A+ and Pi 3B+.

These are the only members of the Pi 3 range still readily available and in terms of price only the A+, costing $25, has any advantage as the 3B+ at $35 costs the same as a Pi 4 B with the same amount (1GB) of memory.

Pi 3A+
802.11 b/g/n/ac wireless LAN 2.4 GHz and 5.0 GHz
Bluetooth 4.2
Bluetooth Low Energy (BLE)
1.4GHz, quad-core CPU 64-bit CPU
512MB RAM
One USB 2 port
No Ethernet

The Pi 3A

Until the arrival of the Pi 5, the Pi 4 was the fastest Pi available. The cheapest version with 1GB of RAM is the same price as a 3B+ ($35). At the top end of the range the 8GB version costs $75, which is starting to be expensive for IoT applications – even so you get a lot of computing power for the money. It also supports dual HDMI monitors, making it ideal for development purposes. You can also buy a P400 ($70) which is a Pi 4 with 4GB of RAM built into a keyboard, ready to use as a desktop computer.

Pi 4
802.11 b/g/n/ac wireless LAN 2.4 GHz and 5.0 GHz
Bluetooth 4.2
Bluetooth Low Energy (BLE)
1.8 GHz, quad-core 64-bit CPU
1, 2, 4 or 8 GB RAM
USB 2 and 3
Gigabit Ethernet

The Pi 4

The Pi 5 is currently the top of the range. Its specifications don't really tell the whole story. It has improved I/O connectivity, which speeds up the USB and Ethernet. It is roughly twice as fast as the Pi 4 and costs $60 with 4GB of RAM and $80 for 8GB. Although it represents excellent value, $60 per unit is starting to sound expensive for IoT deployments. It is still worth considering using one for software development, even if the application eventually ends up running on a less powerful device.

Pi 5
802.11 b/g/n/ac wireless LAN 2.4GHz and 5Ghz.
Bluetooth 5
Bluetooth Low Energy (BLE)
2.4GHz, quad-core CPU
4 or 8GB RAM
Gigabit Ethernet
USB 3

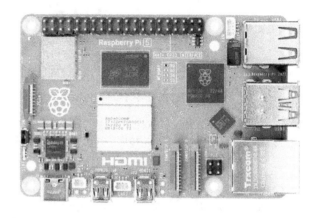

The Pi 5

The use of a custom interface chip, the RP1, makes the Pi 5 incompatible with all previous Pis from the point of view of peripherals including the GPIO lines. The memory map and the registers that control the standard peripherals are different. In fact, the Pi 5 uses a modified Pico to provide its peripherals and as such is quite different from all the other Pis in the family. These differences are largely covered up by the supplied Linux drivers, which work in the same way across devices.

At the time of writing there is no indication of when a P500 self-contained computer version is likely to launch.

Compute Module 4

The Compute Module 4, CM4, is a cut down Pi 4. All of the external connectors have been removed and signals are only available on a high density connector on the bottom of the board. This is a full Pi 4 and the software you write for a main Pi model needs little, if any, change to run on it, but you will need to design a PCB motherboard for it to use to connect to the outside world. At the moment there is no CM5, but one is in the works and should be available sometime in 2024.

The Compute Module is only necessary if you are planning to develop hardware to complement the Pi as well as custom software.

The CM4

The Raspberry Pi Pico

Despite its name, the Pico isn't in the same family as either the Pi Zeros or the Pi 3/4/5s. It is a small device about the same size as the Pi Zero, but it is very different in that it uses a custom, two-core, CPU and doesn't run Linux. If you plan to create an IoT program that doesn't need Linux, then you are probably much better off moving to the Pico. It is low-cost and powerful and the fact that it doesn't host an operating system often makes developing code easier than trying to fit in with the way an operating system works. On the other hand, if you want local user interaction by way of a display, keyboard, touch screen, mouse, etc, then the Pico might not be the right choice.

In short, the Pico is a microcontroller capable of sensing and control tasks and communicating via the network, whereas those in the Pi family are full computers running Linux capable of sensing and control tasks. The book to get you started with the Pico is *Programming The Raspberry Pi Pico/W in C*, 2nd Ed, ISBN:9781871962796 and if you want to go further into the Pico's Wifi capabilities, see *Master the Raspberry Pi Pico in C: WiFi with lwIP & mbedtls*, ISBN:9781871962819.

The Pico W

Pi OS

One additional complication is the choice of operating system for the Pi. The latest Pi OS is based on Debian Bookworm and is available in 32- and 64-bit versions for the Pi 4 and 5. For all the other Pis currently the only OS available is the "legacy" Debian Bullseye. It is possible that Bookworm will become available on these "smaller" Pis in the future, but the main differences between the two aren't important for programmers intending to use Linux drivers. There are some minor irritations in that some drivers have been renamed, but this is relatively easy to cope with. A bigger difference affects any program planning to make use of graphics. Bookworm has taken the big step of using Wayland in place of the X graphics system that Bullseye uses. In most cases you can isolate your programs from this change by using a suitable graphics library, but if you plan to interact at a low level with graphics you need to find out more about Wayland.

Any differences between Bookworm and Bullseye will be pointed out where relevant.

What To Expect

There are no complete projects in this book – although some examples come very close and it is clear that some of them could be used together to create finished projects. The focus here is on learning how things work so that you can move on and do things that are non-standard. What matters is that you can reason about what the processor is doing and how it interacts with the real world in real time. This is the key difference between desktop and embedded programming: timing matters in embedded programming, but not so much in desktop programming.

This is a book about understanding the general principle and making things work. If you read to the end of this book you will have a good understanding of what is going on when you make use of a range of different types of interfacing that typically go together to make a complete system.

What Do You Need?

To follow the examples in this book you will need either a Pi Zero/W/2W or a Pi 3/4/5. You can use an earlier Pi as long as you make allowances for the difference in pin assignments and other minor hardware changes.

It is also worth knowing that while the Pi 4 and Pi 5 are capable of running a development environment and running IoT programs, the Pi Zero makes things hard work. If you want the simplicity of local development, discussed in Chapter 2, use a Pi 4 or 5.

Whichever model of Pi you use, you need it set up with Pi OS, the new name for Raspbian, and you need to know how to connect to it and use it via a serial console. You also need to be comfortable with Linux in the sense that while you might not know how to do something, you know how to look it up and follow the instructions. It is also assumed that you are able to program in C. There isn't enough space to teach the elements of the C programming language in this book. If you need to learn C first or brush up on some of the finer points of C and Linux then see *Fundamental C*, ISBN: 9781871962604 and *Applying C for the IoT with Linux*, ISBN: 9781871962611.

As to additional hardware over and above the Pi you will need a solderless prototype board and some hookup wires – known as Dupoint wires. You will also need some LEDs, a selection of resistors, some 2N2222 or other general purpose transistors and any of the sensors used in later chapters. It is probably better to buy what you need as you choose to implement one of the projects, but an alternative is to buy one of the many "getting started" kits for the Raspberry Pi. You will probably still need to buy some extra components, however.

A solderless prototype board and some Dupoint wires

You don't need to know how to solder, but you will need to be able to hook up a circuit on a prototyping board. A multimeter (less than $10) is useful, but if you are serious about building IoT devices investing in a logic analyzer (less than $50) will repay itself in no time at all. You can get small analyzers that plug in via a USB port and use an application to show you what is happening. It is only with a multichannel logic analyzer can you have any hope of understanding what is happening. Without one and the slight skill involved in using it, you are essentially flying blind and left to just guess what might be wrong.

A Low Cost Logic Analyzer

Finally, if you are even more serious, then a low-cost pocket oscilloscope is also worth investing in to check out the analog nature of the supposedly digital signals that microcontrollers put out. However, if you have to choose between these two instruments the logic analyzer should be your first acquisition.

It is worth noting that the Pi can generate signals that are too fast to be reliably detected by low-cost oscilloscopes and logic analyzers which work at between 1MHz and 25MHz. This can mean that working with pulses much faster than 1 microsecond can be difficult as you cannot rely on your instruments.

Safety In Numbers

A final point to make about the Raspberry Pi and its ecosystem regards the size of its user base. According to the Raspberry Pi Foundation, by August 2023 the Pi had sold more than 50 million units and while these aren't all exactly the same device they are all compatible enough to ensure that your programs have a good chance of running on any of them.

The large numbers of Pis in the world means that you have a good chance of finding the answer to any problem by a simple internet search, although it has to be said that the quality of answers available vary from misleading to excellent. Always make sure you evaluate what you are being advised in the light of what you know. You also need to keep in mind that the advice is also usually offered from a reasonably biased point of view. The C programmer will give you an answer that suits a system that already uses C, and electronics beginners will offer you solutions that are based on "off the shelf" modules when a simple cheap solution is available based on a few cheap components. Even when the advice you get is 100% correct, it still isn't necessarily the right advice for you.

The large numbers of Raspberry Pis in circulation also means that it is unlikely that the device will become obsolete. This isn't something you can assume about other less popular single-board computers. It is reasonable to suppose that any programs you write today will work into the foreseeable future on a device that might not look like today's Raspberry Pi's but will be backward compatible.

In short, the Raspberry Pi provides a secure and non-threatening environment for your development work.

An Information Gap

One of the problems in using Linux device drivers is finding information about them. A search of the web reveals lots of sources, but many are old and there is a great deal of duplication. Here are useful links on specific topics:

Configuration:

https://www.raspberrypi.org/documentation/configuration/config-txt/README.md

Overlay Source:

https://github.com/raspberrypi/firmware/tree/master/boot

Overlay Documentation:

https://github.com/raspberrypi/firmware/blob/master/boot/overlays/README

GitHub Pi OS Repository:

https://github.com/raspberrypi/linux

Hardware details:

https://www.raspberrypi.org/documentation/hardware/raspberrypi/datasheets.md

You can find these links on this book's webpage at www.iopress.info.

Summary

- The cost of computing hardware has fallen to the point where many applications that would have used low-cost and less-powerful microcontrollers can now make use of Raspberry Pi hardware, which is powerful enough to run a full version of Linux.

- The smallest member of the Pi family is the Pi Zero. It has a single-core processor with a minimal number of connectors. The Pi Zero W has built-in WiFi which makes it easy to use in situations where you want connectivity. As well as WiFi, the Pi Zero 2W has four cores.

- The Pi 5 is currently the most powerful of the Pi models. Like the Pi 4, it is a quad-core device with up to 8Gb of RAM, but it is at least twice the speed of the Pi 4.

- As neither the Pi 5 or 4 isn't currently available as a "cut down" model A, the Pi 3A+ is still a viable choice for IoT applications.

- The Compute Module 4 (CM4) is a Pi 4 packaged as a credit card sized industrial device. It needs a custom I/O board or a development board to make use of it. The corresponding CM 5 should be available sometime in 2024

- The Pi 400 is a faster Pi 4 with 4GB of RAM packaged into a keyboard. You can use it as an IoT development system. Currently there is no indication if and when a Pi 500 will be available.

- To work with electronics you will need a solderless prototyping board, some hookup wires and some components. It's also good to have a multimeter and preferably a logic analyzer. After these basic instruments, you can add what you can afford.

- With more than 50 million devices sold and a very large community of users, the Raspberry Pi is a very stable platform and one you can use with reasonable assurance that it will be available in the future.

- Finding accurate and up-to-date information about the availability of Linux drivers on the Internet is difficult. Useful links are updated on the book's page on www.iopress.info.

Chapter 2
C and Visual Studio Code

C is a good language to use for low-level apps. It is the language that Linux is written in, as are all of the Linux drivers that we are going to use in the rest of the book. It is fast and efficient and you can tailor your code to make the best of the hardware you have. You can describe C as a machine-independent assembly language and hence when you learn it you get deeper into the system than with other languages and discover what is really going on. This makes it a good way to improve your understanding of computers and computing in general. If you need to learn C as it is used in IoT programming then see *Fundamental C: Getting Closer To The Machine,* ISBN: 9781871962604.

Sometimes you don't need speed, even in an IoT application. For example, if you just want to flash a few LEDs or read a temperature sensor in a human timescale, then you can program in almost any language. Even so, it is good to have plenty of headroom when it comes to speed and memory demands and C excels in these respects. Only when it comes to complex high-level data processing and implementing a sophisticated UI do other languages offer a more compact solution than C. In such cases, a mixed language approach often works. However, for the remainder of this book programming in C is our focus.

Getting Started In C

You can program in C in many different ways. All of the software you need to run a C program is already installed on a standard Pi running Pi OS, formerly known as Raspbian. You can use an editor on the Pi to create your program and then compile and run it using the command line. However, there are easy-to-use IDEs that make programming in C fast and painless, and they provide debugging facilities that make finding errors much quicker.

You could use Genny, Eclipse, Code::Blocks or NetBeans, all of which are open source. Genny has the advantage of being installed by default on the Pi, but the others are easy enough to install.

Because of its popularity and ubiquity, Visual Studio Code, VS Code, is the code editor used in the rest of this book. This is a free, open-source, multi-language, multi-platform code editor that is worth the time to get to know.

Local Or Remote

There are two distinct ways you can work with any development environment:

- Install VS Code on a Raspberry Pi and work with it via the GUI desktop, i.e. directly on the Pi. In this case you are using the Pi as if it was a full desktop computer and it is your development and test machine.

- You could connect the Pi to a desktop machine and make use of it to write your program and then download and run it on the Pi. In this case the desktop machine is your development machine and the Pi is your test machine.

Remote development can be implemented in a number of ways. For example a cross compiler could be used on the desktop machine and the compiled program could be downloaded to the Pi to be tested. This is not a common approach to Pi remote development as the Pi is powerful enough to do its own compiling. In general what happens is that the source code is downloaded to the Pi which then compiles and runs it.

In practice, the remote development approach tends to work better because the desktop machine has the power to run the editor reasonably fast. Another advantage of remote development is that you can easily change the Pi that you are testing the code on, preserving all of the code stored on the desktop machine. This is very useful because you can try out your program on a range of Raspberry Pis and swap machines simply by changing the build host used for the project.

Put simply, local development is easier, but remote development is more flexible.

VS Code On A Pi

VS Code can be installed on some Raspberry Pis and used to develop programs that run on the same machine, i.e. as local development. This isn't the best way to work, but it is the simplest.

The Pi Zero and Pi Zero W are ruled as it isn't possible to install VS Code on them. While installation is possible for a Pi Zero 2W, with only 512K of RAM it is so slow that it is virtually unusable – you can see screen refreshes being performed and many of the extensions don't work.

Installing VS Code is a reasonable thing to do on a Pi 4/5. For the others, you are better off using remote development with VS Code installed on a desktop machine.

The simplest way to install VS Code is to use the Recommended Software utility from the desktop.

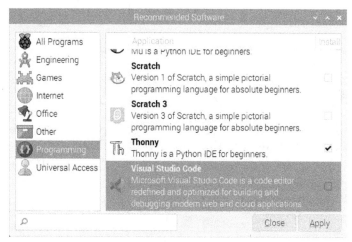

You can also install it using the package manager:

```
sudo apt install code
```

or from the VS Code web site using the Debian release.

After installing VS Code, either on your desktop machine or a Pi, your next step has to be to install the Microsoft C/C++ code extension:

Once you have VS Code installed, you can try a simple hello world program running on the local machine. First select `File` and click the `Open Folder` menu option, navigate to a suitable location and, using right-click and `New`, create a folder called `CPROJECTS`, open it and create another folder called `HelloWorld`:

Finally create a file called `hello.c` in the `HelloWorld` folder and enter:

```c
#include <stdio.h>
#include <stdlib.h>
int main(int argc, char **argv)
{
        printf("Hello C World");
        int test = 42;
        printf("%d\n", test);
        return (EXIT_SUCCESS);
}
```

You don't have to organize your projects in this way, but it is easier if each C program has its own folder within a top-level workspace folder.

When you come to run the program for the first time you will have to select a compiler. If you are running on a Pi then you can use the latest GCC compiler as it is already installed.

This creates a `tasks.json` file in the `.vscode` directory which you can edit to customize the way the compiler and linker run. In most cases this isn't necessary.

Remote Development

If you can use VS Code on a Pi to develop and run code on the Pi then this is as simple as it gets. A possibly better approach is that of full remote C development. That is, you write your program on a, generally a more powerful. desktop machine, and run it on a Pi connected over SSH.

Again, you can't do this with any of the Pi Zeros as they have insufficient memory.

The only other problem with this is that VS Code has more facilities than you need to just run C and this can make it confusing. However, after you have run your first program, it all becomes so much easier. If you are going to be doing much programming on Pis, it is worth the effort in setting up and mastering remote development.

A more useful, but slightly more complicated, approach is to make use of VS Code Tasks to provide remote build and debug. This works with all versions of the Pi, including the Pi Zero range, or indeed any Linux-based device, and it keeps all of the files on the local machine. It also has the advantage of making testing programs running with root privileges, something you need to do if you are accessing the hardware, easier.

Before we can get started with VS Code remote development we need to setup SSH.

SSH Without A Password

Before trying to make any of the following work, you need to have set up SSH access using a Key file. Some of the commands work if you simply supply a password, but the debugging commands don't.

Using a password to connect over SSH is fine when you are just testing the installation, but the number of times you are asked to provide it quickly becomes irritating. The solution is to create a key pair to use. If you look up the instructions for doing this, you might conclude that it is very difficult. This is because every effort is make to ensure security is enforced. If you simply want to use a key as a way of avoiding having to supply a password then you can take shortcuts. As long as you keep your private key safe, the setup is secure.

The first step is generating a key pair on the local machine. As long as you have OpenSSH installed, this is easy. The steps described here will work on Windows, Mac and Linux. If you are using Windows, start a PowerShell session:

```
cd ~\.ssh
ssh-keygen -t rsa
```

This generates a default RSA key in the .ssh directory within the current user's home directory. You can provide a name for the key files and in this example the name pi is used, although this doesn't affect what device you can use them for. There are advantages in using the default name.

You will see output something like:

```
Generating public/private rsa key pair.
Enter file in which to save the key (C:\Users\
userhome/.ssh/id_rsa): pi
Enter passphrase (empty for no passphrase):
Enter same passphrase again:
Your identification has been saved in pi.
Your public key has been saved in pi.pub.
The key fingerprint is:
SHA256:UtiQ3RMYpluJb+nx8n5pqsbLXHgiYv2hKs1EVoF7vqQ user@Rockrose
```

```
The key's randomart image is:
+---[RSA 2048]----+
|     .o+o+..     |
|    . oBo.o      |
|     o+ =  .     |
|    + .= .       |
|   o oo S        |
|   ..o+ +        |
|   +oooo* +  .   |
|  ..E..*oB  +    |
|  .....*+++      |
+----[SHA256]-----+
```

If you really are using the keys for security purposes you should supply a passphrase, which is requested when the key pair is used. If you are simply using the keys to avoid entering a password then leave the passphrase blank for simplicity.

The key generation will leave two files in the .ssh directory – in this case pi and pi.pub. The first is the private key and this you keep to yourself as it is what proves that the machine is the one that the public key belongs to. The pi.pub file contains the public key and this the one that has to be copied to the remote machine. The remote machine uses the public key to challenge the local machine to decode something which can only be done with the private key, so proving that the machine is legitimate, or rather that it has the private key.

You can use the public key with as many remote machines as you need to. The key identifies you as being allowed to connect to a machine that has it using SSH. To make this happen, you have to enter the details of the file into .ssh/authorized_keys. You can do this any way you know how to, but the public key file has to be copied to ~/.ssh/ on the remote machine and renamed authorized_keys. As you have SSH working, the simplest thing to do is:

```
scp pi.pub pi@192.168.11.151:~/.ssh/authorized_keys
```

You might have to make the .ssh folder first. You will have to provide the user's, pi in this case, password. If this works you will find authorized_keys in the .ssh directory. If you want to store more public keys in authorized_keys so that more than one user can log on, you have to append additional public key files to authorized_keys.

SSH will not use the key file if ~/.ssh or ~ are writable by Group or Others. One way of ensuring this is not the case:

```
chmod 700 ~/.ssh
chmod 600 ~/.ssh/authorized_keys
```

As long as the permissions are set correctly, you should be able to connect without a password using:

```
ssh -i ~/.ssh/pi pi@192.168.11.151
```

If you don't use `-i ~/.ssh/pi` to specify the private key file, you might be asked for a password as well as the key file. You also have to specify the correct user name.

If you want to log on and not specify the key file, i.e. just using:

```
pi@192.168.11.151
```

then you need to make sure your key files have the correct default names. For protocol 2 the keys have to be called `id_rsa` and `id_rsa.pub`. If you use these default names for RSA keys then the SSH agent will use them automatically. If you use any other names, like `pi` and `pi.pub`, you will need an Identity file specified in `.ssh config`.

Open the file `config` in the `C:\Users\user\.ssh directory` on the local machine (`~/.ssh` under Linux) and enter:

```
Host 192.168.11.151
    HostName 192.168.11.151
    User pi
    PubKeyAuthentication yes
    IdentityFile ~/.ssh/pi
```

Of course, you have to change the IP address, user name and the location of the key file to be correct for the machine you are trying to connect to. You can enter additional Host specifications for each machine you want to connect to.

After this you should be able to connect and work with the remote Pi without providing a password when using VS Code. You can also just use:

```
ssh pi@192.168.11.151
```

at the command line.

Notice that this is low security as we didn't specify a passphrase to use with the private key. If you need security from the outside world, you need to create a key with a passphrase and then you need to use the SSH agent to supply it automatically.

Remote SSH

To run the remote development extension you need to have an OpenSSH client running on the development machine. Windows 10 has its own version of OpenSSH client. You next need to install the remote development pack. You only need to install Remote SSH.

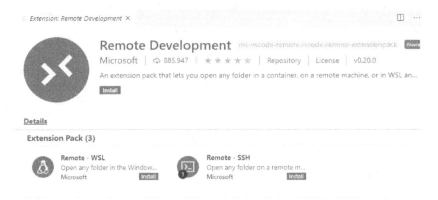

After you have installed Remote SSH you can add the details of the Pi you want to use to develop programs on. To do this click on the `Remote Explorer` icon in the left panel and you will see that there are no SSH clients installed.

As already mentioned, this doesn't work on the Pi Zero/W as the CPU is unsupported and it is unworkable on the Pi Zero 2W because of the small amount of memory available.

Next click on the + that appears when you hover over SSH Targets and enter the details for the Pi you want to connect to:

You specify the host using the format:

`ssh user@ipaddress`

When you press Enter, select a configuration file to use and you are ready to connect to the new host. Right-click on the new host and select "Connect in this window". Next, you will be asked for your password. You will be asked for the password each time you connect unless you create a private key and use it for authentication as detailed earlier.

When you open the file explorer and select `Open Folder` you will see a list of folders stored in your home folder on the host machine. Create a new folder suitable for storing your C programs and create a file called `hello.c` in it. You will be prompted to install the C extensions on the remote machine. If not you need to install them manually. After this you will be able to run the program on the remote machine.

Notice that the program files are stored and compiled on the remote machine. A code server is installed on the remote machine the first time you connect to it.

From here on you can learn about Visual Studio Code and slowly customize it to make your work easier.

Local Remote Synchronization

It is important to realize that the C programs you create are stored on the remote host. This means that, if you do nothing about it, your entire program could be stored solely on a Pi, waiting for something bad to happen to it. Even if you consider this a safe option, you have the problem of transferring the program to another Pi if you want to run it there. The best solution is to keep a copy of your programs on a machine that you consider safe, and share them with any Pi you might want to run them on.

The most attractive option is to use source code management. Visual Studio Code supports Git without you having to install any extensions. Once you have it all set up this works well, but setting it up is a time-consuming process and it requires that you understand how Git, and usually GitHub, works. For small and simple projects this is generally more than you need and you could spend a lot of valuable programming time learning to use a tool that you barely make use of. This said, if you are planning a large project, or a collaborative project, then source code management is your best option, even if it does involve additional initial work.

In most cases we can achieve what we need using simpler tools. You can copy a single file or folder from a remote machine by drag-and-dropping it from the Explorer to the folder in the local machine. Unfortunately, this doesn't work for remote Linux machines, and this includes Pi OS, so it isn't a method that works for us. However, you can drag-and-drop files and folders from the local machine to the Explorer window on the remote machine. See the next section for an automatic way of doing this.

Now we only have the problem of copying files from the remote machine to the local machine. This can be done by selecting a file or folder in the VS Code Explorer and right-clicking to display the context menu. You will see Download in the same section as Copy. Selecting this downloads the entire folder and its contents or the single file. You can pick where you want the file or folder to be copied to and so manually maintain a central copy of anything you are working on.

An alternative way of saving a remote file on the local machine is to use the File, Save As menu option and select the Show Local button.

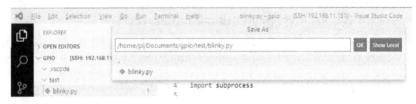

This allows you to save the file on the local machine under whatever name you want to use.

There are ways of automating the copying of files, but manual copying works well and most of the automatic synchronizing methods have their own drawbacks.

Remote Development Using Tasks

Unfortunately VS Code's remote development stores, and works with, the code on the remote machine. This makes moving to another remote machine more difficult. You have to arrange to copy the project to the local machine and then copy it to the new remote machine. This is not the best way of working. When you add in the fact that the remote development extension doesn't work with the Pi Zero range, exactly the device you most want use in remote development mode, you can see that this is not attractive.

The solution adopted here is to create a custom launch file to implement remote running and remote debugging. The basic idea is to use the facility in VS Code to run tasks to create a program on a local machine and then automatically upload the files to the remote machine where they are compiled and run. This is the approach used in the rest of this book with the set of custom tasks provided. Full listings of the tasks and an explanation of how they work can be found in Appendix II. The files used have been tested on Windows, but they should work on Mac OS and Linux with changes to the folders specified. You can also download the files from this book's page on www.iopress.info.

To develop in C on a remote machine you first need to have SSH set up and be able to log in without supplying a password. If you can't do this then remote development tasks will fail unless you switch to the terminal window and enter the password each time you are asked for it. Sometimes the terminal window may not appear or be hard to find pass-wordless SSH makes things simple.

Next you need to create some files in the .vscode folder. All of the files listed below are available from this book's webpage on the I/O Press website, www.iopress.info and you can simply download .vscode and copy the whole folder to the local machine. You will need to customize some of the files to be correct for the folders and remote machine you are using.

Create a folder on the local machine to act as the top level project folder – all of your C projects will be stored in sub-folders of this one. It is important that this project folder is the one that you always open in VS Code as the tasks use this to construct the relevant paths. If you run a task and it can't find a folder or a file then the most common cause is that you have opened the wrong folder.

Within your project folder, create a folder called .vscode if it doesn't already exist and create a custom settings.json file in it. Make sure that this is in the top-level folder as it is intended to apply to all of the subfolders containing your projects.

.vscode contains the details of the remote machine and the folders you want to use on the remote:

```
{
    "sshUser": "pi",
    "sshEndpoint": "192.168.11.151",
    "remoteDirectory": "/home/pi/Documents/
                               ${workspaceFolderBasename}",
    "std": "c99",
    "libs":"",
    "header":""
}
```

Of course, you need to change the data to correspond to the remote machine you are actually using – the IP address, user name and so on. The remoteDirectory variable specifies the directory on the remote machine that you want to store all of the project folders in. In this example it is:

/home/pi/Documents/CProjects

On the local machine your projects should be stored in a folder of the same name, i.e. CProjects. Each project should have its own subfolder, e.g. Blinky, but always open the top-level folder and navigate to the subfolder in VS Code.

As the project folder has to exist on the remote, there is an automatic task that will create it for you, see later. The std variable specifies the version of C you want to use with the compiler, libs specifies any library files you want the compiler to use and header specifies a single custom header file on the remote machine. In this case we can leave them both as null strings until they are needed.

Next, you need to create launch.json, tasks.json and c_cpp_properties.json in the .vscode folder. They are listed in full in Appendix II or you can download them from www.iopress.info.

The launch.json file specifies the location of all the files on the local and remote machine and how to connect to the remote machine. The preLaunchTask runs a task called CopyBuildRemote. As its name suggests, this copies the files in the current folder and uses GCC to build an executable with debug information. You could create a special launch file that runs the program without building and compiling it by changing the preLaunchTask. This is the file that allows you to run and debug the program.

Third, you need the `tasks.json` file which contains the definitions of a number of tasks that are used to run and debug the program. They are listed in Appendix I and on the book's web page. Some of them are useful as standalone tasks:

- copyToRemote
  Copies the files in the folder that the current file open in the editor is stored in. It copies all of the files, even if they haven't changed.

- copyHeader
  Copies the single file specified in `settings.json` from the remote machine to the workspace of the file currently open in the editor. This has to be invoked manually to make sure that the local machine has access to the header for debugging and IntelliSense purposes.

- buildRemote
  Runs GCC to create the .exe file. If the current file is `helloworld.c` the command is:

```
gcc  -g -std=c99
   /home/pi/Documents/Cprojects/HelloWorld/helloworld.c
    -o/home/pi/Documents/Cprojects/HelloWorld/helloworld
```

- runRemote
  Runs the file created by buildRemote.

- CopyBuildRunRemote
  A compound task which uses copyToRemote, buildRemote and runRemote to build and run a remote program. This runs the program without the debugger.

- CopyBuildRemote
  A compound task which uses copyToRemote and buildRemote to build a remote program so that another command can run it.

- StopRemoteC
  Stops all processes with the same name as the program being developed. This is sometimes used manually to stop programs that have been started manually.

The final file is `c_cpp_properties.json` This sets the environment for the local C tools. The `cStandard` variable sets the version of C used for IntelliSense syntax checking and has no effect on the compiler. You need to set the version in two different places - `settings.json` for the compiler and `c_cpp_properties.json` for the editor. The `includePath` variable sets the folders where the editor looks for header files. If you are using a Windows machine as the local editor and you want IntelliSense to work, you need to install MinGW and specify the `mingw` directory for all the standard headers and the workspace folders for custom headers. If you don't do this you will see errors in your program about missing headers, but this doesn't have any effect on the compilation on the remote machine.

Running and Debugging Remotely

With the files given above stored in .vscode, we can now run a
helloworld.c program on the remote machine. Create a HelloWorld folder
within your top-level project folder and create a helloworld.c file within it.
If you just want to build and run the program all you have to do is open it in
the editor and select Terminal, Run Build Task or, as this task is the default
Build task press Ctrl+Shift+B. The program will be automatically copied,
built and run and you will see the output in the Terminal window. If the
program you run is an infinite loop you may need to manually run
StopRemoteC to stop it.

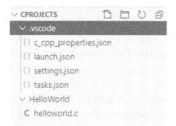

Running it using the default Build doesn't start the debugger – it simply runs
the compiled program. To debug the program you need to use the Run and
Debug icon at the left-hand side of the screen. This uses the launch.json file
to run the program and in this case the Remote C Debug option runs the
program using the remote debugger.

To try this out place some breakpoints in the program:

```
1   #include <stdio.h>
2   #include <stdlib.h>
3   int main(int argc, char **argv)
4   {
5       printf("Hello C World\n\r");
6       int test = 42;
7       printf("%d\n\r", test);
8       return (EXIT_SUCCESS);
9   }
```

Click the Run icon, select Remote C Debug and then click on the Start Debugging icon.

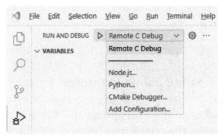

The program is automatically copied, built and run in debug mode. The debugger will pause at the first breakpoint and you can single-step and examine variables. When you are finished click the Stop icon.

It is worth spending some time understanding the tasks and customizing them to make your remote development more efficient.

Using Library and Header Files

Sometimes you need to specify a library file for the program to use. You have to include the appropriate header file and you also have to specify the name of the library, pthreads say, that you want the linker to add to your program. If you are using VS Code to do remote development using tasks, change settings.json to read:

```
{
    "sshUser": "pi",
    "sshEndpoint": "192.168.11.170",
    "remoteDirectory": "/home/pi/Documents/
                        ${workspaceFolderBasename}",
    "std": "c99",
    "libs":"-lpthread,
    "header":""
}
```

The remote machine has the library installed and the compiler can make use of it just by using the -lpthread option, but the local machine doesn't have it installed and doesn't need to as the program is never run there.

Another problem is making use of headers that exist on the remote machine, but not on the local machine. It is very easy to copy the header from the remote machine to the local machine using the copyHeaders task. This creates a headers directory and copies any headers that you list in settings.json into it. Now the reported error should disappear and you should be able run and debug the program in the usual way. In a more general case, you may have to copy multiple header files to the local machine, but you only need the header files as the program is actually compiled on the remote machine.

If you want to make sure that you have all of the standard ARM headers for your program, you can enter and run the `copyARMheaders` task. This copies all of the headers to a new `include` folder. You also need to add:

```
#define __ARM_PCS_VFP
```

to the start of some of your programs to make all of the spurious IntelliSense errors go away. This symbol is defined by the compiler at runtime to select hardware or software floating point operations. Programs that use headers that depend on the hardware specification generate errors on the local machine as they don't know the configuration. Notice that none of this has any effect on the program that runs on the remote machine. It simply suppresses errors that you see on the local machine as VS Code attempts to find pre-compile errors.

Running As Root

There are many hardware facilities that a C program cannot access unless it is running with root privileges. Security is a big problem for Linux programmers, and IoT programmers in particular, because it tends to get in the way of what we are trying to do. For example, running a program as `root` is considered to be very bad practice, but if that program wants to access hardware directly it has no choice but to require root privileges and you have no choice but to supply them, no matter what less well-informed programmers have to say about security risks.

The usual way of running a program with root privileges is to use `sudo`. If the program is called `HelloWorld` then all you have to do to run it as root is:

```
sudo ./HelloWorld
```

You might well be asked to supply your password and your account needs to be a member of the root group.

At the time of writing, using `sudo` to run VS Code as `root` doesn't work. It might in a future version and it is worth checking, but for the moment the only workable solution is to log on as `root`. Exactly how this works depends on whether you are working with VS Code locally or remotely. In either case, you first need to allow root to log on with a password.

To set a password for root:

```
sudo passwd root
```

and enter the new password.

With this change you can now log on as `root`. However, when the desktop starts up, you will notice that there is no taskbar. This is another security mechanism, but why it is necessary isn't clear.

You can start VS Code using Ctrl-Alt-T to open a terminal and then use the command:

```
code --no-sandbox —user-data-dir=/root/.data
```

This is necessary because VS Code applies more security when running as root. The `user-data-dir` you specify is created and used to store session data for VS Code and you can mostly ignore it. Once you have VS Code loaded you can use it as normal and your programs will be run with root permissions.

You can also start a file manager using:

```
pcmanfm
```

at the command prompt.

If you want to work remotely then you also need to allow root login via SSH. To do this use:

```
sudo nano /etc/ssh/sshd_config
```

and add the line:

```
PermitRootLogin yes
```

After a reboot you can log in with the name "root" with the password you set.

Logging in as root using a password is considered insecure and inconvenient. The best advice is to copy the public key, see earlier, using the usual `scp` command at the SSH prompt:

```
scp pi.pub root@192.168.11.151:~/.ssh/authorized_keys
```

You will have to provide the root password and, of course, modify the IP address and the path to the public key. You also need to modify the `.ssh/config` file on the local machine to associate the key to the remote machine.

After you have done this, you can remove the permission to log in using a password by using:

```
sudo nano /etc/ssh/sshd_config
```

and changing the line to read:

```
PermitRootLogin without-password
```

Make sure you can log in using the public key first.

At this point you can start VS Code and set up a remote connection using the root user. This works in exactly the same way as described earlier for a general user and will allow you to run and debug programs with root privileges.

If you want to use the VS Code tasks for remote development then simply change the user to `root` in `settings.json`. You will also have to create the `Documents` directory in `/root` if you want to make use of it.

Summary

- C is a good choice of language for IoT applications – it is the language of Linux and it is efficient and easy to use.

- You can use either local or remote development environments. Local is where you use the same machine to create and run a program. Remote is where the development and machine used to run the program are different.

- For IoT work, remote development has big advantages.

- If you want to use local development you can install and use any of Genny, Eclipse, Code::Blocks, NetBeans or VS Code.

- VS Code can be installed on Windows, Linux or OSX.

- VS Code has many advantages when it comes to remote development, but its own remote development tools don't work on the Pi Zeros and don't work in the best way for IoT.

- A better, though slightly more complicated solution, is to use VS Code tasks to copy the program to the remote machine and then build it on the remote machine using the compilers already installed.

- The complete set of tasks needed for remote development that have been created for this book is listed in Appendix I and you can download them from this book's webpage on www.iopress.info.

- The remote tasks allow you to run or debug your programs and store them on the local machine. Deployment to another remote machine is just a matter of changing a configuration file.

- You also might need to provide copies of header files on the local machine and specify library files to use.

- To access hardware, programs often to run with root permissions and the simplest way to do this is to log in as root. However, this can be tricky as the system doesn't always interact well with the root user.

Chapter 3

Drivers: A First Program

This book is about using off-the-shelf Linux device drivers. This approach has the advantage that you don't have to worry about implementing the low-level protocol that is used to "talk" to the device. You might, however, have to implement the commands that make the device work and to read and write data to configure it. Not all of the work is necessarily done for you. Another big advantage is that the driver runs in kernel mode and this means that it can run without interruption by the operating system. The downside is that most Linux device drivers are poorly documented, usually from the point of view of driver writers rather than users, and suffer from either a lack of support or updates that break your existing programs. With care, however, both situations can be managed.

Linux drivers work with almost any programming language as they usually only require file I/O and some limited system calls. This means that to make use of them all you need to know is how to open, close, read and write a file, making use of Linux/POSIX file descriptors rather than C file streams. POSIX file descriptors are covered in *Applying C for the IoT with Linux*, ISBN: 9781871962611.

This makes using drivers sound easy, but there are a lot of fine details. How do you get a custom driver loaded and configured for the particular hardware you are using? How can you do this from within your program rather than having to ask the user to perform the configuration? What files do you read or write to achieve any desired result? Answering these questions is what this book is all about.

The latest version of Pi OS is Bookworm and this is what we will use in this book. However, the Pi Zero/W/2W currently only run Bullseye, the previous version of Pi OS, which has slight differences in the drivers and driver names. Any differences required are pointed out in this and the following chapters.

Using A Driver

A key principle of Unix and Linux is that, as much as possible, every interaction with the outside world is represented as a file. This isn't as crazy as it sounds as reading and writing to a file can be thought of as sending data to and from a device. When you use a standard file you are sending data to and from a disk drive or a storage device. When you send data to a "pseudo" file you are sending the data to and from some more general device, or even an internal part of the operating system.

External devices, such as disk drives, keyboards and so on, are represented as files in the /dev folder. Internal devices such as GPIO lines, timers and so on are represented as files in the /sys folder. This said, there is a great deal of inherited illogicality in the organization.

Most of the devices that we consider in this book have drivers that represent them as folders and files in the /sys folder. The files can be used as if they were perfectly standard files and read and written using the file handling commands available in whatever language you are using. In C it is usually more appropriate to use Linux file descriptors as the buffering isn't appropriate for most devices, as explained in *Applying C for the IoT with Linux*.

When using a driver, the problems are generally just finding out which folders do what and what the allowable values are. The obvious solution to this problem is to find the documentation for the driver, but often this doesn't supply the information you need, in which you need to engage in interactive reverse engineering.

LEDs

It is usual to first write the IoT equivalent of a Hello World program, i.e. Blinky. This is a program that simply flashes an LED. Usually you have to go over the details of connecting an LED to a GPIO line and then how to use software to make it flash at a set rate. Here, however, we want to use a driver to show how this approach to the IoT works and the good news is that there is an LED driver.

If you are familiar with IoT programming you might find this news slightly disturbing. Flashing an LED is the simplest of programs and using a Linux driver by comparison is grossly inefficient, involving layers of intermediate code. This is true, but using a Linux driver has the advantage of being easier to move to another Linux system and is more sophisticated. If you compare what is easy to implement using the LED driver with its equivalent direct implementation, you will see that the inefficient layers are actually doing something useful.

The Linux LED driver, gpio-leds is installed by default and it automatically creates a /sys/class/leds folder which contains a folder for each LED device the system uses. In the case of the Pi Zero there is just one folder. All other Pis have at least two LEDs and hence two folders.

These are called ACT and PWR. They were called led0 and led1 under earlier operating systems. The ACT folder correspond to the green activity LED on all Pis and the PWR folder corresponds to the red power LED on all Pis apart from the Pi Zero. The Pi 5 combines both LEDs in a two-color device. As it is available across all Pis, let's concentrate on ACT, although PWR works in the same way.

If you open the ACT folder you will see a number of folders and files:

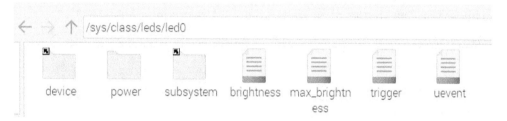

The ones that are important to us at the moment start with brightness, which gets/sets the brightness of the LED. This is a value between 0 and 1, but most LEDs are either on or off and writing anything greater than 0 generally turns the LED full on. The trigger folder sets an association between the LED and various signal sources. By default trigger is set to mmc0 which flashes the LED according to how much memory I/O there is and hence provides an indication of processor activity. It is the ability to connect the LED to a signal source that makes the LED driver more sophisticated than simply connecting an LED to a GPIO line.

Blinky

Time to write a Blinky program for ACT. All we have to do is write none to the trigger and then write a 0 or a 1 to the brightness file:

```c
#include <stdio.h>
#include <errno.h>
#include <unistd.h>
#include <fcntl.h>
int main(int argc, char **argv)
{
    int fd = open("/sys/class/leds/ACT/trigger", O_WRONLY);
    write(fd, "none",4);
    close(fd);
    fd = open("/sys/class/leds/ACT/brightness", O_WRONLY);
    while (1)
    {
        write(fd, "0",1);
        sleep(2);
        write(fd, "1",1);
        sleep(2);
    }
}
```

Unless you have logged in as root, either locally or via remote, see the previous chapter, then this program will not work. To access the LEDs you need root privileges. If you are not logged in as root then simplest way to run your program with root permissions is to use:

```
sudo ./blinky
```

in the terminal after you have compiled it.

You can also try changing the permissions on the driver:

```
sudo chmod -R  a+rwx /sys/class/leds/ACT
```

Following this the program should work in VS Code, but notice that as sys files are not real files they are constructed when the system boots and this is not a permanent change to the permissions.

For all of the programs in the remainder of this book it is assumed that you have root privileges.

A Blinky implementation more in keeping with the LED driver is to use a trigger rather than a loop to flash the on-board LED together with a sleep. When you set trigger to timer the driver automatically creates two more files, delay_on and delay_off which set the on and off time in milliseconds:

```
#include <stdio.h>
import io
from time import sleep

fd = io.open("/sys/class/leds/ACT/trigger","w")
fd.write("timer")
fd.close()

fd = io.open("/sys/class/leds/ACT/delay_on", "w")
fd.write("2000")
fd.close()

fd = io.open("/sys/class/leds/ACT/delay_off", "w")
fd.write("3000")
fd.close()
```

In this case the act LED flashes for two seconds on, three seconds off and doesn't need the program to keep going. Once set up, the trigger controls the LED until it is modified.

Finding Out About Drivers

All of this is very simple, but how do you find the information that you need to use the LED driver? The answer is that it can be challenging. You can look for documentation, but there usually isn't any and if there is then it generally is targeted at driver writers and explains how to make use of the driver's facilities in kernel mode, not user mode. This can be very confusing and can waste time if you try to use drivers in the way described in a user-mode program.

For example, if you look at the documentation for LEDs in the Linux source code tree for the Raspberry Pi, which you can find on the Raspberry Pi GitHub page, i.e. in linux/Documentation/leds/, you will see a lot of files, but which one has the information about basic LED operation is not clear.

There is usually a documentation file for the class or core driver, in this case `leds-class`. If you open this you will find some basic and very general information. It tells you that:

> *"In its simplest form, the LED class just allows control of LEDs from userspace. LEDs appear in /sys/class/leds/. The maximum brightness of the LED is defined in max_brightness file. The brightness file will set the brightness of the LED (taking a value 0-max_brightness). Most LEDs don't have hardware brightness support so will just be turned on for non-zero brightness settings."*

This is enough to get you started, but there is no information about what the actual LEDs in the `leds` folder are. That is, it doesn't help with what ACT and PWR actually are. The documentation does go on to explain the idea of triggers, but it doesn't tell you what triggers are available and there is no documentation for them. The best that you can do is read the source code for the triggers that are available in the `linux/drivers/leds/trigger/` folder:

```
cat trigger
[none] rc-feedback kbd-scrolllock kbd-numlock kbd-capslock kbd-
kanalock kbd-shiftlock kbd-altgrlock kbd-ctrllock kbd-altlock kbd-
shiftllock kbd-shiftrlock kbd-ctrlllock kbd-ctrlrlock timer oneshot
heartbeat backlight gpio cpu cpu0 default-on input panic mmc1 mmc0
rfkill-any rfkill-none rfkill0 rfkill1
```

Some of these are obvious, some less so, and working out how to use any of them is a matter of trial and error and reading the relevant driver code.

If you search the web you will find that other programmers have already investigated on your behalf:

```
none                 No trigger
kbd-scrolllock       Keyboard scroll lock
kbd-numlock          Keyboard num lock
kbd-capslock         Keyboard caps lock
kbd-kanalock         Keyboard kana lock
kbd-shiftlock        Keyboard shift
kbd-altgrlock        Keyboard altgr
kbd-ctrllock         Keyboard ctrl
kbd-altlock          Keyboard alt
kbd-shiftllock       Keyboard left shift
kbd-shiftrlock       Keyboard right shift
kbd-ctrlllock        Keyboard left ctrl
kbd-ctrlrlock        Keyboard right ctrl
timer                Flash at 1 second intervals
oneshot              Flash only once
heartbeat            Flash like a heartbeat (1-0-1-00000)
backlight            Always on
gpio                 Flash when a specified GPIO has an event
cpu0                 Flash on cpu0 usage
cpu1                 Flash on cpu1 usage
cpu2                 Flash on cpu2 usage
cpu3                 Flash on cpu3 usage
default-on           Always on
input                Default state
panic                Flash on kernel panic
mmc0                 Flash on mmc0 (primary SD interface) activity
mmc1                 Flash on mmc1 (secondary SD interface) activity
rfkill0              Flash on wifi activity
rfkill1              Flash on bluetooth activity
```

A lot more information about devices and drivers can be found via the device tree, which is the subject of Chapters 7 and 16.

Summary

- Blinky, flashing an LED, is the IoT's Hello World program and usually this involves wiring an LED and writing code to change the state of a GPIO line.

- Using the Linux LED driver you can create a Blinky program that flashes an onboard LED, so avoiding the need for extra hardware.

- A full Linux driver just to flash an LED may seem like overkill, but it has advantages in that you can connect it to any of a set of triggers that make it flash according to a range of sensors.

- The LED driver is typical of Linux drivers in general in that it creates a set of folders and files which you open and read and write to control the LED.

- The big problem with all drivers is finding documentation on how to use the driver and how to configure it.

Chapter 4

The GPIO Character Driver

As far as IoT goes, the fundamental Linux driver is the GPIO driver, which gives you access to the individual GPIO lines. This is another built-in driver and so is like the LED driver introduced in the previous chapter, but it is a character driver and used in a slightly different way.

In most cases, when a device is connected via a set of GPIO lines, you usually use a specific device driver. In this way you can almost ignore the GPIO lines and what they are doing. However, there are still simple situations where a full driver would be overkill. If you want to interface a button or an LED, then direct control over the GPIO lines is the most direct way to do the job even if there are Linux LED drivers – see the previous chapter – and even an input driver.

The standard way to work with GPIO in Linux used to be via the sysfs interface and you will still find articles advocating its use and you will also encounter many programs making use of it. GPIO sysfs was, however, deprecated in Linux 4.8 at the end of 2016 and was due for removal from the kernel in 2020. At the time of writing, Pi OS is using Linux 6.2.21 and it still includes Sysfs gpio. As it could be removed at any time you shouldn't use it for new projects, however you may still need to know about it to cope with legacy software. You can find out how it works in Appendix I.

Its replacement is the GPIO character device and, while this looks superficially like the old sysfs interface, it has many major differences. While it has some advantages, it also is slightly more complex and can no longer be used from the command line – it is a program-only interface. This said, there are some simple utility programs that are fairly standard and allow GPIO control from the command line. These are covered in the first part of the chapter, even though they are unlikely to be the main way that you work with the new interface. There is also a wrapper library called libgpiod. Although it isn't necessary for simple access to the GPIO lines, it is described in this chapter.

GPIO Character Device

The new approach to working with GPIO comes pre-installed in recent versions of Pi OS, but it isn't supported in versions earlier than Buster. If you look in the /dev directory you will find files corresponding to each GPIO controller installed. You will see at least:

/dev/gpiochip0

This represents the main GPIO controller and all of the GPIO lines it provides. In the case of the Pi 5 the GPIO controller is represented by gpiochip4.

If you know how sysfs works you might well be expecting instructions on how to read and write to the file from the console. In this case, reading and writing to the file will do you little good as most of the work is carried out using the input/output control system call, ioctl() which cannot be used from the command line. The use of ioctl is typical of a character driver, but it does mean that using the GPIO driver is very different from other file-oriented drivers described later. The next chapter looks at the use of ioctl to directly control the GPIO character device.

If you want to explore the GPIO from the command line, you need to install some tools that have been created mainly as examples of using the new device interface. To do this you need to first install them and libgpoid. the gpiod library that you will use later:

sudo apt-get install gpiod libgpiod-dev libgpiod-doc

Notice that, if you don't want to use the library to access the driver, you don't have to install it – the GPIO driver is loaded as part of the Linux kernel and is ready to use.

The Utilities

The standalone applications that are installed are:

◆ gpiodetect

Lists all of the GPIO controllers that are installed:

```
pi@raspberrypi:~ $ gpiodetect
gpiochip0 [pinctrl-bcm2835] (54 lines)
pi@raspberrypi:~ $ ▌
```

Notice that on the Pi 5 it is gpiochip4 that controls the external GPIO lines whereas it is gpiochip0 for other Pis.

- gpioinfo

  Lists all of the GPIO lines provided by the named GPIO controller:

```
pi@raspberrypi:~ $ gpioinfo gpiochip0
gpiochip0 - 54 lines:
        line   0:      unnamed       unused   input  active-high
        line   1:      unnamed       unused   input  active-high
        line   2:      unnamed       unused   input  active-high
        line   3:      unnamed       unused   input  active-high
        line   4:      unnamed       unused   output active-high
        line   5:      unnamed       unused   input  active-high
        line   6:      unnamed       unused   input  active-high
        line   7:      unnamed       unused   input  active-high
        line   8:      unnamed       unused   input  active-high
```

- gpiofind

  You can give particular lines names by editing the device tree. If you do give them appropriate fixed names then gpiofind *name* returns the number of the GPIO line.

- gpioset

  You can set any number of GPIO lines in one operation with:

  gpioset *options chip name/number* <offset1>=<value1>

  <offset2>=<value2> ...

  where *options* are:

-l, --active-low		Sets the line's active state to low
-m, --mode =		Choice of what to do after setting values:
	exit	Exit immediately, the default
	wait	Wait for user to press ENTER
	time	Sleep for a specified amount of time
	signal	Wait for SIGINT or SIGTERM
-s, --sec = *SEC*		Number of seconds to wait
-u, --usec = *USEC*		Number of microseconds to wait
-b, --background		Detaches from the controlling terminal

  The change in the line's state only persists while the command is executing. This means you have to use wait or time to see the effect. For example:

  gpioset -m wait 0 4=0 17=1

  sets gpiochip 0 GPIO4 to 0 and GPIO17 to 1 and waits until the user presses ENTER.

- gpioget

  The gpioget command returns the state of the lines specified as text:

  gpioget *chip name/number* *<offset 1> <offset 2>*

  For example:

  gpioget 0 4 17

  displays the current state of GPIO4 and GPIO17 on gpiochip0.

- gpiomon

  The gpiomon command lets you monitor changes in input lines using a poll system call:

  gpiomon *options chip name/number* *<offset 1> <offset 2> …*

  where *options* are:

-n, --num-events = *NUM*		Exit after processing *NUM* events
-s, --silent		Don't print event info
-r, --rising-edge		Only process rising edge events
-f, --falling-edge		Only process falling edge events
-F, --format =		Specify custom output format
	%o	GPIO line offset
	%e	event type (0 - falling edge, 1 - rising edge)
	%s	seconds part of the event timestamp
	%n	nanoseconds part of the event timestamp

  For example, to monitor GPIO4 and GPIO17 for any changes:

```
pi@raspberrypi:~ $ gpiomon 0 4 17
event:  RISING EDGE offset: 4 timestamp: [1589563313.974056272]
event:  RISING EDGE offset: 17 timestamp: [1589563313.974694285]
```

These utilities are useful and they can be used in scripts to control GPIO lines. For example, if you save:

```
while true
do
 gpioset -m time -s 1 0 4=0 17=1
 gpioset -m time -s 1 0 4=1 17=0
done
```

in a text file called binky.sh and set its execution permission to owner then you can run it in a console and flash a pair of LEDs connected to GPIO4 and GPIO17. Notice that if any of the GPIO lines are in use, the script will return an error message. You also need to keep in mind that the GPIO line is only in use while the gpioset command is running – that is, the line is opened at the start of the command and closed when it ends, so returning the line to input. For the Pi 5, remember to change gpiochip0 to gpiochip4.

You can get a long way with shell scripts and the GPIO utilities, but sooner or later you are going to want to work with C.

Installing The GPIOD Library

The GPIOD library is installed along with the tools discussed at the start of the chapter, but you don't have to use it if you are happy with the ioctl system calls described in the next chapter.

The library splits into two parts, the context-less functions and the lower-level functions, which can be considered context-using. In nearly all cases you will want to use the lower-level functions as the contextless functions have some serious drawbacks. Let's take a look at each in turn.

To use the library you need to install it if you haven't already done so:

```
sudo apt-get install gpiod libgpiod-dev libgpiod-doc
```

You also need to add the headers:

```
#define _GNU_SOURCE
#include <gpiod.h>
```

and you will need to load a library file.

If you are using VS Code you will need to edit settings.json to load the file:

```
{
    "sshUser": "pi",
    "sshEndpoint": "192.168.11.170",
    "remoteDirectory": "/home/pi/Documents/
                        ${workspaceFolderBasename}",
    "std": "c99",
    "libs":"-lgpiod",
    "header":""
}
```

adding "libs":"-lgpiod". By editing the settings.json file in the top-level folder, the setting will apply to all of the subfolders. If you don't want this to be the case, you need to look into VS Code Workspaces, which allow you to set individual settings in each folder.

If you see error messages in VS Code concerning the new header file, you can either ignore them or copy the ARM headers into a sub-folder using the copyARMheaders task. This copies all of the standard headers to a sub-folder called include on the local machine. Notice that this is only necessary to satisfy the local machine's error checking - the program will run on the remote machine without any problems as long as the header is available there.

If you want to do the same job on the command line, add the option:

```
-lgpiod
```

to the compiler command line.

Contextless Functions

The contextless functions all have ctxless in their names and they work by opening the necessary files, performing the operation and then closing them again. This means you don't have to keep track of what files are open and what GPIO lines are in use, but you have the overhead and side effects of repeatedly opening and closing files.

There are two simple get/set functions:

- gpiod_ctxless_get_value(*"device"*, *offset*, active_low, *"consumer"*);
- gpiod_ctxless_set_value(*"device"*, *offset*, value, active_low, *"consumer"*, callback, param)

where *device* is the name, path, number or label of the gpiochip, usually just 0, and *offset* is the GPIO number of the line you want to use, value is 0 or 1 according to whether you want the GPIO line set high or low, and active_low sets the state of the line regarded as active. If set to true, 1 sets the line low and vice versa. You usually want to set this to 0 so that 1 sets it high.

Replace *consumer* with the name of the program/user/entity using the GPIO line. The attributes callback and param work together to define a callback function and the parameters passed to it. The callback function is called immediately before the line is closed. The get version of the function returns the current state of the line as a 0 or 1 according to the line state and the setting of active_low.

As an example of using the contextless functions, simply toggle GPIO 4 as fast as possible:

```
#define _GNU_SOURCE
#include <gpiod.h>
#include <stdio.h>
#include <unistd.h>
#include <stdlib.h>
int res;
int main(int argc, char **argv) {
    for (;;) {
        res = gpiod_ctxless_set_value("0", 4, 1, 1,
                                "output test", NULL, NULL);
        res = gpiod_ctxless_set_value("0", 4, 0, 1,
                                "output test", NULL, NULL);
    }
}
```

If you run this program you will see reasonably equal pulses:

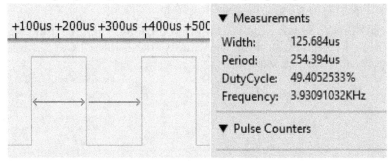

The trace is for a Pi Zero 2W and you can see that the pulses are $125\mu s$ wide. For a Pi 4 pulses are also $125\mu s$ wide. A Pi 5 has pulses that are $46\mu s$ wide.

To set the pulse width you have to use a callback function to delay the closing of the file:

```
#define _DEFAULT_SOURCE
#include <gpiod.h>
#include <stdio.h>
#include <unistd.h>
#include <stdlib.h>
#include <time.h>
int res;

int delayms(int ms) {
    struct timespec delay = {0, ms * 1000*1000};
    return nanosleep(&delay, NULL);
}

int main(int argc, char **argv) {

    for (;;) {
        res = gpiod_ctxless_set_value("0", 4, 1, 1, "output test",
                (gpiod_ctxless_set_value_cb) delayms, (void *) 100);
        res = gpiod_ctxless_set_value("0", 4, 0, 1, "output test",
                (gpiod_ctxless_set_value_cb) delayms, (void *) 100);
    }
}
```

Change "0" to "4" for the Pi 5. Notice that the final parameter isn't actually being used as a pointer, it is just a way of passing an untyped value and the parameter isn't dereferenced in the callback. This version of the program is more useful in that it does produce pulses of around 100ms. Also notice the wrapper for nanosleep because we can only pass a single parameter to the callback function. The first set makes the line go high and it stays high for the duration of the nanosleep and then the close operation resets it to input. The second set makes the line go low for the duration of the nanosleep and it stays low while the line is closed again. What this all means is that the time that the line is low is still longer than the nanosleep time because it includes the time to close and open the file.

You can see that the high time is around 100ms, but the low time is a little longer. You can either adjust the low timings or simply put up with it.

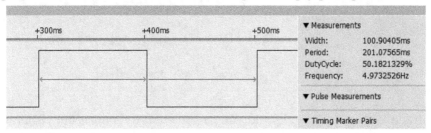

As well as single line get and set functions, there are also multiple line versions:

- gpiod_ctxless_set_value_multiple(*"device"*,offsets[], values[],num_lines,active_low, *"consumer"*,callback,param)
- gpiod_ctxless_get_value_multiple(*"device"*,offsets[], values[],num_lines,active_low, *"consumer"*,callback,param)

These work in the same way, but now you can specify a set of lines as an array of line structs and an array of values to get/set them to. Of course, you have to specify the number of lines and the arrays have to be the correct size. For example, to pulse two lines out of phase you could use:

```
#define _DEFAULT_SOURCE
#include <gpiod.h>
#include <stdio.h>
#include <unistd.h>
#include <stdlib.h>
#include <time.h>
int res;
int delayms(int ms)
{
    struct timespec delay = {0, ms * 1000 * 1000};
    return nanosleep(&delay, NULL);
}
int main(int argc, char **argv)
{
    int offsets[] = {4, 17};
    int state1[] = {1, 0};
    int state2[] = {0, 1};
    for (;;) {
    gpiod_ctxless_set_value_multiple("0", offsets, state1, 2, 1,
    "output test", (gpiod_ctxless_set_value_cb)delayms, (void *)1);
    gpiod_ctxless_set_value_multiple("0", offsets, state2, 2, 1,
    "output test", (gpiod_ctxless_set_value_cb)delayms, (void *)2);
    }
}
```

This pulses lines 4 and 17 so that one is high while the other is low. Even though the function promises to change the lines at the same moment, there is about a 10μs delay between changing the state of lines, as can be seen in the logic analyzer display below:

If you are working in milliseconds, a delay of 10μs probably isn't important, but it is still necessary to know that the lines do not all change together and there are situations in which this matters.

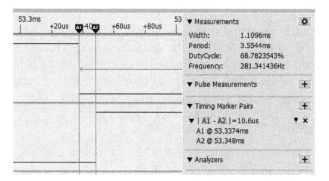

The context-less functions are rarely helpful and they are only slightly easier to use than the much more powerful context-using functions.

Context Functions

The only real difference in using the context functions is that you have to open the resources, use them and close them. This isn't difficult, it generally corresponds to what you actually want to do, and it follows the steps in using the ioctl system call directly as explained in the next chapter.

You have to:

1) Open the GPIO chip you want to use

2) Get the GPIO line or lines you want to use

3) Configure and use the lines

4) Close the GPIO chip

GPIO Chip

First you have to open the GPIO chip of your choice and there are various functions that allow you to specify the chip in different ways:

```
gpiod_chip_open("path")
gpiod_chip_open_by_name("name")
gpiod_chip_open_by_number(num)
gpiod_chip_open_by_label("label");
```

In each case NULL is returned if the open fails, otherwise a pointer is returned to a struct, gpiod_chip, which has the information about the chip. However, you are not given direct access to the fields of the struct as is the way in modern C apis. Instead there are a small number of access functions:

```
const char * name=gpiod_chip_name(chip)
const char * label=gpiod_chip_label(chip)
int number= gpiod_chip_num_lines(chip)
```

where chip is a pointer to struct gpiod_chip. Of course, when you are finished with the chip, you have to close it:

```
gpiod_chip_close(chip)
```

For example:

```
#define _GNU_SOURCE
#include <gpiod.h>
#include <stdio.h>
#include <unistd.h>
#include <stdlib.h>

int main(int argc, char **argv) {
    int res;
    struct gpiod_chip *chip = gpiod_chip_open_by_number(0);
    const char *name = gpiod_chip_name(chip);
    int num = gpiod_chip_num_lines(chip);
    printf("%s %d", name, num);
    gpiod_chip_close(chip);
}
```

This displays the name and number of lines supported by GPIO chip 0 (change to chip 4 for the Pi 5).

Getting Lines

The main purpose of getting a gpiod_chip struct is to get gpiod_line structs. There are different ways of doing this. First, there are two functions that return a pointer to a gpiod_line struct:

```
struct gpiod_line  *line = gpiod_chip_get_line(chip, offset)
struct gpiod_line  *line = gpiod_chip_find_line(chip,"name")
```

where chip is a pointer to struct gpiod_chip and the GPIO line is either specified by number or name.

You can also close the line:

```
void gpiod_line_release(struct gpiod_line *line);
```

There are also three functions that work with groups of GPIO lines:

* gpiod_chip_get_lines(chip, offsets[], num_offsets, bulk)
* gpiod_chip_find_lines(chip, names[], bulk)
* gpiod_chip_get_all_lines(chip, bulk)

All three functions return a pointer to a bulk struct which contains an array of gpiod_line structs.

The fields of the gpiod_line structs are hidden from you, but there are a range of access functions:

* int offset = gpiod_line_offset(line)
* const char *name = gpiod_line_name(line)
* const char *consumer = gpiod_line_consumer(line)
* int direction = gpiod_line_direction(line)
* int active_state = gpiod_line_active_state(line)
* bool used = gpiod_line_is_used(line)
* bool open_drain = gpiod_line_is_open_drain(line)
* bool open_source = gpiod_line_is_open_source(line)

where line is a pointer to a line struct.

There is also the small matter of whether a line is already in use. The old sysfs GPIO driver used export and unexport to reserve and release lines. The new driver simply reserves the line when you open it as a file or, using the GPIOD library, when you get the line from the GPIO chip, and unreserves it when you release it. Notice that many other Linux drivers use the GPIO driver to access lines and hence using a device via a driver might well reserve the GPIO lines it uses.

You can test to see if a line is free using:

```
bool gpiod_line_is_used(line)
```

which returns true if the line is in use. Notice that you cannot find out why a line is in use – it might be the operating system or another process. The only point is that you can only use a line when it isn't already in use. It could even be that the current process already has the line in use. You can check for this condition using:

```
bool gpiod_line_is_requested(struct gpiod_line *line)
```

If this returns true the current process has ownership of the line and can use it without getting it.

Using Lines

Once you have a struct gpiod_line you can use it to configure the line. There are two simple configuration functions:

- gpiod_line_request_input(line, "consumer")
- gpiod_line_request_output(line, "consumer", default_val)

where line is a pointer to struct gpiod_line and the second parameter assigns a label. For output, you can also set a default or initial value.

Once you have a line set to output you can set it using:

```
gpiod_line_set_value(line, value)
```

Once you have a line set to input you can read it using:

```
int value = gpiod_line_get_value(line)
```

For example, a simple program to toggle GPIO4 as fast as possible is:

```
#define _GNU_SOURCE
#include <gpiod.h>
#include <stdio.h>
#include <unistd.h>
#include <stdlib.h>

int main(int argc, char **argv) {
    int res;
    struct gpiod_chip *chip = gpiod_chip_open_by_number(0);
    struct gpiod_line *line4 = gpiod_chip_get_line(chip, 4);
    res=gpiod_line_request_output(line4, "test output", 0);

    for(;;){
        res=gpiod_line_set_value(line4,  1);
        res=gpiod_line_set_value(line4,  0);
    };
}
```

Remember to change the chip number to 4 if you are running this on a Pi 5.

The first part of the program opens the GPIO chip and retrieves GPIO 4 which is set to output. Finally the infinite loop simply toggles the line. Notice that you cannot close the GPIO chip and continue to use the line. You can close/release the line and continue to use the chip. There is also a combined line and chip close function:

```
gpiod_line_close_chip(line)
```

In this case we didn't close the lines or the chip for simplicity, but in principle you always should. It is only when the line is closed does its status change from used to unused and another process can make use of it. In nearly all cases, however, the line is closed when your program ends.

If you try the program, you will discover that the pulses produced are around $0.6\mu s$ to $0.8\mu s$ on Pi 4, and $2.0\mu s$ to $2.2\mu s$ on a Pi Zero which is similar in speed to using ioctl system calls directly, see the next chapter.

You can also configure a line in more detail using:

```
gpiod_line_request(line, config, default_val)
```

where config is a pointer to a gpiod_line_request_config struct:

```
struct gpiod_line_request_config {
        const char *consumer;
        int request_type;
        int flags;
};
```

The request_type is any of:

- GPIOD_LINE_REQUEST_DIRECTION_AS_IS
- GPIOD_LINE_REQUEST_DIRECTION_INPUT
- GPIOD_LINE_REQUEST_DIRECTION_OUTPUT
- GPIOD_LINE_REQUEST_EVENT_FALLING_EDGE
- GPIOD_LINE_REQUEST_EVENT_RISING_EDGE
- GPIOD_LINE_REQUEST_EVENT_BOTH_EDGES

The event requests are discussed in more detail later and flags are:

- GPIOD_LINE_REQUEST_FLAG_OPEN_DRAIN
- GPIOD_LINE_REQUEST_FLAG_OPEN_SOURCE
- GPIOD_LINE_REQUEST_FLAG_ACTIVE_LOW

A future version of the library will also support:

- GPIOD_LINE_REQUEST_FLAG_BIAS_DISABLE
- GPIOD_LINE_REQUEST_FLAG_BIAS_PULL_DOWN
- GPIOD_LINE_REQUEST_FLAG_BIAS_PULL_UP

You will also find a set of functions which perform a request using only flags and a preset request type. Essentially these are just shortcuts that mean you don't have to fill in a gpiod_line_request_config struct:

```
gpiod_line_request_input(struct gpiod_line *line,
                                const char *consumer);
gpiod_line_request_output(struct gpiod_line *line,
                        const char *consumer, int default_val);
gpiod_line_request_rising_edge_events(struct gpiod_line *line,
                                const char *consumer);
gpiod_line_request_falling_edge_events(struct gpiod_line *line,
                                const char *consumer);
gpiod_line_request_both_edges_events(struct gpiod_line *line,
                                const char *consumer);
```

There are also a set of functions that do the same thing, but let you set the flags as well. Again, the only advantage is not having to create a gpiod_line_request_config struct:

```
int gpiod_line_request_input_flags(struct gpiod_line *line,
                               const char *consumer, int flags);
int gpiod_line_request_output_flags(struct gpiod_line *line,
                     const char *consumer, int flags,int default_val);
int gpiod_line_request_rising_edge_events_flags(
           truct gpiod_line *line,const char *consumer,int flags);
int gpiod_line_request_falling_edge_events_flags(
           struct gpiod_line *line,const char *consumer,int flags);
int gpiod_line_request_both_edges_events_flags(
           struct gpiod_line *line,const char *consumer,int flags);
```

Working With More Than One Line

There are also "bulk" versions of the line functions which work with a set of lines at one time. The key to understanding these is the gpiod_line_bulk struct:

```
struct gpiod_line_bulk {
      struct gpiod_line *lines[GPIOD_LINE_BULK_MAX_LINES];
      unsigned int num_lines;
};
```

This is essentially an array of gpiod_line structs with the number of lines in use recorded in a separate field. Again a set of functions are provided to let you work with the struct:

```
gpiod_line_bulk_init(struct gpiod_line_bulk *bulk)
gpiod_line_bulk_add(struct gpiod_line_bulk *bulk,
                                      struct gpiod_line * line)
gpiod_line* gpiod_line_bulk_get_line(struct gpiod_line_bulk *bulk,
                                         unsigned int offset)
unsigned int gpiod_line_bulk_num_lines(
                                struct gpiod_line_bulk *bulk)
```

You can use these to initialize, add and retrieve line structs from the bulk struct. There is a general initialization function:

```
int gpiod_line_request_bulk(struct gpiod_line_bulk *bulk,
          const struct gpiod_line_request_config *config,
                             const int *default_vals);
```

This configures each line according to the array of config structs and, for output, sets the initial values to the elements of the default_vals array.

As in the case of a single line, there are functions that set all of the lines to a particular configuration:

```
int gpiod_line_request_bulk_input(
        struct gpiod_line_bulk *bulk,const char *consumer);
int gpiod_line_request_bulk_output(
        struct gpiod_line_bulk *bulk,const char *consumer,
                                    const int *default_vals);
int gpiod_line_request_bulk_rising_edge_events(
        struct gpiod_line_bulk *bulk,const char *consumer);
int gpiod_line_request_bulk_falling_edge_events(
        struct gpiod_line_bulk *bulk,const char *consumer);
int gpiod_line_request_bulk_both_edges_events(
        struct gpiod_line_bulk *bulk,const char *consumer);
```

Likewise, there are extended functions that let you also set the flags:

```
int gpiod_line_request_bulk_input_flags(
    struct gpiod_line_bulk *bulk,const char *consumer,int flags);
int gpiod_line_request_bulk_output_flags(
    struct gpiod_line_bulk *bulk,const char *consumer,
                            int flags,const int *default_vals);
int gpiod_line_request_bulk_rising_edge_events_flags(
    struct gpiod_line_bulk *bulk,const char *consumer,int flags);
int gpiod_line_request_bulk_falling_edge_events_flags(
    struct gpiod_line_bulk *bulk,const char *consumer,int flags);
int gpiod_line_request_bulk_both_edges_events_flags(
    struct gpiod_line_bulk *bulk,const char *consumer,int flags);
```

If you use any of these functions, all of the lines in the gpiod_line_bulk array are set to the same configuration.

There is also a function what will close all of the lines that you have been working with:

```
void gpiod_line_release_bulk(struct gpiod_line_bulk *bulk);
```

Once you have set up the bulk lines you can get and set them:

```
int gpiod_line_get_value_bulk(struct gpiod_line_bulk *bulk,
                                            int *values);
```

```
int gpiod_line_set_value_bulk(struct gpiod_line_bulk *bulk,
                                    const int *values);
```

For the get function the values array is set to the state of all of the lines, including output lines and for the set function the values array is written to the lines.

How these functions all work is easy to understand after you see an example. In this case the program pulses two lines that are out of phase:

```
#define _GNU_SOURCE
#include <gpiod.h>
#include <stdio.h>
#include <unistd.h>
#include <stdlib.h>

int main(int argc, char **argv) {
    int res;
    struct gpiod_chip *chip = gpiod_chip_open_by_number(0);

    struct gpiod_line_bulk bulk;
    gpiod_line_bulk_init(&bulk);
    gpiod_line_bulk_add(&bulk, gpiod_chip_get_line(chip, 4));
    gpiod_line_bulk_add(&bulk, gpiod_chip_get_line(chip, 17));

    res=gpiod_line_request_bulk_output(&bulk, "test", 0);
    for (;;) {
        gpiod_line_set_value_bulk(&bulk,(int[2]){0,1});
        gpiod_line_set_value_bulk(&bulk,(int[2]){1,0});

    };
}
```

Remember to use gpiochip4 in place of gpioghip0 if you are running this on a Pi 5.

The new steps are the creation of a gpio_line_bulk struct and the use of gpiod_line_bulk_add to add lines to it. Once we have the gpio_line_bulk struct set up, the gpiod_line_request_bulk_output is called to set the lines to output and finally the loop sets the lines to different values. The use of an array literal in the gpiod_line_set_value_bulk call only works in C99 and later. In earlier versions of C you need to create two separate arrays.

Overall, the GPIOD library isn't a huge advance over using the raw ioctl calls. Use whichever approach you prefer. In Chapter 6 we will look at some of the interrupt-like features that the GPIO driver provides.

Using GPIO Lines – Measuring R and C

There is a simple way to measure either the resistance of a circuit or its capacitance. The idea is to set up a circuit with a capacitor and a resistor in series and a GPIO line:

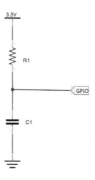

When the GPIO line is set to input the capacitor charges via R1 and eventually reaches 3.3V. In this state, the GPIO line reads the state as a high, i.e. a 1. If the GPIO line changes to an output and is set low, the capacitor discharges to 0V. The current through the GPIO line settles to 3.3/R1 and this should be less than 3mA, although the current when the capacitor first discharges will be much greater, it only flows for a short time. When the GPIO line reverts to input, the capacitor starts to charge again through the resistor R1. Eventually the capacitor reaches a high enough voltage for the GPIO line to read 1. The time it takes to read 1 is proportional to R1C1 and hence, if C1 is fixed, you can use the time to work out R1. If R1 is fixed, you can use the time to work out C1. You can see that you can use time-to-charge to measure either the resistance or the capacitance. Any sensor that varies its resistance or capacitance in response to external conditions can be used with this arrangement. For example, a thermistor, a temperature-dependent resistor, and can be read and so can an LDR, a very common light-sensitive resistor.

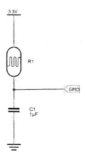

You can create a presence sensor by using a metal plate as one side of a capacitor. As people move closer, or further way, its capacitance changes. It is also possible to measure soil moisture content by measuring the resistance, or the capacitance, of two soil probes as both vary according to water content.

Using GPIOD functions it is easy to create a program that measures resistance or capacitance:

```
#define _GNU_SOURCE
#include <gpiod.h>
#include <stdio.h>
#include <unistd.h>
#include <stdlib.h>
#include <time.h>

int main(int argc, char **argv)
{
    int res;
    struct timespec delay = {0, 10 * 1000 * 1000};
    struct timespec time1, time2;

    struct gpiod_chip *chip = gpiod_chip_open_by_number(0);
    struct gpiod_line *line4 = gpiod_chip_get_line(chip, 4);

    res = gpiod_line_request_input(line4, "RMeasure");
    nanosleep(&delay, NULL);
    gpiod_line_release(line4);

    res = gpiod_line_request_output(line4, "RMeasure", 0);
    nanosleep(&delay, NULL);
    gpiod_line_release(line4);

    clock_gettime(CLOCK_REALTIME, &time1);
    gpiod_line_request_input(line4, "RMeasure");
    while (gpiod_line_get_value(line4) == 0)
    {
    };
    clock_gettime(CLOCK_REALTIME, &time2);
    printf("Time=%d", (time2.tv_nsec - time1.tv_nsec) / 1000);
}
```

The program starts by setting up the GPIO chip on GPIO 4. Remember to change the GPIO chip from 0 to 4 for the Pi 5. Next we set the line to input and wait 10ms for things to settle. The line is then released and opened as an output set to 0. Again we wait 10ms for things to settle and then release the line again and set it to input. The time is recorded and we now wait till the line reads 1 and take the time again. The difference between the two times is the value we need.

If you try this out you will find the measurement is fairly noisy. This is probably due to the slow charging of the capacitor which causes the input to bounce:

Exactly when reading the line returns a 1 is a matter of chance. If you want to increase the accuracy, you could take ten or more measurements and average them.

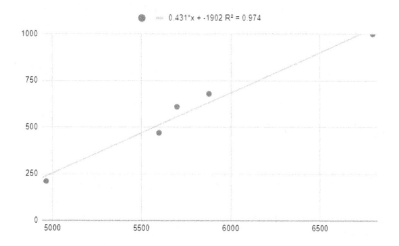

Typical result of measurements of 200K 1000kΩ resistor using a 1μF capacitor – resistance in ohms along the y-axis and time in ms on the x-axis.

If you want to use this approach, you can easily package the code into an easy-to-use function.

Summary

- The GPIO character driver replaces the sysfs GPIO driver and it is the one to use for all future projects.

- The GPIOD library provides a higher level way of using the GPIO character driver, but if you don't want the overhead of using it then the direct ioctl interface is easy to use.

- After the library has been installed there are a number of utilities that are sometimes useful at the command line or in scripts.

- The library has two types of function, context-less and context-using. The contextless functions can be used in an ad-hoc fashion, but the context-using functions have to be used in an organized manner.

- The contextless functions set GPIO lines to input or output without opening them or reserving them in any way. This makes them slow and you need to use callback functions to control their output.

- The context-using functions require you to open the GPIO line and configure it before you use it. Once used you have to close the line to allow another process to make use of it.

- Context-using functions are not difficult to use and are much more flexible and fast.

- You can work with multiple GPIO lines in a single function call. However, there are still delays between setting lines to particular values.

- The context-using functions can create pulses as fast as $1\mu s$ to $2.0\mu s$.

- Using time-to-charge you can measure either the resistance or the capacitance of a circuit using a single GPIO line.

Chapter 5

GPIO Using I/O Control

The GPIOD library is fairly easy to use but so is the underlying ioctl, input/output control, interface. The main reasons for wanting to use it is that it is slightly faster and slightly more efficient in that you don't need to load a library. There is also the benefit of working directly with the ioctl driver and understanding what is going on.

Raw GPIO Character Device In C

You don't need anything special to work with a character device. All you need is the standard ioctl system call and for this you simply need to add:

```
#include <sys/ioctl.h>
```

The call varies according to the device it is being used with. Its general form is:

```
ioctl(fd, request, pstruct)
```

where `fd` is a file descriptor that returns the device being used and `request` is an unsigned long variable that specifies the request or operation to be performed. The third parameter is usually a pointer to a struct or an area of memory. Some ioctl calls have additional parameters.

The request number was never formalized and driver writers tended to invent their own, but there was an impromptu move to apply an organization and many request numbers follow a regular pattern. The most recent scheme uses two direction bits (`00`: none, `01`: write, `10`: read, `11`: read/write) followed by 14 size bits (giving the size of the argument), followed by an 8-bit type (collecting the ioctls in groups for a common purpose or a common driver), and an 8-bit serial number. A set of macros is provided so that the request number can be built up from its parts:

```
_IOR(type,nr,size)
_IOW(type,nr,size)
_IOWR(type,nr,size)
_IO(type,nr)
```

These are optional in that, if you know the request number, you can simply use it in the ioctl call.

The GPIO character device works entirely in terms of the ioctl system call – not by reading or writing the files. What you need to know to use the driver directly are the request codes and the structures that are passed. These are all defined in the gpio.h header:

```
#include <linux/gpio.h>
```

Working with the GPIO chip and the GPIO lines follows the same standard steps:

1. Find the request constant you need to use
2. Find the struct that is used with that constant
3. Open the appropriate file
4. Make an ioctl call using the constant and the struct.

Getting Chip Info

As a first simple example, let's get some information about the GPIO chip. If you look through the header file you will find:

```
GPIO_GET_CHIPINFO_IOCTL
```

which is the request constant. You will also find:

```
struct gpiochip_info {
        char name[32];
        char label[32];
        __u32 lines;
};
```

which is used to hold information about the GPIO chip.

With this information we can open the file and make the ioctl call:

```
#include <stdio.h>
#include <errno.h>
#include <unistd.h>
#include <fcntl.h>
#include <sys/ioctl.h>
#include <linux/gpio.h>
int main(int argc, char **argv) {
    int fd;
    struct gpiochip_info info;
    fd = open("/dev/gpiochip0", O_RDONLY);
    int ret = ioctl(fd, GPIO_GET_CHIPINFO_IOCTL, &info);
    close(fd);
    printf("label: %s\n name: %s\n number of lines: %u\n",
                            info.label,info.name,info.lines);
    return 0;
}
```

As with all good, easy-to-understand examples, error handling has been omitted. If you run this program you will see something like :

```
label: pinctrl-bcm2835
name: gpiochip0
number of lines: 54
```

If you run this on a Pi 5 change gpiochip0 to gpiochip4.

GPIO Output

The next step is to set a GPIO line to output and use it. This involves only a few more ideas than the previous example. We need to go through the same steps, but in this case we first use the GPIO chip to make a GPIO handler device. This represents multiple GPIO lines, i.e. you can work with a group of lines, not just one line at a time. This is a two-stage process. First get the GPIO chip and then ask it to configure the GPIO lines and return a new file descriptor to the GPIO lines. The request constant for setting a line to a particular state and returning a new file descriptor that references the set line is:

GPIO_GET_LINEHANDLE_IOCTL

The appropriate struct is:

```
struct gpiohandle_request {
        __u32 lineoffsets[GPIOHANDLES_MAX];
        __u32 flags;
        __u8 default_values[GPIOHANDLES_MAX];
        char consumer_label[32];
        __u32 lines;
        int fd;
};
```

This has to be initialized to sensible values before the ioctl call. The lineoffsets array is simply a list of GPIO line numbers that you want to set.

The flags field is one of:

- GPIOHANDLE_REQUEST_OUTPUT
- GPIOHANDLE_REQUEST_INPUT
- GPIOHANDLE_REQUEST_ACTIVE_LOW
- GPIOHANDLE_REQUEST_OPEN_DRAIN
- GPIOHANDLE_REQUEST_OPEN_SOURCE

All of the lines specified in lineoffsets are set to the same state. Notice that you can OR the flags together where this makes sense, for example to request an active low output with an open drain. Two additional flags will be made available in the future:

- GPIOHANDLE_REQUEST_PULL_UP
- GPIOHANDLE_REQUEST_PULL_DOWN

The default_values array sets output lines to high or low, depending on whether you store 1 or 0 in each element.

The consumer_label assigns a label to each of the lines, which can be retrieved using a GPIO_GET_LINEINFO_IOCTL request and the struct:

```
struct gpioline_info {
        __u32 line_offset;
        __u32 flags;
        char name[32];
        char consumer[32];
};
```

Finally the lines field determines the number of lines being used, i.e. the number of elements of the lineoffsets array that contain meaningful data. The final fd field is used to return a file descriptor for the lines.

Now we are ready to write the program. First we set up the gpiohandle_request struct:

```
struct gpiohandle_request req;
req.lineoffsets[0] = 4;
req.lineoffsets[1] = 17;
req.flags = GPIOHANDLE_REQUEST_OUTPUT;
req.default_values[0] = 0;
req.default_values[1] = 0;
strcpy(req.consumer_label, "Output test");
req.lines = 2;
```

You can see that we are using GPIO4 and GPIO17 and setting both to output. They are also both set to start at 0 and are labeled Output test.

To actually set up these lines and get a file descriptor to them we need to call ioctl():

```
fd = open("/dev/gpiochip0", O_RDONLY);
ret = ioctl(fd, GPIO_GET_LINEHANDLE_IOCTL, &req);
close(fd);
```

Again, no error checking is included. Notice that we can close the GPIO chip as we now have the file descriptor to the lines that have been set up. Opening the line returns a file descriptor in the gpiohandle_request struct – in this case req.fd. You don't export or unexport a line, but you have ownership of the line until you close the file:

```
close(req.fd);
```

Notice that you have to close the file if you want to open the line in a different configuration.

Now we have the lines set up as outputs, we can use the request:

```
GPIOHANDLE_SET_LINE_VALUES_IOCTL
```

to set the line states.

It should come as no surprise that there is also a corresponding GET request and both use the struct:

```
struct gpiohandle_data {
        __u8 values[GPIOHANDLES_MAX];
};
```

When you use SET the values array specifies what the lines should be set to. When you use GET the values returned are the states of the lines.

Now we can write a loop that toggles the GPIO lines we have set up:

```
struct gpiohandle_data data;
data.values[0] = 0;
data.values[1] = 1;
while (1) {
  data.values[0] = !data.values[0];
  data.values[1] = !data.values[1];
  ret = ioctl(req.fd, GPIOHANDLE_SET_LINE_VALUES_IOCTL, &data);
}
```

Again, error handling has been ignored for the sake of simplicity.

Putting all this together gives:

```
#include <string.h>
#include <stdio.h>
#include <errno.h>
#include <unistd.h>
#include <fcntl.h>
#include <sys/ioctl.h>
#include <linux/gpio.h>

int main(int argc, char **argv) {
    int fd, ret;

    struct gpiohandle_request req;
    req.lineoffsets[0] = 4;
    req.lineoffsets[1] = 17;
    req.flags = GPIOHANDLE_REQUEST_OUTPUT;
    req.default_values[0] = 0;
    req.default_values[1] = 0;
    strcpy(req.consumer_label, "Output test");
    req.lines = 2;

    fd = open("/dev/gpiochip0", O_RDONLY);
    ret = ioctl(fd, GPIO_GET_LINEHANDLE_IOCTL, &req);
    close(fd);

    struct gpiohandle_data data;
    data.values[0] = 0;
    data.values[1] = 1;
    while (1) {
        data.values[0] = !data.values[0];
        data.values[1] = !data.values[1];
        ret = ioctl(req.fd, GPIOHANDLE_SET_LINE_VALUES_IOCTL,
                                              &data);

    }
    return 0;
}
```

Remember to change gpiochip0 to gpiochip4 if you are running on a Pi 5.

If you try this out on a Pi Zero you will find that the pulses are faster than you might expect – pulse width 1.5μs giving a frequency of 325kHz. Notice that the switching of the two lines is not in sync. There is a 135ns lag between switching each line. On a Pi 4 the pulse is 0.64μs and 766kHz with a lag of 75ns. On a Pi 5 the pulse is 0.92μs and 540kHz with a lag of around 50ns.

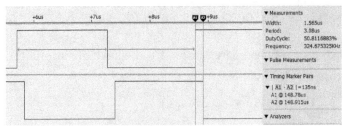

These figures should be compared to the performance of the obsolete sysfs approach, which produced 130kHz and a pulse width of 3.6μs on a Pi Zero and 450kHz and 1.1μs on a Pi 4, i.e. the new system is roughly twice as fast as sysfs. However, compared to using the hardware directly from C, when the Pi Zero pulses at about 70ns and Pi 4 pulses around 75ns, it is more than ten times slower.

GPIO Input

Reading data from GPIO lines follow the same steps as writing, but with obvious changes:

```
#include <string.h>
#include <stdio.h>
#include <errno.h>
#include <unistd.h>
#include <fcntl.h>
#include <sys/ioctl.h>
#include <linux/gpio.h>
int main(int argc, char **argv) {
    int fd, ret;
    struct gpiohandle_request req;
    req.lineoffsets[0] = 4;
    req.lineoffsets[1] = 17;
    req.flags = GPIOHANDLE_REQUEST_INPUT;
    strcpy(req.consumer_label, "Input test");
    req.lines = 2;
    fd = open("/dev/gpiochip0", O_RDONLY);
    ret = ioctl(fd, GPIO_GET_LINEHANDLE_IOCTL, &req);
    close(fd);
    struct gpiohandle_data data;
    ret = ioctl(req.fd, GPIOHANDLE_GET_LINE_VALUES_IOCTL, &data);
    printf("%hhu , %hhu",data.values[0],data.values[1]);
    close(req.fd);
    return 0;
}
```

Remember to change `gpiochip0` to `gpiochip4` if you are running on a Pi 5. You can see that now the request is to set an input line and the reading part of the program uses the GET and then displays the values in the data structure.

Measuring R and C Using I/O Control

The use of a gpio line to measure the time a capacitor took to charge implemented at the end of the previous chapter using GPIOD is easy to implement using nothing but ioctl calls.

Using ioctl calls it is easy to create a program that measures resistance or capacitance:

```
#define _GNU_SOURCE
#include <string.h>
#include <stdio.h>
#include <errno.h>
#include <unistd.h>
#include <fcntl.h>
#include <linux/gpio.h>
#include <sys/ioctl.h>
#include <time.h>
int main(int argc, char **argv){
    int fd, ret;
    struct timespec delay = {0, 10 * 1000 * 1000};
    struct timespec time1, time2;
    fd = open("/dev/gpiochip0", O_RDONLY);
    struct gpiohandle_request req;
    req.lineoffsets[0] = 4;
    strcpy(req.consumer_label, "RC Measure");
    req.lines = 1;

    req.flags = GPIOHANDLE_REQUEST_INPUT;
    ret = ioctl(fd, GPIO_GET_LINEHANDLE_IOCTL, &req);
    nanosleep(&delay, NULL);
    close(req.fd);

    req.flags = GPIOHANDLE_REQUEST_OUTPUT;
    struct gpiohandle_data data;
    data.values[0] = 0;
    ret = ioctl(fd, GPIO_GET_LINEHANDLE_IOCTL, &req);
    ret = ioctl(req.fd, GPIOHANDLE_SET_LINE_VALUES_IOCTL, &data);
    nanosleep(&delay, NULL);
    close(req.fd);

    req.flags = GPIOHANDLE_REQUEST_INPUT;
    clock_gettime(CLOCK_REALTIME,&time1);
    ret = ioctl(fd, GPIO_GET_LINEHANDLE_IOCTL, &req);
    ret = ioctl(req.fd, GPIOHANDLE_GET_LINE_VALUES_IOCTL, &data);
```

```
while (data.values[0] == 0){
    ret = ioctl(req.fd, GPIOHANDLE_GET_LINE_VALUES_IOCTL,
                                                    &data)
}
clock_gettime(CLOCK_REALTIME,&time2);
printf("Time=%d",(time2.tv_nsec-time1.tv_nsec)/1000);
return 0;
}
```

Remember to change gpiochip0 to gpiochip4 if you are running on a Pi 5. The program opens the GPIO chip and uses its file descriptor to open GPIO4 for input. After 10ms it closes the line and opens it again for output and sets it to zero. After 10ms it closes the line and reopens it for input. It then reads the line waiting for it to go to 1. The times are taken and used to calculate the recharge time for the capacitor.

Note: If you are using VS Code you may see header errors – these are due to IntelliSense not being able to find a header file on the local machine. The program will run perfectly on the remote machine.

Summary

- The raw GPIO character driver is easy to use once you know the ioctl operations supported and their structs.

- The big problem with using ioctl is finding out the request numbers to use for any particular driver. Despite attempts to organize the allocation of values, this hasn't really worked.

- The GPIO lines have to remain open while you use them and you need to remember to close them when you have finished using them.

- You can set and read multiple GPIO lines in a single function call.

- The GPIO character driver is about twice as fast as the deprecated sysfs-based interface, but still ten times slower than direct access.

Chapter 6
GPIO Events

The new GPIO character driver supports events and this is perhaps its biggest advantage over older and competing methods of working with the GPIO lines. Using it you can respond to events well after they have happened and determine the time they occurred more accurately than using a polling loop.

Something you quickly discover in an IoT, or any electronics-related context, is that output is easy but input is difficult. The reason is that when working with output your program determines when something will happen. You can pulse a line every second by arranging for your program to do something every second using a timer. Input is quite different – when things happen is completely out of your control. When a line is set high all you can do is read its state as frequently as possible in an attempt to determine when it made the transition from low to high. The straightforward way of doing this is to set up a polling loop and test the line's state periodically. The problem with this approach is ensuring that the polling loop tests the line often enough and this becomes increasingly difficult as the other work the loop has to do increases.

The polling loop is a perfectly valid way to approach the input problem and it has the advantage of changing the problem from asynchronous to synchronous – your program determines when the input will be read. There are two important alternatives to the polling loop – events and interrupts. Many IoT programmers are convinced that interrupts are a really good idea. However, they are really only applicable to situations where things happen infrequently, but need to be dealt with quickly – low frequency/low latency - and exactly what these terms mean varies according to the situation. In general, low frequency means a rate of occurring that gives time for the action needed to be completed before it happens again.

As interrupts are not available to user mode programs, the GPIO character drivers implements a system of events, which if used carefully is more useful than an interrupt.

Events

An event is like a latch or a memory that something happened. Imagine that there is a flag that will be automatically set when an input line changes state. The flag is set without the involvement of software, or at least any software that you have control over. It is useful to imagine an entirely hardware-based setting of the flag, even if this is not always the case. With the help of an event, you can avoid missing an input because the polling loop was busy doing something else. Now the polling loop can read the state of the flag, rather than the actual state of the input line, and hence it can detect if the line has changed since it was last polled. The polling loop resets the event flag and processes the event. You can even arrange for the flag to store the time that the event happened and so increase the resolution of the polling loop.

A simple event can avoid the loss of a single input, but what if there is more than one input while the polling loop is unavailable? The most common solution is to create an event queue – that is, a FIFO (first in, first out) queue of events as they occur. The polling loop now reads the event at the front of the queue, processes it and reads the next. It continues like this until the queue is empty, when it simply waits for an event. As long as the queue is big enough, an event queue means you don't miss any input, but input events are not necessarily processed close to the time that they occurred.

Interrupts Considered Harmful?

As user mode Linux programs have no access to interrupts, this is an important but academic discussion as far as most Linux IoT programs are concerned.

Interrupts are often confused with events, but they are very different. An interrupt is a hardware mechanism that stops the computer doing whatever it is currently doing and makes it transfer its attention to running an interrupt handler. You can think of an interrupt as an event flag that, when it is set, interrupts the current program to run the assigned interrupt handler.

Using interrupts means the outside world decides when the computer should pay attention to input and there is no need for a polling loop. Most hardware people think that interrupts are the solution to everything and polling is inelegant and only to be used when you can't use an interrupt. This is far from the reality.

There is a general feeling that real-time programming and interrupts go together and if you are not using an interrupt you are probably doing something wrong. The truth is that if you are using an interrupt you are probably doing something wrong. Indeed, some organizations are convinced that interrupts are so dangerous that they are banned from being used at all.

Interrupts are only really useful when you have a low frequency condition that needs to be dealt with on a high-priority basis. Interrupts can simplify the logic of your program, but rarely does using an interrupt speed things up because the overhead involved in interrupt handling is usually quite high.

If you have a polling loop that takes 100ms to poll all inputs and there is an input that demands attention in under 60ms, then clearly the polling loop is not going to be good enough. Using an interrupt allows the high-priority event to interrupt the polling loop and be processed in less than 100ms. However, if this happens very often the polling loop will cease to work as intended. Notice an alternative is to simply make the polling loop check the input twice per loop.

For a more real-world example, suppose you want to react to a doorbell push button. You could write a polling loop that simply checks the button status repeatedly and forever or you could write an interrupt service routine (ISR) to respond to the doorbell. The processor would be free to get on with other things until the doorbell was pushed, when it would stop what it was doing and transfer its attention to the ISR.

How good a design this is depends on how much the doorbell has to interact with the rest of the program and how many doorbell pushes you are expecting. It takes time to respond to the doorbell push and then the ISR has to run to completion. What is going to happen if another doorbell push happens while the first push is still being processed? Some processors have provision for forming a queue of interrupts, but it doesn't help with the fact that the process can only handle one interrupt at a time.

Despite their attraction, interrupts are usually a poor choice for anything other than low-frequency events that need to be dealt with quickly.

Events and the GPIOD Library

The GPIOD library provides a set of functions that wrap the lower-level interrupt handling provided by the GPIO character driver. These are marginally slower than using the ioctl system call directly, but they are slightly easier to use. There are two possible event types, rising or falling edge, and you can set a line to work with either or both.

You can set a line to respond to events using:

```
gpiod_line_request(line, config, default_val)
```

where config is a pointer to a gpiod_line_request_config struct:

```
struct gpiod_line_request_config {
        const char *consumer;
        int request_type;
        int flags;
};
```

The `request_type` is any of:

- GPIOD_LINE_REQUEST_EVENT_FALLING_EDGE
- GPIOD_LINE_REQUEST_EVENT_RISING_EDGE
- GPIOD_LINE_REQUEST_EVENT_BOTH_EDGES

Each of these implies that the line is set to input. You can set pull-ups using the flags in the usual way.

There are also functions that will set event handling without needing a `gpiod_line_request_config` struct and a set of bulk functions, see Chapter 4 for a full list.

Once you have set a line to respond to events, there are some basic functions that let you handle the event:

```
gpiod_line_event_wait(line,timeout)
gpiod_line_event_wait_bulk(bulk,timeout, event_bulk)
gpiod_line_event_read(line, event)
```

where `gpiod_line_event_wait` and `gpiod_line_event_wait_bulk` wait for a single line to generate an event or a set of lines. The parameters are:

- line   Pointer to a `gpiod_line` struct
- event   Pointer to a `gpiod_line_event` struct
- timeout   Pointer to a `timespec` struct
- bulk   Pointer to a `gpiod_line_bulk` struct
- event_bulk   Pointer to a second `gpiod_line_bulk` struct which holds the details of the lines that generated an event.

The `gpiod_line_event_read` function blocks until an event occurs and returns it in event, a pointer to a `gpiod_line_event` struct:

```
struct gpiod_line_event {
     struct timespec ts;
     int event_type;
};
```

Notice that this mechanism really does use an interrupt generated by the GPIO line which is handled by the kernel. For this to work, you have to make sure that the line:

```
dtoverlay=gpio-no-irq
```

isn't present in, or is commented out of, the /boot/config.txt file. The no-irq state was the default until recently and was changed to accommodate the event handling of the GPIOD library.

The simplest event program is:

```
#define _GNU_SOURCE
#include <gpiod.h>
#include <stdio.h>
#include <unistd.h>
#include <stdlib.h>

int main(int argc, char **argv) {
    int res;
    struct gpiod_chip *chip = gpiod_chip_open_by_number(0);
    struct gpiod_line *line4 = gpiod_chip_get_line(chip, 4);
    gpiod_line_request_both_edges_events(line4, "event test");
    gpiod_line_event_wait(line4, NULL);
    printf("Event on line 4");
}
```

Remember to change gpiochip0 to gpiochip4 if you are running on a Pi 5.

This waits until an event, a rising or falling edge, occurs on GPIO4 and then prints a message. If you want details of the event, you can use a gpiod_line_event_read, which blocks until there is some event data to read:

```
struct gpiod_line_event event;
gpiod_line_event_read(line4, &event);
printf("Event on line 4 %d,%d", event.event_type,event.ts.tv_nsec);
```

You can also read multiple events from the line, which have happened since the last read.

```
int gpiod_line_event_read_multiple(struct gpiod_line *line,
        struct gpiod_line_event *events,unsigned int num_events)
```

You have to state the maximum number of items to read and you have to make sure that the gpiod_line_event struct array has enough elements. The system uses a 16-event ring buffer so if more events than this occur the earliest events are lost. You can also only read a maximum of 16 events at a time. This will block until there is at least one event to read.

Measuring R and C Using Events

To discover how events can improve the accuracy of a program, we can revisit the R/C measuring example first introduced at the end of Chapter 4. The first part of the program is as before. We open the GPIO chip and GPIO4. Next we set GPIO4 to input and wait 100ms for things to settle and then set it to output with a value of zero and after a 100ms delay the line is released. This is where the program differs. Instead of polling the line waiting for a 1, we simply set a rising edge event and wait for it to occur. When it happens the read returns with the time it occurred.

An event driven program is:

```
#define _GNU_SOURCE
#include <gpiod.h>
#include <stdio.h>
#include <unistd.h>
#include <stdlib.h>
#include <time.h>

void gpiod_line_release(struct gpiod_line *line);
int main(int argc, char **argv)
{
  int res;

  struct timespec delay = {0, 10 * 1000 * 1000};
  struct timespec time1;

  struct gpiod_chip *chip = gpiod_chip_open_by_number(0);
  struct gpiod_line *line4 = gpiod_chip_get_line(chip, 4);

  res = gpiod_line_request_input(line4, "RMeasure");
  nanosleep(&delay, NULL);
  gpiod_line_release(line4);

  res = gpiod_line_request_output(line4, "RMeasure", 0);
  nanosleep(&delay, NULL);
  gpiod_line_release(line4);
  clock_gettime(CLOCK_REALTIME, &time1);

  gpiod_line_request_rising_edge_events(line4, "RMeasuret");
  struct gpiod_line_event event;
  gpiod_line_event_read(line4, &event);
  printf("Event on line 4 %d, %d", event.event_type,
                  (event.ts.tv_nsec-time1.tv_nsec)/1000);
}
```

Remember to change gpiochip0 to gpiochip4 if you are running on a Pi 5.

As the read is waiting for the first transition from 0 to 1, the timing is more accurate and not dependent on when the timing loop decides to read the line.

Measuring Pulses With Events

Now we have all of the functions we need to implement a pulse measurement program using events, we can measure the width of any pulse as the distance between a rising and a falling edge or a falling and a rising edge. We need to make sure that we have a rising edge by waiting for one:

```
do{
    res = gpiod_line_event_read(line4, &event);
  } while (event.event_type != GPIOD_LINE_EVENT_RISING_EDGE);
```

84

We then record the time of the event and wait for a falling edge:

```
do{
    res = gpiod_line_event_read(line4, &event);
  } while (event.event_type != GPIOD_LINE_EVENT_FALLING_EDGE);
```

and use both times to compute the pulse width.

The complete program is:

```
#define _GNU_SOURCE
#include <gpiod.h>
#include <stdio.h>
#include <unistd.h>
#include <stdlib.h>
#include <time.h>

void gpiod_line_release(struct gpiod_line *line);
int main(int argc, char **argv)
{
  int res;
  struct timespec time1;
  struct gpiod_chip *chip = gpiod_chip_open_by_number(0);
  struct gpiod_line *line4 = gpiod_chip_get_line(chip, 4);
  res = gpiod_line_request_both_edges_events(line4, "Measure");
  struct gpiod_line_event event;
  while (true)
  {
    do
    {
      res = gpiod_line_event_read(line4, &event);
    } while (event.event_type != GPIOD_LINE_EVENT_RISING_EDGE);

    time1.tv_nsec = event.ts.tv_nsec;

    do
    {
      res = gpiod_line_event_read(line4, &event);
    } while (event.event_type != GPIOD_LINE_EVENT_FALLING_EDGE);

    printf("Pulse Width %d \r\n",
                    (event.ts.tv_nsec - time1.tv_nsec) / 1000);
    fflush(stdout);
  }
}
```

Remember to change gpiochip0 to gpiochip4 if you are running on a Pi 5.

There are many variations on this program. You could set the line to respond only to a rising edge and then only to a falling edge, but this would mean closing the line and reopening it, which is potentially slow. If you are sure that a falling event always occurs after a rising event, you could remove the test for it and simply accept the next event as the one used to take the time.

If you try this out on a Pi Zero you will find that it is reliable up to 3kHz, but starts to miss events at 4kHz. It still manages to measure some pulses accurately up to 10kHz, but it misses some of the following falling edges and so returns a result that is too big. On a Pi 4 you can get reasonably accurate measurements up to about 40kHz. The marked difference between the two is due to the number of cores available to run threads. As the loading of the Pi 4 increases, it will start to behave like the Pi Zero and miss falling edges.

An Edgy Button

To clarify the difference between reading the line to detect a change of state and using the events, let's consider a simple non-event program that responds to the press of a button. In this case the GPIO line is set up for input and a message to press the button is printed. Then the program waits for 20s and finally tests the state of the line. Even if the user has pressed the button lots of times during the 20-second interval, all that matters is the final state of the line, read when the sleep(20) ends:

```
#define _GNU_SOURCE
#include <gpiod.h>
#include <stdio.h>
#include <unistd.h>
#include <stdlib.h>
#include <time.h>
void gpiod_line_release(struct gpiod_line *line);
int main(int argc, char **argv)
{
    int res;
    struct gpiod_chip *chip = gpiod_chip_open_by_number(0);
    struct gpiod_line *line4 = gpiod_chip_get_line(chip, 4);
    res = gpiod_line_request_input(line4,"button");
    printf("Press button \n\r");
    fflush(stdout);
    sleep(20);
    if (gpiod_line_get_value(line4) == 1)
    {
        printf("button pressed");
    }
    else
    {
        printf("button not pressed");
    }
}
```

In other words, this program misses any button presses during the 20-second pause.

Now compare this to the same program using edge events:

```
#define _GNU_SOURCE
#include <gpiod.h>
#include <stdio.h>
#include <unistd.h>
#include <stdlib.h>
#include <time.h>

void gpiod_line_release(struct gpiod_line *line);
int main(int argc, char **argv)
{
    int res;
    struct timespec timeout = {0, 0};
    struct gpiod_chip *chip = gpiod_chip_open_by_number(0);
    struct gpiod_line *line4 = gpiod_chip_get_line(chip, 4);
    res = gpiod_line_request_both_edges_events(line4, "button");
    printf("Press button \n\r");
    fflush(stdout);
    sleep(20);
    struct gpiod_line_event event;

    res=gpiod_line_event_wait(line4,&timeout);
    if (res>0)
    {
        res = gpiod_line_event_read(line4, &event);
        printf("button pressed %d",event.ts.tv_nsec);
    }
    else
    {
        printf("button not pressed");
    }

}
```

Again, remember to change gpiochip0 to gpiochip4 for a Pi 5.

In this case the GPIO line is set up as an input with a pull-up and it fires an event on the falling edge of a signal. The state of the event is discovered using gpiod_line_event_wait with a timeout of 0. This means the wait returns immediately and res is set to -1 if it timed out and 1 if at least one event occurs. Notice that now the if statement tests not the state of the line, but the state of the event. The difference is that if the user presses the button at any time during the 20-second sleep, the event occurs and is remembered and as a result the program registers the button press. The event occurs no matter what the program is doing, so instead of sleeping it could be getting on with some work, confident that it won't miss a button press. You can even know when the event occurred by calling gpiod_line_event_read which you know will return at once because you have already tested for an event.

Event Polling

Notice that the technique, used in the previous example, of calling gpiod_line_event_wait with a timeout of 0 gives you a way of testing for events in a polling loop. In many cases, using an event within a polling loop means that you can get on with other tasks without the risk of missing an event that occurs while the program is otherwise occupied. Given that the system will keep multiple events, you could even rely on it to record more than one event and time, although it is better to try to handle one event at a time.

You can easily create an event polling function:

```
int gpiod_line_event_poll(struct gpiod_line *line, struct
gpiod_line_event *event)
{
    struct timespec timeout = {0, 0};
    int res = gpiod_line_event_wait(line, &timeout);
    if (res > 0)
        res = gpiod_line_event_read(line, event);
    if (res == 0)
        res = -1;
    return res;
}
```

When you call this function, if it returns 1 then you can use the gpiod_line_event struct to determine when the event occurred. If it returns 0 then no event has occurred and the struct gpiod_line_event is unchanged and if it returns -1, there was an error.

A complete program that polls for an edge event is also easy:

```
#define _GNU_SOURCE
#include <gpiod.h>
#include <stdio.h>
#include <unistd.h>
#include <stdlib.h>
#include <time.h>

int gpiod_line_event_poll(struct gpiod_line *line,
                          struct gpiod_line_event *event);

int main(int argc, char **argv)
{
    int res;

    struct gpiod_chip *chip = gpiod_chip_open_by_number(0);
    struct gpiod_line *line4 = gpiod_chip_get_line(chip, 4);

    res = gpiod_line_request_both_edges_events(line4, "button");

    struct gpiod_line_event event;
```

```
    while (true)
    {
        res = gpiod_line_event_poll(line4, &event);
        if (res > 0)
        {
            gpiod_line_event_read(line4, &event);
            printf("Event on line 4 %d,%d \n\r ",
                            event.event_type, event.ts);
            fflush(stdout);
        }
    }

}

int gpiod_line_event_poll(struct gpiod_line *line,
                        struct gpiod_line_event *event)
{
    struct timespec timeout = {0, 0};
    int res = gpiod_line_event_wait(line, &timeout);
    if (res > 0)
        res = gpiod_line_event_read(line, event);
    if (res == 0)
        res = 1;
    return res;
}
```

To run this on a Pi 5, change `gpiochip0` to `gpiochip4` at the start.

There are many other functions in the library, but we have covered the different varieties and you should find it easy to make use of any that have been ignored by reading the `gpiod.h` file for the function definitions.

Low-Level I/O Control Events

Advanced: Skip unless you need to use it.

It is worth knowing how the gpiod library wraps the lower-level ioctl operation of the GPIO character driver and its events, as you will encounter a general Linux principle that crops up in other places. Linux files can generate interrupts to tell the kernel when they change state – for example, have some data to read. User-mode programs often need to wait on files to be ready and there are special commands that do the job - `select`, `poll` or `epoll`. Until recently, `poll` would have been the preferred way to wait for a file to be ready, but today `epoll` is its more sophisticated replacement.

To be clear about what is happening - when your program waits on a file using `epoll` it is suspended and other threads get to use the processor. When the file is ready to be used, it fires an interrupt which the kernel handles and the interrupt service routine that is called wakes up your suspended program. Notice that, while this is a hardware interrupt, your program can't

89

do anything but wait for it to happen, so it is a little more restrictive than a full interrupt. You can make it much more like a full interrupt by waiting for the file to be ready on another thread, while allowing your main program's thread to continue with other work.

What has all this got to do with the GPIO lines? The answer is that the GPIO character driver is a pseudo file and as such you can wait on it using `epoll`. As this makes use of an interrupt generated by the GPIO lines, you need to ensure that the line:

```
dtoverlay = gpio-no-irq
```

isn't present in, or is commented out of, the `/boot/config.txt` file.

To wait for an event on a GPIO line we have to use the `GPIO_GET_LINEEVENT_IOCTL` request to the GPIO character driver and the associated struct:

```
struct gpioevent_request {
        __u32 lineoffset;
        __u32 handleflags;
        __u32 eventflags;
        char consumer_label[32];
        int fd;
};
```

Notice that you can set only a single GPIO number – `lineoffset` isn't an array. The `handleflags` field is the same as the `flags` field and it is usually set to `GPIOHANDLE_REQUEST_INPUT`. The `eventflags` field determines what causes an event:

- `GPIOEVENT_REQUEST_RISING_EDGE`
- `GPIOEVENT_REQUEST_FALLING_EDGE`
- `GPIOEVENT_REQUEST_BOTH_EDGES`

When the ioctl call returns the file descriptor in the `fd` field, it can be used to wait for an event to occur. For example, first we set up the `gpioevent` struct and make the `GPIO_GET_LINEEVENT_IOCTL` request:

```
int fd, ret;

struct gpioevent_request req;
req.lineoffset = 4;
req.handleflags = GPIOHANDLE_REQUEST_INPUT;
req.eventflags = GPIOEVENT_REQUEST_BOTH_EDGES;
strcpy(req.consumer_label, "Event test");

fd = open("/dev/gpiochip0", O_RDONLY);
ret = ioctl(fd, GPIO_GET_LINEEVENT_IOCTL, &req);
close(fd);
```

Now we can use `epoll` to wait on the file having something to read. The `epoll` system call accepts an array of `epoll_event` structs that tells it what it is waiting for and how to return the results.

In this case, we have only a single file descriptor and we are waiting for the file to have something to read:

```
static struct epoll_event ev;
ev.events = EPOLLIN;
ev.data.fd = req.fd;
```

The events field specifies what the poll is waiting for – EPOLLIN means that the file is ready to read. The data.fd field specifies the file that the event is associated with.

Once the array of structs, or just the single element in our example, is set up we can add it to an epoll instance, which also just happens to be a file:

```
int epfd = epoll_create(1);
int res = epoll_ctl(epfd, EPOLL_CTL_ADD, req.fd, &ev);
```

The first instruction creates the epoll entity, which lives in the kernel and returns a file descriptor to it. The single parameter specifies the number of events it will monitor. The second instruction adds the array of structs that specify the events. As well as EPOLL_CTL_ADD, you can also use EPOLL_CTL_MOD and EPOLL_CTL_DEL to modify and delete the elements in the array of structs. In this case, the file descriptor is used to identify which element to modify or delete. Finally, we can wait for the file, or files, to have something ready to read or attend to:

```
int nfds = epoll_wait(epfd, &ev,1,20000);
```

The first parameter gives the epoll entity to use, the second is an array of epoll_event structs used to return the results, the third is the size of the array, and hence the number of events returned at any time, and the final parameter is the timeout in milliseconds. The epoll_wait suspends the thread that it is in and waits for an interrupt from the file or files it is waiting for. If the interrupt corresponds to one of the events being waited for, the epoll function restarts its user mode thread and returns the number of file descriptors that have fired an event – nfds in this case. You can test to detect a timeout when nfds will be 0. If it is greater than 0 you have to process each of the epoll_event structs returned. In this case, we have only one file so we can ignore the returned epoll_event struct and read the GPIO line to retrieve the event data in a gpioevent_data struct, which gives you an event id and a timestamp:

```
struct gpioevent_data edata;
read(req.fd,&edata,sizeof edata);
printf("%u,%llu",edata.id,edata.timestamp);
```

The complete program is:

```c
#include <string.h>
#include <stdio.h>
#include <errno.h>
#include <unistd.h>
#include <fcntl.h>
#include <sys/ioctl.h>
#include <linux/gpio.h>
#include <sys/epoll.h>

int main(int argc, char **argv) {
    int fd, ret;

    struct gpioevent_request req;
    req.lineoffset = 4;
    req.handleflags = GPIOHANDLE_REQUEST_INPUT;
    req.eventflags = GPIOEVENT_REQUEST_RISING_EDGE;
    strcpy(req.consumer_label, "Event test");

    fd = open("/dev/gpiochip0", O_RDONLY);
    ret = ioctl(fd, GPIO_GET_LINEEVENT_IOCTL, &req);
    close(fd);

    static struct epoll_event ev;
    ev.events = EPOLLIN;
    ev.data.fd = req.fd;
    int epfd = epoll_create(1);
    int res = epoll_ctl(epfd, EPOLL_CTL_ADD, req.fd, &ev);

    int nfds = epoll_wait(epfd, &ev, 1, 20000);
    if (nfds != 0) {
        struct gpioevent_data edata;
        read(req.fd, &edata, sizeof edata);
        printf("%u,%llu", edata.id, edata.timestamp);
    }
}
```

Remember to change `gpiochip0` to `gpiochip4` for a Pi 5.

You can set up multiple GPIO lines to generate events. Also notice that the file that triggered the event might have more than one `gpioevent_data` struct ready to read. You have to read the data that is ready to clear the event.

One of the advantages of the new interface is that events are not lost and they are timestamped so you know when they happened.

GPIOD and File Descriptors

Advanced: Skip unless you need to use it.

Of course, the GPIOD library uses the ioctl calls to handle events in exactly the way described above. You can get the file descriptor of the file that gpiod opens using:

```
int gpiod_line_event_get_fd(struct gpiod_line *line)
```

You can also use gpiod to read an event from a file descriptor:

```
int gpiod_line_event_read_fd(int fd,
                        struct gpiod_line_event *event)
```

The event is returned in a gpiod event struct.

To illustrate this, the previous example using `epoll` can be rewritten using gpiod to set up the GPIO line and then using the file descriptor and `epoll` to wait for the event:

```c
#define _GNU_SOURCE
#include <string.h>
#include <stdio.h>
#include <errno.h>
#include <unistd.h>
#include <fcntl.h>
#include <sys/ioctl.h>
#include <linux/gpio.h>
#include <sys/epoll.h>
#include <gpiod.h>

int main(int argc, char **argv)
{
    int res;
    struct gpiod_chip *chip = gpiod_chip_open_by_number(0);
    struct gpiod_line *line4 = gpiod_chip_get_line(chip, 4);
    res = gpiod_line_request_rising_edge_events(line4, "button");
    int fd = gpiod_line_event_get_fd(line4);
    static struct epoll_event ev;
    ev.events = EPOLLIN;
    ev.data.fd = fd;
    int epfd = epoll_create(1);
    res = epoll_ctl(epfd, EPOLL_CTL_ADD, fd, &ev);

    int nfds = epoll_wait(epfd, &ev, 1, 20000);
    if (nfds != 0)
    {
        struct gpioevent_data edata;
        read(fd, &edata, sizeof edata);
        printf("%u,%llu", edata.id, edata.timestamp);
    }
}
```

Remember to change `gpiochip0` to `gpiochip4` if you are running on a Pi 5.

If you want to read an event using gpiod that you have waited for using epoll then you need to use `gpiod_line_event_read_fd`. For example the final `if` statement in the previous example can be rewritten:

```
if (nfds != 0)
{
    struct gpiod_line_event event;
    gpiod_line_event_read_fd(fd, &event);
    printf("%d", event.ts.tv_nsec);
}
```

Simulating Interrupts

Advanced: Skip unless you need to use it.

The `epoll` function or the gpiod `wait` function gets you as close to handling interrupts as you can get in user mode, but there is one thing missing - the thread is suspended while waiting for the interrupt. This is generally not what you want to happen.

You can create a better approximation to a true interrupt by running the `epoll` function or `wait` on another thread. That is, if the main program wants to work with an interrupt you have to define an interrupt-handling function that will be called when the interrupt occurs. Next you have to wait on the event using either `epoll` or gpiod `wait`. This causes your new thread to be suspended, but you don't care because its only purpose is to wait for the interrupt and meanwhile your program's main thread continues to run and do useful work. When the interrupt occurs, the new thread is restarted and it checks that the interrupt was correct and then calls your interrupt handler. When the interrupt handler completes, the thread cleans up and calls `epoll` again to wait for another interrupt. If you want to know more about threads, see Chapter 12 of *Applying C for the IoT with Linux*, ISBN: 9781871962611.

This is all very straightforward conceptually, but it does mean using threads, which is an advanced technique that tends to make programs prone to esoteric errors and more difficult to debug.

The following program provides the basic skeleton of using a thread to simulate a user-mode interrupt using gpiod, without error checking, error recovery or locking for simplicity. If you are going to use this sort of approach in the real world you would have to add code that handles what happens when something goes wrong, whereas this code simply assumes that everything goes right.

First we need to include the pthreads library. This isn't just a matter of adding #include <pthread.h>, you also have to specify the name of the library that you want the linker to add to your program.

94

If you are using VS Code to do remote development change settings.json to read:

```
{
    "sshUser": "pi",
    "sshEndpoint": "192.168.11.170",
    "remoteDirectory": "/home/pi/Documents/$
                        {workspaceFolderBasename}",
    "std": "c99",
    "libs":"-lgpiod -lpthread",
    "header":""
}
```

Make appropriate changes specific to your setup.

The simplest way of implementing this is to create a function waitInterrupt that we can run on another thread:

```
void *waitInterrupt(void *arg)
{
    intVec *intData = (intVec *)arg;
    struct gpiod_line_event event;
    while (true)
    {
        int res = gpiod_line_event_read(intData->line, &event);
        if (res == 0)
            intData->func(&event);
    }
}
```

This casts the input arg to the correct type for use in the function. Then it repeatedly calls gpiod_line_event_read, which suspends the thread until the interrupt occurs. Then it wakes up and checks that it was the interrupt and not an error. If so it calls the interrupt routine which processes the event data and returns as soon as possible, so that the next event can be caught.

The waitInterrupt function accepts a pointer to a struct that contains all of the information about what the call has to wait for and the function to call when an event occurs:

```
typedef struct
{
    struct gpiod_line *line;
    eventHandler func;
} intVec;
```

The line field is just a pointer to a line that has been opened to respond to an event and func is the interrupt handler you want to call when the event occurs.

The eventHandler, the function called when the event occurs, receives a single parameter which is the event struct that informs it of the event. To create and pass a pointer to such a function we need a to define a type:

```
typedef void (*eventHandler)(struct gpiod_line_event *);
```

To try this out we need a main program and an event-handling function.

The interrupt function simply reports the data in the event struct passed to it:

```
void myHandler(struct gpiod_line_event *event)
{
    printf("%d,%d \n\r", event→event_type,
                            event->ts.tv_nsec / 1000);
    fflush(stdout);
}
```

The main program to test this is something like:

```
int main(int argc, char **argv)
{
    int fd, ret, res;
    struct gpiod_chip *chip = gpiod_chip_open_by_number(0);
    struct gpiod_line *line4 = gpiod_chip_get_line(chip, 4);
    res = gpiod_line_request_rising_edge_events(line4, "button");

    intVec intData;
    intData.line = line4;
    intData.func = &myHandler;

    pthread_t intThread;
    if (pthread_create(&intThread, NULL, waitInterrupt,
                            (void *)&intData))
    {
        fprintf(stderr, "Error creating thread\n");
        return 1;
    }
    for (;;)
    {
        printf("Working\n\r");
        fflush(stdout);
        sleep(2);
    }
}
```

For a Pi 5 remember to change the chip number from 0 to 4.

This opens the GPIO line for an event on a rising edge, sets up the intData struct and then runs the waitInterrupt on a new thread. The main program then prints a message every two seconds to show it is still working.

When you run the program, you will see the event details, including a timestamp, in milliseconds, every time there is an interrupt.

It is often argued that this approach to interrupts is second class, but if you think about how this threaded use of polling works, you have to conclude that it provides all of the features of an interrupt. The interrupt routine is idle and not consuming resources until the interrupt happens, when it is activated and starts running. This is how a true interrupt routine behaves. There might even be advantages in a multi-core system, as the interrupt thread could be scheduled on a different core from the main program and hence run concurrently. This might, however, be a disadvantage if you are unsure as to whether the result is well behaved.

There are some other disadvantages of this approach. The main one is that the interrupt routine is run on a different thread and this can cause problems with code that isn't thread-safe - UI components, for example. In our example, the use of printf in both threads is certainly not thread-safe and if you run it often enough you will see some strange output. There are standard library functions that you can use in different threads listed in the documentation. You can make functions thread-safe by using locks, but this introduces another level of complexity.

It is also more difficult to organize interrupts on multiple GPIO lines. It is generally said that you need one thread per GPIO line, but in practice a single thread can wait on any number of GPIO lines using epoll or a bulk read function. If you plan to use this within a real application, you would also need to add functions to pause and remove the interrupt.

The complete program is:

```
#define _GNU_SOURCE
#include <string.h>
#include <stdio.h>
#include <errno.h>
#include <unistd.h>
#include <fcntl.h>
#include <sys/ioctl.h>
#include <gpiod.h>
#include <sys/epoll.h>
#include <pthread.h>

typedef void (*eventHandler)(struct gpiod_line_event *);

typedef struct
{
    struct gpiod_line *line;
    eventHandler func;
} intVec;
```

```
void myHandler(struct gpiod_line_event *event)
{
    printf("%d,%d \n\r", event->event_type,
                                event->ts.tv_nsec / 1000);
    fflush(stdout);
}

void *waitInterrupt(void *arg)
{
    intVec *intData = (intVec *)arg;
    struct gpiod_line_event event;
    while (true)
    {
        int res = gpiod_line_event_read(intData->line, &event);
        if (res == 0)
            intData->func(&event);
    }
}

int main(int argc, char **argv)
{
    int fd, ret, res;

    struct gpiod_chip *chip = gpiod_chip_open_by_number(0);
    struct gpiod_line *line4 = gpiod_chip_get_line(chip, 4);

    res = gpiod_line_request_rising_edge_events(line4, "button");

    intVec intData;
    intData.line = line4;
    intData.func = &myHandler;

    pthread_t intThread;
    if (pthread_create(&intThread, NULL, waitInterrupt,
                                (void *)&intData))
    {
        fprintf(stderr, "Error creating thread\n");
        return 1;
    }
    for (;;)
    {
        printf("Working\n\r");
        fflush(stdout);
        sleep(2);
    }
}
```

Remember to change the number for the chip from 0 to 4 if you are running on a Pi 5.

The Contextless Event Functions

There are also some contextless functions which you probably won't need to use as they are very slow. You can specify a monitor with:

```
gpiod_ctxless_event_monitor("device",event_type, offset,
    active_low,"consumer",*timeout, pollcallback, event_cb, data)
```

and its multiple line counterpart:

```
gpiod_ctxless_event_monitor_multiple("device",event_type,
offsets[],num_lines, active_low, "consumer",*timeout,
                                pollcallback, event_cb, data)
```

The *pollcallback* is used in the polling loop. If you set it to NULL the default poll, or more accurately ppoll, another version of epoll, is used to wait for the file descriptor to be ready. The *event_cb* is a function that is called when an event occurs. Notice that a call to gpiod_ctxless_event_monitor is blocking.

Monitoring a line is easy. If you want to set a timeout you need a timespec struct filled in correctly:

```
int main(int argc, char **argv) {
    int res;
    struct timespec time;
    time.tv_nsec=0;
    time.tv_sec=20;
    res = gpiod_ctxless_event_monitor("0",
            GPIOD_CTXLESS_EVENT_BOTH_EDGES,
            4, 0, "monitor test", &time, NULL, event_cb, NULL);
}
```

This waits for either a rising or falling edge on GPIO4 and calls event_cb when it occurs.

A demonstration event_cb could be:

```
int event_cb(int event, unsigned int offset,
            const struct timespec *timestamp, void *unused)
{
  printf("[%ld.%09ld] %s\n",
      timestamp->tv_sec, timestamp->tv_nsec,
      (event == GPIOD_CTXLESS_EVENT_CB_RISING_EDGE)? "rising":
      (event == GPIOD_CTXLESS_EVENT_CB_FALLING_EDGE)? "falling":
      (event == GPIOD_CTXLESS_EVENT_CB_TIMEOUT) ? "timeout":"??");
  fflush(stdout);
  return GPIOD_CTXLESS_EVENT_CB_RET_OK;
}
```

Notice that the polling loop only comes to an end if there is a timeout. You can also write a custom *pollcallback* which returns GPIOD_CTXLESS_EVENT_POLL_RET_STOP to stop the loop for any reason.

The complete program is:

```
#define _GNU_SOURCE
#include <gpiod.h>
#include <stdio.h>
#include <unistd.h>
#include <stdlib.h>

int event_cb(int event, unsigned int offset,
             const struct timespec *timestamp, void *unused)
{
   printf("[%ld.%09ld] %s\n",
     timestamp->tv_sec, timestamp->tv_nsec,
     (event == GPIOD_CTXLESS_EVENT_CB_RISING_EDGE)? "rising" :
     (event == GPIOD_CTXLESS_EVENT_CB_FALLING_EDGE)? "falling" :
     (event == GPIOD_CTXLESS_EVENT_CB_TIMEOUT) ? "timeout" : "??");
     fflush(stdout);
     return GPIOD_CTXLESS_EVENT_CB_RET_OK;
}


int main(int argc, char **argv) {
    int res;
    struct timespec time;
    time.tv_nsec=0;
    time.tv_sec=20;
    res = gpiod_ctxless_event_monitor("0",
          GPIOD_CTXLESS_EVENT_BOTH_EDGES, 4, 0, "monitor test",
          &time, NULL, event_cb, NULL);
}
```

There are more contextless functions, but they are all fairly straightforward and obvious once you have seen the few described here. In most cases, it isn't worth using the contextless functions as they are slow and, if you are doing almost anything complicated with GPIO lines, it is worth explicitly opening the lines you want to use and closing them once you have finished.

Responding To Input

This look at methods of dealing with the problems of input isn't exhaustive – there are always new ways of doing things, but it does cover the most general ways of implementing input. As already mentioned, the problem with input is that you don't know when it is going to happen. What generally matters is speed of response.

For low-frequency inputs, using interrupts, even Linux user-mode interrupt simulation using threads, is worthwhile. It can leave your program free to get on with other tasks and simplify its overall structure. For high-frequency inputs that need to be serviced regularly, a polling loop is still the best option for maximum throughput. How quickly you can respond to an input depends on how long the polling loop is and how many times you test for it per loop.

Finally, there is the operating system to consider. In all of the examples and measurements of input speeds, the samples were taken when the program had uninterrupted use of the processor. In all cases there were times when the program was suspended by the operating system and then no input occurred for tens of microseconds or more.

Summary

- Events are a stored indication that something has happened.

- Interrupts are events that cause something to happen.

- You can use an event with a polling loop to protect against missing input because the program is busy doing something else.

- If an event occurs before the current event has been cleared then it might be missed. To avoid missing events, you can use an event queue which stores events in the order they happened until they are processed.

- The GPIOD library supports GPIO events. You can configure an event if the GPIO line goes high or low – a rising or falling edge.

- If you use events then you have to turn on GPIO generated event handling or the system will crash.

- Using events in a polling loop hardly slows things down at all.

- You can use events to generate an interrupt that you can wait for using an epoll. To do this you need to use the GPIO character driver to provide the file that the epoll waits on.

- The use of the GPIO character driver slows things down a lot.

- When using epolls the thread simply waits for the interrupt to occur. If you want to continue processing until the interrupt occurs then you have to wait for the interrupt on a new thread. This is slow, but it is the closest approach to a true interrupt that user mode allows.

- The GPIOD library has some commands that will wait for an event to occur and report the timestamp of the event.

- Overall events are useful, but interrupts are not. Neither increases the throughput of a polling loop and an interrupt only decreases response time if the event is infrequent.

Chapter 7

The Device Tree

Up to this point we have been using drivers that are installed and configured. In most cases you will at least need to configure the driver or some aspect of the system. The device tree is the modern way to install and configure drivers and is the subject of this chapter. This is an introduction to the device tree from the point of view of someone wanting to use ready made drivers and ready made driver configurations with minimal customization. Most introductions to the device tree go into much more detail and are often written from the point of view of the device driver writer. This one is about understanding enough about the device tree to use supplied overlays. Chapter 16 picks up this subject again and extends it so that you can write your own overlays.

The Device Tree and Overlays

Linux makes use of a data structure known as the device tree (DT) to describe the hardware it is running on. With the help of the device tree a single Linux kernel can configure itself to run on different hardware. There is some truth in the idea that the device tree was invented to take care of the many small variations found in different ARM processors and when the machine boots up it reads the device tree and modifies its configuration to suit the machine. Device tree files end in .dtbo and they are not human readable. To create a .dtbo file you create a text specification using an XML-like language and then compile it. Exactly how to do this is described in Chapter 16.

From our point of view, what is important about the device tree is that it selects which drivers are loaded and the parameters supplied to the drivers. Some drivers are compiled into the kernel and to remove them or add to them you have to edit the source code and compile the kernel. Most drivers, however, take the form of Linux kernel modules or Loadable Kernel Modules LKMs, which can be linked into the kernel at any point after the system has booted. The device tree determines which drivers are loaded and how they are configured. The original way of doing this is via a set of commands, modprobe, lsmod and so on, which are discussed in Chapter 16. For the moment let's concentrate on the use of the device tree.

There is a "master" device tree which is processed by the firmware loader, start.elf. The device trees appropriate for the hardware of each model of Pi are stored in /boot. The loader determines which of the available device trees should be loaded for the particular model of Pi in use. By selecting a device tree that is right for the hardware, the same Linux Kernel can be used to boot any model of Pi.

The master device tree sets a typical configuration for the machine and any customization is performed by using overlays. An overlay is a fragment of a device tree that the loader reads and merges with the master device tree to add or configure drivers. You can think of it as an editing process where the master device tree is merged with the updates provided by the overlays. There are a lot of overlay files stored in /boot /overlays and not all of them are used to modify the device tree. The file config.txt in the /boot folder has a list of commands that load the overlays you want to use.

The command to load an overlay is dtoverlay. For example:

```
dtoverlay=myoverlay
```

will load myoverlay.dtbo from the /boot /overlays folder. All of the overlays in config.txt are loaded and merged with the master device tree to produce a final device tree which is passed to the kernel.

To make overlays even more flexible, you can define parameters which can be set using the dtparam command. For example, if myoverlay has a gpiopin parameter you could set it to a particular GPIO line using:

```
dtoverlay=myoverlay
dtparam=gpiopin=4
```

If there are multiple parameters you can repeat the dtparam command:

```
dtoverlay=myoverlay
dtparam=gpiopin=4
dtparam=gpio_in_pull=down
```

or you can put the parameters into a single dtparam command:

```
dtoverlay=myoverlay
dtparam=gpiopin=4,gpio_in_pull=down
```

You can also simply put the parameters in the dtoverlay command:

```
dtoverlay=myoverlay,gpiopin=4,gpio_in_pull=down
```

This is a lot of detail but the essentials are:

1) A device tree describes the hardware that the operating system is running on so that it can configure itself and load and configure any drivers required to use the hardware.

2) The loader selects the appropriate device tree for the Pi model that is booting.

3) The loader merges the device tree with the overlays listed in config.txt to produce a customized final device tree used to boot the system.

4) Overlays can themselves be customized by specifying parameters.

Working With Overlays

Most of the time, using a particular piece of hardware is just a matter of using a presupplied overlay to load and configure a driver. For example, in the previous chapter we used the LED driver from C, but you can configure the driver using standard overlays. If you consult the list of overlays in https://github.com/raspberrypi/firmware/blob/master/boot/overlays/README or in the file /boot/overlays/README you will find:

```
Name: act-led
        Info: Pi 3B, 3B+, 3A+ and 4B use a GPIO expander to drive the LEDs
        which can only be accessed from the VPU. There is a special driver
        for this with a separate DT node, which has the unfortunate
        consequence of breaking the act_led_gpio and act_led_activelow
        dtparams. This overlay changes the GPIO controller back to the
        standard one and restores the dtparams.

        Load: dtoverlay=act-led,<param>=<val>
        Params:
                activelow Set to "on" to invert the sense of the LED
                (default "off")

                gpio Set which GPIO to use for the activity LED
```

The important information here is that there is an overlay called act-led.dtbo and you can use it with dtoverlay as shown. You have to use this overlay to return control of the LEDs back to the processor so that other overlays have an effect. To load it you simply add:

```
dtoverlay=act-led
```

to the config.txt file.

As an example of setting a parameter you can now change the trigger for the act LED using:

```
dtoverlay=act-led
dtparam=act_led_trigger=heartbeat
```

in the config.txt file. The changes only take effect after a reboot.

There are similar overlays for the power LED, pwr, for the Pis that support it.

Finding Out About The Device Tree

When the loader parses the device tree and applies all of the overlays that you have specified, the final device tree is represented by the folders in `/proc/device-tree/`. There is a folder for each driver and within that folder, a folder for each device the driver is providing. For example, within `/proc/device-tree/` you will find the `leds` folder which contains at least the `act` folder and possibly more if there are additional LEDs. Within the `act` folder you will see a number of files that contain the values specified as parameters in the device tree:

If you examine the contents you will find `gpios` empty, `label` contains `act`, `linux, default-trigger` contains `heartbeat` and `name` contains `led0`. This information is also repeated in the directory:
`/sys/class/leds/ACT/device/of_node/led-act`

The `of_node` folder shows you the information relating to that particular node in the device tree whereas the `/proc/device-tree` is a complete representation of the active device tree. If you move one level up to `/sys/class/leds/ACT/device/of_node` you will see another useful file – `compatible`. This gives the name of the driver that is used to implement the device. For example, in the case of `act` you will see `gpio-leds` and you can use this information to find the code of the driver in the GitHub repository.

The DHT22 Temperature Humidity Sensor – A Driver Example

As an example of the stages you have to go through in using a driver targeting a single device, we can do no better than the DHT22 Humidity/Temperature sensor, a more accurate version of the DHT11. It is very easy to use, low in cost and hence very popular. It makes use of a custom protocol which means you can't interface it using I2C or the SPI bus – you need something that will work with just it.

The good news is that there is a driver that is easy to use and, while named DHT11, works well with both versions and also with the AM2302, which is equivalent to the DHT22. Notice that the DHT11 is not software compatible with the DHT22 but the driver solves this problem for us.

```
Model AM2302/DHT22
Power supply 3.3-5.5V DC
Output signal digital signal via 1-wire bus
Sensing element Polymer humidity capacitor
Operating range
  humidity 0-100%RH;
  temperature -40~80Celsius
Accuracy
  humidity +-2%RH(Max +-5%RH);
  temperature +-0.5Celsius
Resolution or sensitivity
  humidity 0.1%RH;
  temperature 0.1Celsius
Repeatability
  humidity +-1%RH;
  temperature +-0.2Celsius
```

The device will work at 3.3V and it makes use of a 1-wire open collector-style bus, which makes it very easy to make the physical connection to the Pi.

The 1-Wire bus used isn't standard, being used only by this family of devices, so we have little choice but to implement the protocol in C – or use a driver.

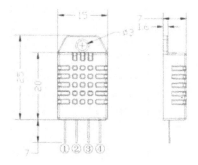

The pinouts are:

1. VDD
2. SDA serial data
3. not used
4. GND

The standard way of connecting the device is:

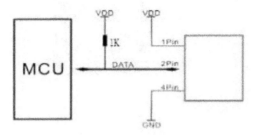

Although the recommended pull-up resistor is 1K, a higher value works better with the Pi - typically 4.7K, but larger will work.

Exactly how you build the circuit is a matter of preference. The basic layout can be seen below.

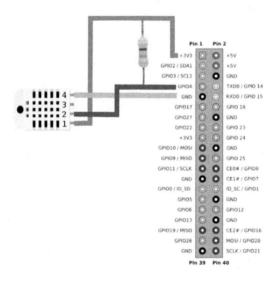

It is very easy to create this circuit using a prototyping board and some jumper wires. You can also put the resistor close to the DHT22 to make a sensor package connected to the Pi using three cables.

If you lookup the details of the dht11 overlay in the ReadMe you will find:

```
Name: dht11
     Info: Overlay for the DHT11/DHT21/DHT22 humidity/temperature
     sensors. Also sometimes found with the part number(s)
     AM230x.
     Load: dtoverlay=dht11,<param>=<val>
     Params: gpiopin GPIO connected to the sensor's DATA output.
     (default 4)
```

This is all very straightforward. If you add:

```
dtoverlay=dht11 gpiopin=4
```

to the `config.txt` file then when you reboot, the driver will be loaded and configured to use GPIO4. Change the `gpiopin` parameter to whichever GPIO line you are using. After a reboot the driver will be ready to use – but where are the device folders? If you look in `/sys/class` you won't find any new or obvious folders, but examining the device tree listed in `/proc/device-tree` you will find a new device, `/proc/device-tree/dht11@0`. However, looking through the information listed there gives you no clue how to find and use the device folders. This is very typical of using a new device driver – its use is more than obvious to its creators, but a potential user is left out in the cold.

The key to using the dht11 device driver is to discover that it is stored in the Pi OS GitHub repository at `/linux/drivers/iio/humidity/dht11.c`. The iio folder is where drivers written to the Industrial I/O standard are stored. This is covered in more detail in Chapter 14, but for now we can ignore this fact and simply use it to find the device folders.

All IIO devices are stored in `/sys/bus/iio/devices/` and if you look you will find `/sys/bus/iio/devices/iio:device0`. This corresponds to the dht11 device you have just added. Of course `iio:device0` isn't a name that is going to ensure that you have the dht11 device. A partial solution is to read the name file to discover the device name. To read the actual data you read `in_temp_input` for the temperature in millidegree Celsius and `in_humidityrelative_input` for the percentage humidity times 1000. There is no easy way to find the names of these files in the documentation, but once you have found the correct folder they are fairly obvious.

A program to read the name, temperature and humidity is:

```c
#include <stdio.h>
#include <errno.h>
#include <unistd.h>
#include <fcntl.h>
int main(int argc, char **argv)
{
    char buffer[25];
    int fd = open("/sys/bus/iio/devices/iio:device0/name",
                                                O_RDONLY);
    read(fd, buffer, 25);
    close(fd);
    printf("%s",buffer);
    fd = open("/sys/bus/iio/devices/iio:device0/in_temp_input",
                                                O_RDONLY);
    read(fd, buffer, 25);
    close(fd);
    int temp;
    sscanf(buffer, "%d", &temp);

    printf("%f\n\r", temp / 1000.0);
    fd=open("/sys/bus/iio/devices/iio:device0/
                        in_humidityrelative_input",O_RDONLY);
    read(fd, buffer, 25);
    close(fd);
    int hum;
    sscanf(buffer, "%d", &hum);
    printf("%f\n\r", hum / 1000.0);
}
```

If you run the program you will see the name dht11@0 and the temperature and humidity. In a more complete program you would check the name to make sure that it is the device you want and if there are multiple devices you would search through the top-level folder to find the device with the correct name.

Dynamic Loading Drivers

There are many problems with using drivers as part of an application and one big one is the need to configure the system to install the driver. The simplest solution is to ask the user to edit the config.txt file, but this could be a roadblock to your app being installed at all and then there is the possibility of user error. A better solution is to include the change in an install script. This is simple but doesn't allow for the user or some other program changing the config.txt file so that your app no longer works. A good solution in some cases is to make use of the new dynamic overlay loading feature. This is fairly recent but it works with the latest version of Pi OS.

Instead of having to load drivers at boot time you can use the dtoverlay or dtparam commands to install and configure drivers. The only problem is that there are some cases where it doesn't work. Essentially you have to try it out to see it if works. The overlays that are dynamically loaded form a stack and, in theory, you can only remove the overlay on the top of the stack. In practice, removing any overlay often results in a memory leak at best and a crashed system at worst.

The dtoverlay command is described in the documentation as:

```
dtoverlay <overlay> [<param>=<val>...]
Add an overlay (with parameters)
dtoverlay -D                        Dry-run(prepare overlay, but don't
                                    apply- save it as dry-run.dtbo)
dtoverlay -r [<overlay>]            Remove an overlay (by name,
                                    index or the last)
dtoverlay -R [<overlay>]            Remove from an overlay (by name,
                                    index or all)
dtoverlay -l                        List active overlays/params
dtoverlay -a                        List all overlays (marking
                                    the active)
dtoverlay -h                        Show this usage message
dtoverlay -h <overlay>              Display help on an overlay
dtoverlay -h <overlay> <param>..    Or its parameters
                                    where <overlay> is the name of an
                                    overlay or 'dtparam' for dtparams
```

Options applicable to most variants:

```
-d <dir>    Specify an alternate location for the overlays
            (defaults to /boot/overlays or /flash/overlays
-p <string> Force a compatible string for the platform
-v          Verbose operation
```

The dtparam command is:

```
 dtparam <param>=<val>…     Add an overlay (with parameters)
 dtparam -D                 Dry-run (prepare overlay, but don't
                            apply -  save it as dry-run.dtbo)
 dtparam -r [<idx>]         Remove an overlay (by index, or the
                            last)
 dtparam -R [<idx>]         Remove from an overlay (by index, or
                            all)
 dtparam -l                 List active overlays/dtparams
 dtparam -a                 List all overlays/dtparams (marking
                            the active)
 dtparam -h                 Show this usage message
 dtparam -h <param>...      Display help on the listed parameters
```

Options applicable to most variants:

```
-d <dir>    Specify an alternate location for the overlays
            (defaults to /boot/overlays or /flash/overlays)
-p <string> Force a compatible string for the platform
-v          Verbose operation
```

The important thing is that you can use the -l option to discover what overlays are already loaded and hence avoid loading the same overlay again.

A function to check for the dht11 overlay and only load it if it isn't already loaded is easy enough with just some string handling and the use of the popen function:

```c
#define _DEFAULT_SOURCE
#include <stdio.h>
#include <stdlib.h>
#include <errno.h>
#include <unistd.h>
#include <string.h>
#include <fcntl.h>

FILE *doCommand(char *cmd)
{
    FILE *fp = popen(cmd, "r");
    if (fp == NULL)
    {
        printf("Failed to run command %s \n\r", cmd);
        exit(1);
    }
    return fp;
}
void checkDht11()
{
    FILE *fd = doCommand("sudo  dtparam -l");
    char output[1024];
    int txfound = 0;

    char indicator[] = "dht11  gpiopin=4";
    char command[] = "sudo dtoverlay dht11 gpiopin=4";
    while (fgets(output, sizeof(output), fd) != NULL)
    {
        printf("%s\n\r", output);
        fflush(stdout);
        if (strstr(output, indicator) != NULL)
        {
            txfound = 1;
        }
    }
    if (txfound == 0)
    {
        fd = doCommand(command);
    }

    pclose(fd);
}
```

```c
int main(int argc, char **argv)
{
    char buffer[25];
    checkDht11();
    int fd = open(
                "/sys/bus/iio/devices/iio:device0/name", O_RDONLY);
    read(fd, buffer, 25);
    close(fd);
    printf("%s", buffer);

    fd = open(
        "/sys/bus/iio/devices/iio:device0/in_temp_input", O_RDONLY);
    read(fd, buffer, 25);
    close(fd);
    int temp;
    sscanf(buffer, "%d", &temp);

    printf("%f\n\r", temp / 1000.0);

    fd = open("/sys/bus/iio/devices/iio:device0/
                        in_humidityrelative_input", O_RDONLY);
    read(fd, buffer, 25);
    close(fd);
    int hum;
    sscanf(buffer, "%d", &hum);
    printf("%f\n\r", hum / 1000.0);
}
```

The indicator string is used to specify the string that is in the overlay listing when the driver is loaded and this isn't necessarily the same as the string in the command string, which is the command to install the driver with any parameters that are needed.

You can run this program without having to change the config.txt file. The driver remains loaded until the next reboot and is reinstalled when you next run the program. Notice that the program has to have root permissions to be able to run sudo, even if the program isn't being run as root.

Summary

- The Device Tree is the modern way to specify the hardware configuration of a machine and to load and configure drivers.

- The boot disk contains device trees for each of the different versions of the Pi and the loader selects the appropriate device tree for the Pi model that is booting.

- The loader merges the device tree with the overlays listed in the config.txt file to produce a customized final device tree used to boot the system.

- Overlays are fragments of the device tree which can be used to modify and add to the basic device tree.

- Overlays can themselves be customized by specifying parameters.

- When the loader parses the device tree and applies all the overlays you have specified, the final device tree is represented by the folders in /proc/device-tree.

- The DHT22 Humidity and Temperature Sensor provides an example of loading and customizing a driver.

- A fairly recent innovation is the ability to load and customize drivers after the system has booted using the dtoverlay and dtparam commands.

- You can easily write a program to load and configure missing drivers at runtime.

- Dynamic loading of overlays doesn't always work and unloading overlays, while possible, isn't a good idea.

Chapter 8

Some Electronics

Now that we have looked at some simple I/O, it is worth spending a little time on the electronics of output and input. First some basics – how transistors can be used as switches. The approach is very simple, but it is enough for the simple circuits that digital electronics makes use of. It isn't enough to design a high-quality audio amplifier or similar analog device, but it might be all you need.

Electrical Drive Characteristics

The basis of all electronics is Ohm's law, $V = IR$, and this prerequisite implies an understanding of voltage, current and resistance. If you are not very familiar with electronics, the important things to know are what voltages are being worked with and how much current can flow. The most important thing to know about the Raspberry Pi is that it works with two voltage levels, 0V and 3.3V. If you have worked with other logic devices you might be more familiar with 0V and 5V as being the low and high levels. The Pi uses a lower output voltage to reduce its power consumption, which is good, but you need to keep in mind that you may have to use some electronics to change the 3.3V to other values. The same is true of inputs, which must not exceed 3.3V or you risk damaging the Pi.

In output mode a single GPIO line can source and sink 16mA, but the situation is a little more complicated than this suggests. Unfortunately, the Pi power supply can only supply enough power for all of the GPIO lines working at around 3mA each. If you use too much current then the 3.3V supply will fail. The safe limit is usually stated as 50mA in total, i.e all of the GPIO lines have to keep their current consumption below a total of 50mA. When you get close to this limit you might find that current spikes cause strange behavior. In addition, no single GPIO line should supply or sink more than 8mA, or 16mA if you configure a high drive current, see later.

In practice, if you are planning to use more than 3mA from multiple GPIO lines, consider using a transistor. If your circuits draw more than 50mA from the 3.3V supply rail, consider a separate power supply. You can use the 5V supply with a regulator if you need even more than the 3.3V supply can source. How much current the 5V pin can source is a difficult question that depends on the USB power supply in use, but 2A is a reasonable estimate if there are no other USB devices connected. The total of all USB, HDMI, Camera, and 5V pin demands has to be less than 2.5A. If in doubt use a separate power supply. Notice that the 16mA limit means that you cannot safely drive a standard 20mA red LED without restricting the current to below 16mA. A better solution is to use a low-power 2mA LED or use a transistor driver.

Driving An LED

One of the first things you need to know how to do is compute the value of a current-limiting resistor. For example, if you just connect an LED across a GPIO line and ground then no current will flow when the line is low and the LED is off, but when the line is high at 3.3V it is highly likely that the current will exceed the safe limit. In most cases nothing terrible will happen as the Pi's GPIO lines are rated very conservatively, but if you keep doing it eventually something will fail. The correct thing to do is to use a current-limiting resistor. Although this is an essential part of using an LED, it is also something you need to keep in mind when connecting any output device. You need to discover the voltage that the device needs and the current it uses and calculate a current-limiting resistor to make sure that is indeed the current it draws from the GPIO line.

An LED is a non-linear electronic component – the voltage across is stays more or less the same irrespective of the current passing through the device. Compare this to a more normal linear, or "Ohmic", device where the current and voltage vary together according to Ohm's law, $V = IR$, which means that if the current doubles, so does the voltage and vice versa. This is not how an LED behaves. It has a fairly constant voltage drop irrespective of the current. (If you are curious, the relationship between current and voltage for an LED is exponential, meaning that big changes in the current hardly change the voltage across the LED.) When you use an LED you need to look up its forward voltage drop, about 1.7V to 2V for a red LED and about 3V for a blue LED, and the maximum current, usually 20mA for small LEDs. You don't have to use the current specified, this is the maximum current and maximum brightness.

To work out the current-limiting resistor you simply calculate the voltage across the resistor and then use Ohm's law to give you the resistor you need for the current required. The LED determines the voltage and the resistor sets the current.

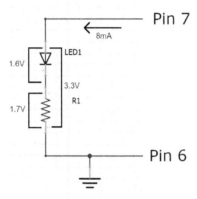

A GPIO line supplies 3.3V and if you assume 1.6V as its forward voltage across the LED that leaves 1.7V across the current-limiting resistor since voltage distributes itself across components connected in series. If we restrict the current to 8mA, which is very conservative, then the resistor we need is given by:

$R = V/I = 1.7/8 = 0.212$

The result is in kilohms, kΩ, because the current is in milliamps, mA. So we need at least a 212Ω resistor. In practice, you can use a range of values as long as the resistor is around 200 ohms – the bigger the resistor the smaller the current, but the dimmer the LED. If you were using multiple GPIO lines then keeping the current down to 3mA would be better, but that would need a transistor.

You need to do this sort of calculation when driving other types of output device. The steps are always the same. The 3.3V distributes itself across the output device and the resistor in some proportion and we know the maximum current. From these values we can compute the resistor needed to keep the actual current below this value.

LED BJT Drive

Often you need to reduce the current drawn from a GPIO line. The Bipolar Junction Transistor (BJT) may be relatively old technology, but it is a current amplifier, low in cost and easy to use. A BJT is a three-terminal device - base, emitter and collector - in which the current that flows through the emitter/collector is controlled by the current in the base:

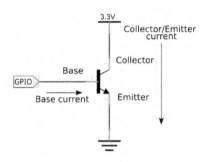

The diagram shows an NPN transistor, which is the most common. This diagram is a simplification in that, in reality, the current in the emitter is slightly larger than that in the collector because you have to add the current flowing in the base.

In most cases, all you have to know are two additional facts. Firstly, the voltage on the base is approximately 0.6V, no matter how much current flows since the base is a diode, a nonlinear device just like the LED in the previous section. Secondly, the current in the collector/emitter is hfe or ß (beta) times the current in the base. That is, hfe or beta is the current gain of the transistor and you look it up for any transistor you want to use. While you are consulting the datasheets, you also need to check the maximum currents and voltages the device will tolerate. In most cases, the beta is between 100 and 200 and hence you can use a transistor to amplify the GPIO current by at least a factor of 100.

Notice that, for the emitter/collector current to be non-zero, the base has to have a current flowing into it. If the base is connected to ground then the transistor is "cut off", i.e. no current flows. What this means is that when the GPIO line is high the transistor is "on" and current is flowing and when the GPIO line is low the transistor is "off" and no current flows.

This high-on/low-off behavior is typical of an NPN transistor. A PNP transistor works the other way round:

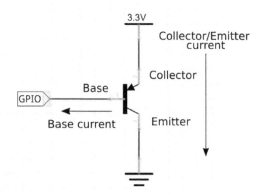

The 0.6V is between the base and the collector and the current flows out of the base. What this means is that the transistor is off when the GPIO line is high and on when it is low.

This complementary behavior of NPN and PNP BJTs is very useful and means that we can use such transistors in pairs. It is also worth knowing that the diagram given above is usually drawn with 0V at the top of the diagram, i.e. flipped vertically, to make it look the same as the NPN diagram. You need to always make sure you know where the +V line is.

A BJT Example

For a simple example we need to connect a standard LED to a GPIO line with a full 20mA drive. Given that all of the Pi's GPIO lines work at 3.3V and ideally only supply a few milliamps, we need a transistor to drive the LED which typically draws 20mA. You could use a Field Effect Transistor (FET) of some sort, but for this type of application an old-fashioned BJT (Bipolar Junction Transistor) works very well and is cheap and available in a thru-hole mount, i.e. it comes with wires.

Almost any general purpose NPN transistor will work, but the 2N2222 is very common. From its datasheet, you can discover that the max collector current is 800mA and beta is at least 50, which makes it suitable for driving a 20mA LED with a GPIO current of at most 20/50mA = 0.4mA.

The circuit is simple but we need two current-limiting resistors:

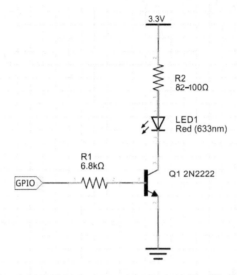

If you connect the base to the GPIO line directly then the current flowing in the base would be unrestricted – it would be similar to connecting the GPIO line to ground. R1 restricts the current to 0.39mA, which is very low and, assuming that the transistor has a minimum gain (hfe) of 50, this provides just short of 20mA to power it. The calculation is that the GPIO supplies 3.3V and the base has 0.6V across it, so the voltage across R1 is 3.3 - 0.6V = 2.7V. To limit the current to 0.4mA would need a resistor of 2.7/0.4kΩ = 6.7kΩ.

The closest preferred value is 6.8kΩ, which gives a slightly smaller current. Without R2 the LED would draw a very large current and burn out. R2 limits the current to 20mA. Assuming a forward voltage drop of 1.6V and a current of 20mA, the resistor is given by (3.3-1.6)/20kΩ = 85Ω. In practice, we could use anything in the range 82Ω to 100Ω.

The calculation just given assumes that the voltage between the collector and emitter is zero, but of course in practice it isn't. Ignoring this results in a current less than 20mA, which is erring on the safe side. The datasheet indicates that the collector emitter voltage is less than 200mV. The point is that you rarely make exact calculations for circuits such as this, you simply arrive at acceptable and safe operating conditions.

You can also use this design to drive something that needs a higher voltage. For example, to drive a 5V dip relay, which needs 10mA to activate it, you would use something like:

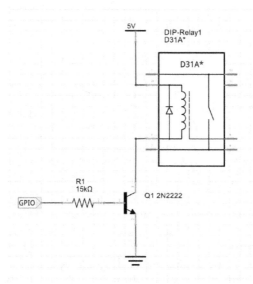

Notice that in this case the transistor isn't needed to increase the drive current – the GPIO line could provide the 10mA directly. Its purpose is to change the voltage from 3.3V to 5V. The same idea works with any larger voltage. If you are using the 2N2222 then the pinouts are:

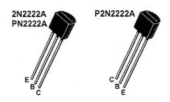

As always, the positive terminal on the LED is the long pin.

MOSFET Driver

There are many who think that the FET (Field Effect Transistor), or more precisely the MOSFET (Metal Oxide Semiconductor FET), is the perfect amplification device and we should ignore BJTs. They are simpler to understand and use, but it can be more difficult to find one with the characteristics you require.

Like the BJT, a MOSFET has three terminals called the gate, drain and source. The current that you want to control flows between the source and drain and it is controlled by the gate. This is analogous to the BJT's base, collector and emitter, but the difference is that it is the voltage on the gate that controls the current between the source and drain.

The gate is essentially a high resistance input and very little current flows in it. This makes it an ideal way to connect a GPIO line to a device that needs more current or a different voltage. When the gate voltage is low the source drain current is very small. When the gate voltage reaches the threshold voltage $V_{GS(th)}$, which is different for different MOSFETs, the source drain current starts to increase exponentially. Basically when the gate is connected to 0V or below $V_{GS(th)}$ the MOSFET is off and when it is above $V_{GS(th)}$ the MOSFET starts to turn on. Don't think of $V_{GS(th)}$ as the gate voltage at which the MOSFET turns on, but as the voltage below which it is turned off. The problem is that the gate voltage to turn a typical MOSFET fully on is in the region of 10V. Special "logic" MOSFETs need a gate voltage around 5V to fully turn on and this makes the 3.3V at which the Raspberry Pi's GPIO lines work a problem. The datasheets usually give the fully on resistance and the minimum gate voltage that produces it, usually listed as Drain-Source On-State Resistance. For digital work this is a more important parameter than the gate threshold voltage.

You can deal with this problem in one of two ways – ignore it or find a MOSFET with a very small $V_{GS(th)}$. In practice, MOSFETs with thresholds low enough to work at 3.3V are hard to find and when you do find them they are generally only available as surface mounts. Ignoring the problem sometimes works if you can tolerate the MOSFET not being fully on. If the current is kept low then, even though the MOSFET might have a resistance of a few ohms, the power loss and voltage drop may be acceptable.

What MOSFETs are useful for is in connecting higher voltages to a GPIO line used as an input, see later.

Also notice that this discussion has been in terms of an N-channel MOSFET. A P-channel works in the same way, but with all polarities reversed. It is cut off when the gate is at the positive voltage and turns on when the gate is grounded. This is exactly the same as the NPN versus PNP for the BJT.

MOSFET LED

A BJT is the easiest way to drive an LED, but as an example of using a common MOSFET we can arrange to drive one using a 2N7000, a low-cost, N-channel device available in a standard TO92 form factor suitable for experimentation:

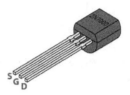

Its datasheet states that it has a $V_{GS(th)}$ of typically 2V, but it could be as low as 0.8V or as high as 3V. Given we are trying to work with a gate voltage of 3.3V you can see that in the worst case this is hardly going to work – the device will only just turn on. The best you can do is to buy a batch of 2N7000 and measure their $V_{GS(th)}$ to weed out any that are too high. This said, the circuit given below does generally work.

Assuming a $V_{GS(th)}$ of 2V and a current of 20mA for the LED, the datasheet gives a rough value of 6Ω for the on resistance with a gate voltage of 3V. The calculation for the current-limiting resistor is the same as in the BJT case and the final circuit is:

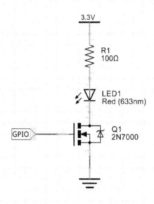

Notice that we don't need a current-limiting resistor for the GPIO line as the gate connection is high impedance and doesn't draw much current. In practice, it is usually a good idea to include a current-limiting resistor in the GPIO line if you plan to switch it on and off rapidly. The problem is that the gate looks like a capacitor and fast changes in voltage can produce high currents.

While there could be devices labeled 2N7000 that will not work in this circuit due to the threshold gate voltage being too high, encountering one is rare. A logic-level MOSFET like the IRLZ44 has a resistance of 0.028Ω at 5V compared to the 2N2222's of 6Ω. It also has a $V_{GS(th)}$ guaranteed to be between 1V and 2V.

Setting Drive Type

The GPIO output can be configured into one of a number of modes, but the most important is pull-up/down. Before we get to the code to do the job, it is worth spending a moment explaining the three basic output modes, push-pull, pull-up and pull-down.

Push-Pull Mode

In push-pull mode two transistors of opposite polarity, one PNP and one NPN, are used:

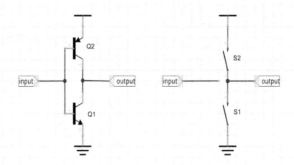

The circuit behaves like the two-switch equivalent shown on the right. Only one of the transistors, or switches, is "closed" at any time. If the input is high then Q1 is saturated and the output is connected to ground - exactly as if S1 was closed. If the input is low then Q2 is saturated, as if S2 was closed, and the output is connected to 3.3V. You can see that this pushes the output line high with the same "force" as it pulls it low. This is the standard configuration for a GPIO output.

Pull-Up Mode

In pull-up mode one of the transistors is replaced by a resistor:

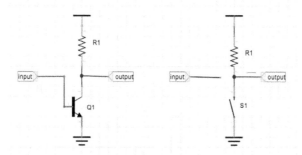

In this case the circuit is equivalent to having a single switch. When the switch is closed, the output line is connected to ground and hence driven low. When the switch is open, the output line is pulled high by the resistor. You can see that in this case the degree of pull-down is greater than the pull-up, where the current is limited by the resistor. The advantage of this mode is that it can be used in an AND configuration. If multiple GPIO or other lines are connected to the output, then any one of them being low will pull the output line low. Only when all of them are off does the resistor succeed in pulling the line high. This is used, for example, in a serial bus configuration like the SPI bus.

Pull-Down Mode

Finally, pull-down mode, which is the best mode for driving general loads, motors, LEDs, etc, is exactly the same as pull-up, only now the resistor is used to pull the output line low.

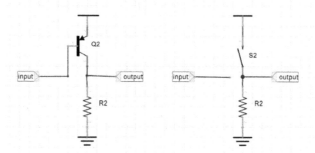

The line is held high by the transistor and pulled low by the resistor only when all the switches are open. Putting this the other way round, the line is high if any one switch is closed. This is the OR version of the shared bus idea.

Basic Input Circuit - The Switch

Now it is time to turn our attention to the electrical characteristics of GPIO lines as inputs. One of the most common input circuits is the switch or button. Many beginners make the mistake of wiring a GPIO line to a switch something like:

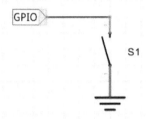

The problem with this is that, if the switch is pressed, the GPIO line is connected to ground and will read as zero. The question is, what does it read when the switch is open? A GPIO line configured as an input has a very high resistance. It isn't connected to any particular voltage and the voltage on it varies due to the static it picks up. The jargon is that the unconnected line is "floating". When the switch is open the line is floating and, if you read it, the result, zero or one, depends on whatever noise it has picked up.

The correct way to do the job is to tie the input line either high or low when the switch is open using a resistor. A pull-up arrangement would be something like:

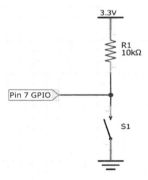

The value of the resistor used isn't critical. It simply pulls the GPIO line high when the switch isn't pressed. When it is pressed a current of a little more than 0.3mA flows in the resistor. If this is too much, increase the resistance to 100kΩ or even more, but notice that the higher the resistor value the noisier the input to the GPIO and the more it is susceptible to RF interference. This circuit gives a zero when the switch is pressed.

If you want a switch that pulls the line high instead of low, reverse the logic by swapping the positions of the resistor and the switch in the diagram to create a pull-down:

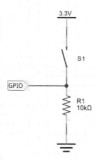

This gives a one when the switch is pressed.

The good news is that the Raspberry Pi has built-in pull-up and pull-down resistors which you can enable in software. This means that you can connect a switch directly to the GPIO and set a pull-up or pull-down configuration in software.

Setting Pull Mode

Currently the GPIO character device driver, see Chapter 4, only supports two pull mode configurations:

```
GPIOD_LINE_REQUEST_FLAG_OPEN_DRAIN
GPIOD_LINE_REQUEST_FLAG_OPEN_SOURCE
```

This basically sets things up so that you can add an external pull-up or pull-down resistor to the GPIO line. Open drain corresponds to a pull-up configuration without a resistor in place and open source corresponds to a pull-down configuration without a resistor in place.

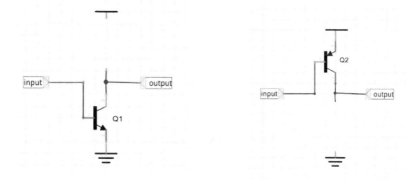

There are also external 1.8kΩ pull-ups on pins 3 and 5. The only way to remove them is to unsolder them from the board and for these pins the open drain and open source correspond to pull-up and pull-down without having to add external resistors.

A future version of the library/driver will also support:

```
GPIOD_LINE_REQUEST_FLAG_BIAS_DISABLE
GPIOD_LINE_REQUEST_FLAG_BIAS_PULL_DOWN
GPIOD_LINE_REQUEST_FLAG_BIAS_PULL_UP
```

Debounce

Although the switch is the simplest input device, it is very difficult to get right. When a user clicks a switch of any sort, the action isn't clean - the switch bounces. What this means is that the logic level on the GPIO line goes high then low and high again and bounces between the two until it settles down. There are electronic ways of debouncing switches, but software does the job much better. All you have to do is insert a delay of a millisecond or so after detecting a switch press and read the line again - if it is still low then record a switch press. Similarly, when the switch is released, read the state twice with a delay. You can vary the delay to modify the perceived characteristics of the switch.

A more sophisticated algorithm for debouncing a switch is based on the idea of integration. All you have to do is read the state multiple times, every few milliseconds say, and keep a running sum of values. If you sum ten values each time then a total of between 6 and 10 can be taken as an indication that the switch is high. A total less than this indicates that the switch is low. You can think of this as a majority vote in the time period for the switch being high or low.

The Potential Divider

If you have an input that is outside of the range of 0V to 3.3V you can reduce it using a simple potential divider. In the diagram V is the input from the external logic and Vout is the connection to the GPIO input line:

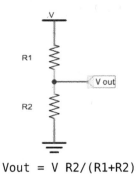

Vout = V R2/(R1+R2)

You can spend a lot of time working out good values of R1 and R2. For loads that take a lot of current you need R1+R2 to be small and divided in the same ratio as the voltages. For example, for a 5V device R1=18 or 20KΩ and R2=33KΩ work well to drop the voltage to 3.3V.

A simpler approach that works for a 5V signal is to notice that the ratio R1:R2 has to be the same as (5-3.3):3.3, i.e. the voltage divides itself across the resistors in proportion to their value, which is roughly 1:2. What this means is that you can take any resistor and use it for R1 and use two of the same value in series for R2 and the Vout will be 3.33333V.

The problem with a resistive divider is that it can round off fast pulses due to the small capacitive effects. This usually isn't a problem, but if it is then the solution is to use a FET or a BJT as an active buffer:

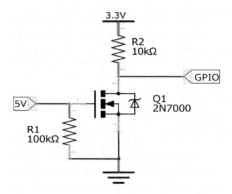

Notice that this is an inverting buffer, the output is low when the input is high, but you can usually ignore this and simply correct it in software, i.e. read a 1 as a low state and a 0 as a high state. The role of R1 is to make sure the FET is off when the 5V signal is absent and R2 limits the current in the FET to about 0.3mA. In most cases you should try the simple voltage divider and only move to an active buffer if it doesn't work.

This very basic look at electronics isn't all that you need to know, but it is enough for you to see some of the problems and find some answers. In general, this sort of electronics is all about making sure that voltages and currents are within limits. As switching speeds increase you have additional problems, which are mainly concerned with making sure that your circuits aren't slowing things down. This is where things get more subtle.

Summary

- You can get a long way with only a small understanding of electronics, but you do need to know enough to protect the Pi and things you connect to it.

- The maximum current from any GPIO line should be less than 16mA and the total current should be less than 50mA.

- All of the GPIO lines work at 3.3V and you should avoid directly connecting any other voltage.

- You can drive an LED directly from a GPIO line, but only at 16mA rather than the nominal 20mA needed for full brightness.

- Calculating a current-limiting resistor always follows the same steps – find out the current in the device, find out the voltage across the device, and work out the resistor that supplies that current when the remainder of the voltage is applied to it.

- For any load you connect to a GPIO output you generally need a current-limiting resistor.

- In many cases you need a transistor, a BJT, to increase the current supplied by the GPIO line.

- To use a BJT you need to calculate a current-limiting resistor in the base and, generally, one in the collector.

- MOSFETs are popular alternatives to BJTs, but it is difficult to find a MOSFET that works reliably at 3.3V.

- GPIO output lines can be set to active push-pull mode, where a transistor is used to pull the line high or low, or passive pull-up or pull-down mode, where one transistor is used and a resistor pulls the line high or low when the transistor is inactive.

- GPIO lines have built-in pull-up and pull-down resistors which can be selected or disabled under software control and can be used in input mode.

- When used as inputs, GPIO lines have a very high resistance and in most cases you need pull-up or pull-down resistors to stop the line floating. The built-in pull-up or pull-down resistors can be used in input mode.

- Mechanical input devices have to be debounced to stop spurious input.

- If you need to connect an input to something bigger than 3.3V, you need a potential divider to reduce the voltage back to 3.3V. You can also use a transistor.

Chapter 9

Pulse Width Modulation

One way around the problem of getting a fast response from a microcontroller is to move the problem away from the processor. In the case of the Pi's processor there are some built-in devices that can use GPIO lines to implement protocols without the CPU being involved. In this chapter we take a close look at pulse width modulation (PWM) including generating sound and driving LEDs.

When performing their most basic function, i.e. output, the GPIO lines can be set high or low by the processor. How quickly they can be set high or low depends on the speed of the processor.

Using the GPIO line in its Pulse Width Modulation (PWM) mode you can generate pulse trains up to 4.8MHz, i.e. pulses just a little more than $0.08\mu s$. The reason for the increase in speed, a factor of at least 100, is that the GPIO is connected to a pulse generator and, once set to generate pulses of a specific type, the pulse generator just gets on with it without needing any intervention from the GPIO line or the processor. In fact, the pulse output can continue after your program has ended if you forget to reset it.

Of course, even though the PWM line can generate pulses as short as $0.1\mu s$, it can only change the pulses it produces each time that the processor can modify them. For example, you can't use PWM to produce a single $0.1\mu s$ pulse because you can't disable the PWM generator in just $0.1\mu s$. This said, hardware generated PWM is available on the Pi and there is a good PWM driver that makes it very easy to use.

Some Basic Pi PWM Facts

There are some facts worth getting clear right from the start, although their full significance will only become clear as we progress.

First, what is PWM? The simple answer is that a Pulse Width Modulated signal has pulses that repeat at a fixed rate, say, one pulse every millisecond, but the width of the pulse can be changed.

There are two basic things to specify about the pulse train that is generated, its repetition rate and the width of each pulse. Usually the repetition rate is set as a simple repeat period and the width of each pulse is specified as a percentage of the repeat period, referred to as the duty cycle. So, for example, a 1ms repeat and a 50% duty cycle specifies a 1ms period, which is high for 50% of the time, i.e. a pulse width of 0.5ms.

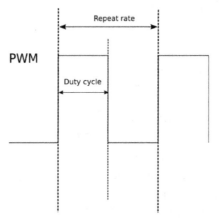

The two extremes are 100% duty cycle, i.e. the line is always high, and 0% duty cycle, i.e. the line is always low. The duty cycle is simply the proportion of time the line is set high. Notice it is the duty cycle that carries the information in PWM and not the frequency. What this means is that, generally, you select a repeat rate and stick to it and what you change as the program runs is the duty cycle.

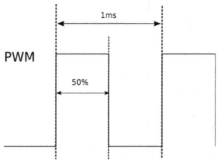

There are many ways to specify a PWM signal – frequency and duty cycle, time high and time low and so on. It is easy to convert between these different representations.

As you can guess, there are no PWM inputs, just output. If for some reason you need to decode, or respond to, a PWM input then you need to program it using the GPIO input lines and the pulse measuring techniques introduced in previous chapters.

Software PWM

The alternative to dedicated PWM hardware is to implement it in software. You can quite easily work out how to do this. All you need is to set a timing loop to set the line high at the repetition rate and then set it low again according to the duty cycle. You can easily implement software PWM using the GPIO character driver:

```c
#define _GNU_SOURCE
#include <gpiod.h>
#include <stdio.h>
#include <unistd.h>
#include <stdlib.h>
#include <time.h>

void pwm(struct gpiod_line *line, int);

int main(int argc, char **argv)
{
    int period = 20;
    int duty = 25;
    int res;
    struct gpiod_chip *chip = gpiod_chip_open_by_number(0);
    struct gpiod_line *line4 = gpiod_chip_get_line(chip, 4);
    res = gpiod_line_request_output(line4, "test output", 0);

    struct timespec ontime = {0, 0};
    struct timespec offtime = {0, 0};
    ontime.tv_nsec = period * duty * 10 * 1000;
    offtime.tv_nsec = (period - period * duty / 100) * 1000 * 1000;

    for (;;)
    {
        res = gpiod_line_set_value(line4, 1);
        nanosleep(&ontime, NULL);
        res = gpiod_line_set_value(line4, 0);
        nanosleep(&offtime, NULL);
    };
}
```

Remember to change "0" to "4" if you are running on a Pi 5.

The basic idea is to take the period in ms and the duty cycle as a percentage and work out the on and off time.

A more advanced version of the same program makes use of a thread to implement the toggling of the PWM line.

To understand how this works you need to be happy with threads and you have to compile with the pthreads library:

```c
#define _GNU_SOURCE
#include <gpiod.h>
#include <stdio.h>
#include <unistd.h>
#include <stdlib.h>
#include <time.h>
#include <pthread.h>

struct pwmargs
{
    struct gpiod_line *line;
    struct timespec ontime;
    struct timespec offtime;
};

void *pwmrun(void *arg)
{
    struct pwmargs *pwmdata = (struct pwmargs *)arg;
    int res;
    for (;;)
    {
        res = gpiod_line_set_value(pwmdata->line, 1);
        nanosleep(&(pwmdata->ontime), NULL);
        res = gpiod_line_set_value(pwmdata->line, 0);
        nanosleep(&(pwmdata->offtime), NULL);
    };
}

int pwm(struct gpiod_line *line, int period, int duty)
{
    static struct pwmargs pwmdata;
    pwmdata.line = line;
    pwmdata.ontime.tv_sec = 0;
    pwmdata.ontime.tv_nsec = period * duty * 10;
    pwmdata.offtime.tv_sec = 0;
    pwmdata.offtime.tv_nsec = (period-period * duty/100) * 1000;

    pthread_t pwmThread;
    if (pthread_create(&pwmThread, NULL, pwmrun, (void *)&pwmdata))
    {
        fprintf(stderr, "Error creating thread\n");
        return 1;
    }
    return 0;
};
```

```
int main(int argc, char **argv)
{
    int res;
    struct gpiod_chip *chip = gpiod_chip_open_by_number(0);
    struct gpiod_line *line4 = gpiod_chip_get_line(chip, 4);
    res = gpiod_line_request_output(line4, "test output", 0);

    pwm(line4, 20*1000, 25);
    for (;;)
    {
    };
}
```

Remember to change 0 to 4 if you are running on a Pi 5.

This will generate the PWM signal on the specified gpio line independent of the main program. If you want to use this in production you would need to add error handling and some functions to pause and stop the thread.

The accuracy of the PWM signal goes down as the frequency increases. At a period of 20ms and a duty cycle of 25% the frequency and duty cycle are typically 49.5Hz and 25.1%, i.e. around 1% accuracy, but at 2ms the figures are 450Hz and 27% i.e. around 10% accuracy. It becomes increasingly inaccurate and becomes unusable at around 2kHz. The reason is that nanosleep is used for the timing. This suspends the thread and relies on the operating system to restart it. The problem is that as the requested sleep time becomes shorter the operating system fails to restart the thread early enough due to it running other threads while the PWM thread is suspended. You could replace the nanosleep call by a busy wait loop to make the timing more accurate, but this wouldn't allow the operating system to run another thread while waiting. This would work well on a quad-core Pi 5/4/3 and Pi Zero 2W, but would be not so good on a single-core Pi Zero/W.

Software implemented PWM isn't workable for higher frequencies. It is, however, good enough to work at 50Hz, which is suitable for driving servos – see later.

The PWM Driver

All Pi models have two PWM channels implemented in hardware, but on models earlier than the Pi 4 these are also used to generate audio. What this means is that if you want to use hardware PWM on a Pi Zero or earlier you have to disable or at least not use audio at the same time. You can use both on a Pi 4, but notice that the PWM channels and the audio share the same clock signal and this can still cause problems. The Pi 5 has four PWM channels, but only two can be used via the driver.

The two PWM hardware modules can be configured to drive different GPIO lines. For the Pi the standard configuration is to have PWM0 drive either GPIO18 or GPIO12 and PWM1 drive either GPIO13 or GPIO19.

There are two PWM drivers available. One that activates a single PWM channel and one that activates both the available channels. The documentation for both is:

```
Name:   pwm
Info:   Configures a single PWM channel
        Legal pin,function combinations for each channel:
        PWM0:12,4(Alt0) 18,2(Alt5) 40,4(Alt0) 52,5(Alt1)
        PWM1:13,4(Alt0) 19,2(Alt5) 41,4(Alt0) 45,4(Alt0) 53,5(Alt1)
        N.B.:
          1) Pin 18 is the only one available on all platforms, and
             it is the one used by the I2S audio interface.
             Pins 12 and 13 might be better choices on an A+/B+/Pi2.
          2) The onboard analogue audio output uses both PWM channels.
          3) So be careful mixing audio and PWM.
          4) Currently the clock must have been enabled and configured
             by other means.
Load:   dtoverlay=pwm,<param>=<val>
Params:pin            Output pin (default 18) - see table
       func           Pin function (default 2 = Alt5) - see above
       clock          PWM clock frequency (informational)

Name:   pwm-2chan
Info:   Configures both PWM channels
        Legal pin,function combinations for each channel:
        PWM0: 12,4(Alt0) 18,2(Alt5) 40,4(Alt0) 52,5(Alt1)
        PWM1: 13,4(Alt0) 19,2(Alt5) 41,4(Alt0) 45,4(Alt0) 53,5(Alt1)
        N.B.:
          1) Pin 18 is the only one available on all platforms, and
             it is the one used by the I2S audio interface.
             Pins 12 and 13 might be better choices on an A+/B+/Pi2.
          2) The onboard analogue audio output uses both PWM channels.
          3) So be careful mixing audio and PWM.
          4) Currently the clock must have been enabled and configured
             by other means.
Load:   dtoverlay=pwm-2chan,<param>=<val>
Params: pin           Output pin (default 18) - see table
        pin2          Output pin for other channel (default 19)
        func          Pin function (default 2 = Alt5) - see above
        func2         Function for pin2 (default 2 = Alt5)
        clock         PWM clock frequency (informational)
```

In simple terms, you can use one or two channels of PWM and you would be well advised to use GPIO18 for PWM0 and GPIO19 for PWM1 on all recent Pis. Notice that you cannot currently use the driver to set the frequency of the PWM clock, but this is automatically enabled at a default frequency. You can find what the frequency is using:

```
vcgencmd measure_clock pwm
```

at the command prompt. It only reports an accurate value if the PWM driver is loaded and enabled. On a Pi Zero and a Pi 4 it reports 99995000, i.e. approximately 100Mhz, and empirical measurements give the effective clock rate, after division by 5, as 20MHz for both the Pi 4 and Pi Zero. The clock rate is important because it determines the resolution of the duty cycle, as explained later.

If you load either driver by adding:

```
dtoverlay=pwm
```

or

```
dtoverlay=pwm-2chan
```

to `boot/config.txt`, you will discover that on reboot you have a new `pwmchip0 folder` in the `/sys/pwm` folder.

The driver is configured to see the PWM hardware as a single PWM "chip". To work with either PWM channel you have to export it. In this context exporting means that you claim sole use of the channel. To do this you have to write a "0" or a "1" to the `export` file in the `pwmchip0` folder. To unexport you do the same to the `unexport` file in the `pwmchip0` folder.

After you have exported the channel you will see new folders, `pwm0` and `pwm1` in the `pwmchip0` folder. Of course you only see the folders you have exported and you can only export `pwm0` if you have used the `PWM` driver.

Within the `pwmx` folder you will find the following important files:

- ♦ `period`   Period in nanoseconds
- ♦ `duty_cycle`   Duty cycle in nanoseconds
- ♦ `enable`   Write "1" to enable, "0" to disable

So all you have to do is:

1. Export the channel bv writing its number to `export`.
2. Write to `period`
3. Write to `duty_cycle`
4. Write "1" to `enable`

Notice that as this is hardware PWM, once you have set and enabled the channel, the PWM generation continues after the program ends.

A simple program to use `pwm0` is:

```c
#define _DEFAULT_SOURCE
#include <stdio.h>
#include <stdlib.h>
#include <errno.h>
#include <unistd.h>
#include <fcntl.h>
#include <string.h>
#include <fcntl.h>
```

```c
FILE *doCommand(char *cmd)
{
    FILE *fp = popen(cmd, "r");
    if (fp == NULL)
    {
        printf("Failed to run command %s \n\r", cmd);
        exit(1);
    }
    return fp;
}
void checkPWM()
{
    FILE *fd = doCommand("sudo  dtparam -l");
    char output[1024];
    int txfound = 0;

    char indicator[] = "pwm-2chan";
    char command[] = "sudo dtoverlay pwm-2chan";
    while (fgets(output, sizeof(output), fd) != NULL)
    {
        printf("%s\n\r", output);
        fflush(stdout);
        if (strstr(output, indicator) != NULL)
        {
            txfound = 1;
        }
    }
    if (txfound == 0)
    {
        fd = doCommand(command);
        sleep(2);
    }
    pclose(fd);
}

int main(int argc, char **argv)
{
    checkPWM();
    int fd = open("/sys/class/pwm/pwmchip0/export", O_WRONLY);
    write(fd, "0", 1);
    close(fd);
    sleep(2);
    fd = open("/sys/class/pwm/pwmchip0/pwm0/period", O_WRONLY);
    write(fd, "10000000", 8);
    close(fd);
    fd = open("/sys/class/pwm/pwmchip0/pwm0/duty_cycle", O_WRONLY);
    write(fd, "8000000", 7);
    close(fd);
    fd = open("/sys/class/pwm/pwmchip0/pwm0/enable", O_WRONLY);
    write(fd, "1", 1);
    close(fd);
}
```

The checkPWM function dynamically loads the `pwm-2chan` driver – you can change it to `pwm` if you only need one channel. It exports the channel and then sets the period to 100Hz with an 80% duty cycle. A delay of 1 second is included after the export to allow the system to create the folders and files. A better solution is to test for an error on the first open and keep looping until it works. This program doesn't need root permissions to run, only to dynamically install the driver. You can use the other channel in the same way.

It seems relatively safe to dynamically remove the `pwm` and `pwm-2wchan` overlays.

PWM On The Pi 5

The Pi 5 has a different implementation of PWM hardware and has four channels which can be used via the driver. At the time of writing, overlays were only available to use two channels at most.

The first important difference is that the PWM chip is `pwmchip2` and the four channels are `pwm0` to `pwm3`. You can use the `pwm` or `pwm-2chan` overlays and the channels are selected by the number that you write to `export`. Apart from this everything works in the same way, but the GPIO lines and function modes associated with each channel are:

```
pwm0 GPIO12  mode 4
pwm1 GPIO13  mode 4
pwm2 GPIO18  mode 2
pwm3 GPIO19  mode 2
```

Notice that on a Pi 5 the indicated modes are legacy GPIO modes, not the GPIO functions provided by the Pi 5.

For example, to use GPIO18 and GPIO12 you would use:

```c
#define _DEFAULT_SOURCE
#include <stdio.h>
#include <stdlib.h>
#include <errno.h>
#include <unistd.h>
#include <fcntl.h>
#include <string.h>
#include <fcntl.h>
FILE *doCommand(char *cmd)
{
    FILE *fp = popen(cmd, "r");
    if (fp == NULL)
    {
        printf("Failed to run command %s \n\r", cmd);
        exit(1);
    }
    return fp;
}
```

```c
void checkPWM()
{
    FILE *fd = doCommand("sudo  dtparam -l");
    char output[1024];
    int txfound = 0;

    char indicator[] = "pwm";
    char command[] = "sudo dtoverlay pwm-2chan,
                                pin=18 func=2 pin2=12 func2=4";
    while (fgets(output, sizeof(output), fd) != NULL)
    {
        printf("%s\n\r", output);
        fflush(stdout);
        if (strstr(output, indicator) != NULL)
        {
            txfound = 1;
            printf("Overlay already loaded\n\r");
        }
    }
    if (txfound == 0)
    {
        fd = doCommand(command);
        sleep(2);
    }
    pclose(fd);
}
int main(int argc, char **argv)
{
    checkPWM();
    int fd = open("/sys/class/pwm/pwmchip2/export", O_WRONLY);
    write(fd, "0", 1);
    close(fd);
    sleep(2);
    fd = open("/sys/class/pwm/pwmchip2/pwm0/period", O_WRONLY);
    write(fd, "10000000", 8);
    close(fd);
    fd = open("/sys/class/pwm/pwmchip2/pwm0/duty_cycle", O_WRONLY);
    write(fd, "8000000", 7);
    close(fd);
    fd = open("/sys/class/pwm/pwmchip2/pwm0/enable", O_WRONLY);
    write(fd, "1", 1);
    close(fd);
    fd = open("/sys/class/pwm/pwmchip2/export", O_WRONLY);
    write(fd, "2", 1);
    close(fd);
    sleep(2);
    fd = open("/sys/class/pwm/pwmchip2/pwm2/period", O_WRONLY);
    write(fd, "10000000", 8);
    close(fd);
    fd = open("/sys/class/pwm/pwmchip2/pwm2/duty_cycle", O_WRONLY);
    write(fd, "5000000", 7);
    close(fd);
```

```
    fd = open("/sys/class/pwm/pwmchip2/pwm2/enable", O_WRONLY);
    write(fd, "1", 1);
    close(fd);
}
```

Notice the two blocks of file commands differ only by the use of "0" and "2" for pwm0 and pwm2 respectively. Notice that the channels that you select use the GPIO lines indicated earlier.

As long as the overlay isn't already loaded, this will generate a PWM signal on GPIO12 and GPIO18. Otherwise nothing will happen. You can remove the overlay, before running the program, using:

```
sudo dtoverlay -R  pwm-2chan
```

either at the command line or as part of the program.

Simple PWM Functions

The big problem in using the PWM driver is in avoiding opening and closing files, which is a slow operation. A better idea is to implement a function that can work with the driver without closing the frequency and duty cycle files until they are no longer needed. It is possible to write this so that it will work on the Pi 5 as well as the other devices by simply changing "/sys/class/pwm/pwmchip0/" to "/sys/class/pwm/pwmchip2/" and selecting a set of GPIO lines that works with both. If you use:

```
sudo dtoverlay pwm-2chan pin=12 func=4 pin2=13 func2=4
```

then this works with pwm0 and pwm1 on all Pis. The only complication is the amount of string handling you need to use to make sure that the paths to the directories are correct. If the symbol Pi5 is defined the paths are correct for the Pi 5 otherwise they are correct for all other Pis.

```
#define _DEFAULT_SOURCE
#include <stdio.h>
#include <stdlib.h>
#include <errno.h>
#include <unistd.h>
#include <fcntl.h>
#include <string.h>
#define Pi5
FILE *doCommand(char *cmd)
{
    FILE *fp = popen(cmd, "r");
    if (fp == NULL)
    {
        printf("Failed to run command %s \n\r", cmd);
        exit(1);
    }
    return fp;
}
```

```c
void checkPWM()
{
    FILE *fd = doCommand("sudo  dtparam -l");
    char output[1024];
    int txfound = 0;

    char indicator[] = "pwm-2chan";
    char command[] = "sudo dtoverlay pwm-2chan pin=12
                                    func=4 pin2=13 func2=4";
    while (fgets(output, sizeof(output), fd) != NULL)
    {
        printf("%s\n\r", output);
        fflush(stdout);
        if (strstr(output, indicator) != NULL)
        {
            txfound = 1;
        }
    }
    if (txfound == 0)
    {
        pclose(fd);
        fd = doCommand(command);
    }

    pclose(fd);
}
enum pwm
{
    OpenChan,
    SetFreq,
    SetDuty,
    EnableChan,
    DisableChan,
    CloseChan
};

int pwmAction(enum pwm action, int chan, int param)
{
    static int fdf[2];
    static int fdd[2];
    int fd;
    char buf[150];
    char schan[6];

    if (chan != 0 && chan != 1)
        return -1;

#if defined(Pi5)
    char path[] = "/sys/class/pwm/pwmchip2/";
#else
    char path[] = "/sys/class/pwm/pwmchip0/";
#endif
```

```c
    char chanNum[2];
    snprintf(schan, 6, "%s%d","pwm",chan);
    snprintf(chanNum,2,"%d",chan);
    int L;
    switch (action)
    {
    case OpenChan:
        checkPWM();
        snprintf(buf, 150, "%s%s", path, "export");
        fd = open(buf, O_WRONLY);
        write(fd,chanNum , 1);
        close(fd);
        sleep(2);
        snprintf(buf, 150, "%s%s%s", path, schan, "/period");
        fdf[chan] = open(buf, O_WRONLY);
        snprintf(buf, 150, "%s%s%s", path, schan, "/duty_cycle");
        fdd[chan] = open(buf, O_WRONLY);
        break;
    case SetFreq:
        L = snprintf(buf, 150, "%d", param);
        write(fdf[chan], buf, L);
        break;
    case SetDuty:
        L = snprintf(buf, 150, "%d", param);
        write(fdd[chan], buf, L);
        break;
    case EnableChan:
        snprintf(buf, 150, "%s%s%s", path, schan, "/enable");
        fd = open(buf, O_WRONLY);
        write(fd, "1", 1);
        close(fd);
        break;
    case DisableChan:
        snprintf(buf, 150, "%s%s%s", path, schan, "/enable");
        fd = open(buf, O_WRONLY);
        write(fd, "0", 1);
        close(fd);
        break;
    case CloseChan:
        close(fdf[chan]);
        close(fdd[chan]);
        snprintf(buf, 150, "%s%s%s", path, "/unexport");
        printf("%s\n",buf);
        fd = open(buf, O_WRONLY);
        write(fd, chanNum, 1);
        close(fd);
        break;
    }
    return 0;
}
```

The pwmAction function accepts an initial command parameter which controls what it does. The command can be one of:

```
enum pwm
{
    OpenChan,
    SetFreq,
    SetDuty,
    EnableChan,
    DisableChan,
    CloseChan
};
```

If you open a channel then the frequency and duty cycle files are opened and the file descriptors saved for the other commands to use. After opening a channel you can set the frequency and the duty cycle and then enable the channel. Using the function is easy, you simply supply the action as the first parameter, the channel 0 or 1 as the second, and the third is either the frequency or the duty cycle or ignored.

For example:

```
int main(int argc, char **argv)
{

    pwmAction(OpenChan, 1, 0);
    pwmAction(SetFreq, 1, 10000000);
    pwmAction(SetDuty, 1, 8000000);
    pwmAction(EnableChan, 1, 0);

    pwmAction(OpenChan, 0, 0);
    pwmAction(SetFreq, 0, 10000000);
    pwmAction(SetDuty, 0, 2000000);
    pwmAction(EnableChan, 0, 0);
}
```

If you don't like having to supply extra parameters you can use C90's variable parameters. Change the function definition to:

```
int pwmAction(enum pwm action, int chan, ...)
{
    static int fdf[2];
    static int fdd[2];

    int fd;
    int param;
    char buf[150];
    char schan[2];
    va_list params;

    int L;
```

and change the `SetFreq` and `SetDuty` case clauses to:

```
case SetFreq:
    va_start(params, chan);
    param = va_arg(params, int);
    L = snprintf(buf, 150, "%d", param);
    write(fdf[chan], buf, L);
    break;

case SetDuty:
    va_start(params, chan);
    param = va_arg(params, int);
    L = snprintf(buf, 150, "%d", param);
    write(fdd[chan], buf, L);
    break;
    return 0;
```

You will also need to add:

```
#include <stdarg.h>
```

Now you only need to supply the third parameter when the action makes use of it.

The full variable parameter version can be found on the book's webpage on www.iopress.info.

Clocks and Duty Cycle Resolution

If you just take the PWM driver at face value then you might believe that you can set any frequency and any duty cycle – this is not the case. Due to hardware limitations, the resolution of the duty cycle depends on the PWM clock frequency and this also governs the highest frequency PWM signal you can create. The situation with the Raspberry Pi is complicated by the fact that the PWM clock is set once when the device is booted. Any changes to the clock that occur after boot are not reset by loading the PWM driver and any changes can result in the driver setting the wrong frequency and duty cycle.

The effective PWM clock is 20MHz in an unmodified just rebooted Pi Zero and Pi 4. The importance of the clock is that the PWM signal can only change once per clock pulse. What this means is that the highest frequency that you can use is 10MHz with a 50% duty cycle:

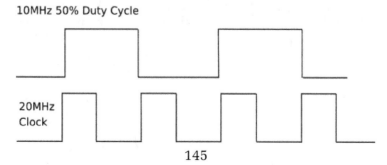

145

If you select a duty cycle other than 50% then you will get either 100%, 50% or 0% depending on which value is closer to the desired value. In practice, you will also see some strange behavior for anything other than 50%. A program to produce the highest frequency is:

```
int main(int argc, char **argv)
{
    pwmAction(OpenChan, 0, 0);
    int t =100;
    pwmAction(SetFreq, 0, t);
    int d = t/2;
    pwmAction(SetDuty, 0, d);
    pwmAction(EnableChan, 0, 0);
}
```

The number of different duty cycles you can achieve depends on the number of clock pulses in the total period. At 10MHz there are just two clock pulses and so just three duty cycles 0%, 50% and 100%.

You can easily work out the number of duty cycles available at any given frequency:

PWM Frequency	Number of clock pulses	Number of different duty cycles	Resolution in bits
10MHz	2	3	1.6
5MHz	4	5	2.3
2.5MHz	8	9	3.2
1.25MHz	16	17	4.1
625kHz	32	33	5.0
312.5kHz	64	65	6.0
156.25kHz	128	129	7.0
nkHz	20000/n	20000/n - 1	$Log_2(20000/n -1)$

In many applications 8-bit resolution for the duty cycle is considered the minimum acceptable and this sets the highest frequency to about 75kHz, which is high enough for most things. For example, if you want to control a servo motor, see later, then you need a PWM signal with a frequency of 50Hz and at this frequency you can specify the duty cycle down to about 25 bits or around 40 million increments, more than enough for any real servo motor.

Controlling An LED

You can use PWM to generate physical quantities such as the brightness of an LED or the rotation rate of a DC motor. The only differences required by these applications are to do with the voltage and current you need and the way the duty cycle relates to whatever the physical effect is. In other words, if you want to change some effect by 50%, how much do you need to change the duty cycle? For example, how do we "dim" an LED?

By changing the duty cycle of the PWM pulse train you can set the amount of power delivered to an LED, or any other device, and hence change its brightness. In the case of an LED, the connection between duty cycle and brightness is a complicated matter, but the simplest approach uses the fact that the perceived brightness is roughly proportional to the cube of the input power. The exact relationship is more complicated, but this is good enough for most applications.

As the power supplied to the LED is proportional to the duty cycle we have:

$$b = kd^3$$

where b is the perceived brightness and d is the duty cycle. The constant k depends on the LED.

Notice that, as the LED when powered by a PWM signal is either full on or full off, there is no effect of the change in LED light output with current - the LED is always run at the same current.

What all of this means is that if you want an LED to fade in a linear fashion you need to change the duty cycle in a non-linear fashion. Intuitively it means that changes when the duty cycle is small produce bigger changes in brightness than when the duty cycle is large.

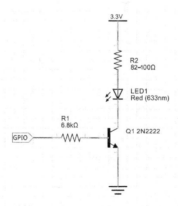

For a simple example, let's connect a standard LED to the PWM line and then use the BJT driver circuit introduced in Chapter 5.

Assuming that you have this circuit constructed, then a simple PWM program to modify its brightness from low to high and back to low in a loop is:

```
int main(int argc, char **argv)
{
    pwmAction(OpenChan, 0, 0);
    int t = 1000000;
    pwmAction(SetFreq, 0, t);
    int d = 0;
    pwmAction(SetDuty, 0, d);
    pwmAction(EnableChan, 0, 0);

    struct timespec delay = {0, 50000 * 1000};

    int inc = 100000;
    for (;;)
    {
        pwmAction(SetDuty, 0, d);
        d = d + inc;
        if (d > t)
        {
            d = t;
            inc = -inc;
        }

        if (d <= 0)
        {
            d = 0;
            inc = -inc;
        }
        nanosleep(&delay, NULL);
    }
}
```

Note: This program is to be used with the pwmAction function given earlier. The basic idea is to set up a pulse train with a period of 1ms. Next, in the for loop, the duty cycle is set to 0% to 100% and then back down to 0%. If you watch the flashing you will see that it changes brightness very quickly and then seems to spend a long time "stuck" at almost full brightness and then suddenly starts to dim rapidly. This is a consequence of the way the human eye perceives light output as a function of input power. For a linear change you have to vary the duty cycle as a cubic power, but in most cases a simple flash works just as well.

How Fast Can You Modulate?

For reasons that will be discussed later, in most cases, the whole point is to vary the duty cycle, or the period, of the pulse train. This means that the next question is how fast can you change the characteristic of a PWM line? In other words, how fast can you change the duty cycle? There is no easy way to give an exact answer and, in most applications, an exact answer isn't of much value. The reason is that for a PWM signal to convey information it generally has to deliver a number of complete cycles with a given duty cycle. This is because of the way pulses are often averaged in applications.

We also have another problem, synchronization. There is no way to swap from one duty cycle to another exactly when a complete duty cycle has just finished. All you can do is use a timer to estimate when the pulse is high or low. What this means is that there is going to be a glitch when you switch from one duty cycle to another. Of course, this glitch becomes less important as you slow the rate of duty cycle change and exactly what is usable depends on the application. For example, set up the 150kHz, which provides an 8-bit duty cycle resolution. We can change the duty cycle from 25% to 75% as quickly as possible:

```
int main(int argc, char **argv)
{
    pwmAction(OpenChan, 0, 0);
    int freqkHz = 150;
    int dutyPc = 75;

    int t = 1000000000 / (freqkHz * 1000);
    pwmAction(SetFreq, 0, t);

    int d1 = t * 75 / 100;
    int d2 = t * 25 / 100;

    pwmAction(EnableChan, 0, 0);

    for (;;)
    {
        pwmAction(SetDuty, 0, d1);
        pwmAction(SetDuty, 0, d2);
    }
}
```

The result looks fairly good, but notice that the changeover time is around two pulses. It is sometimes too short and then you only get a single pulse before the duty cycle changes.

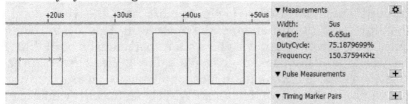

The fastest PWM repetition rate that you can use is $26.6\mu s$ for an 8-bit resolution and you can change the duty cycle as frequently as once per pulse.

Controlling a Servo

Hobby servos, the sort used in radio control models, are very cheap and easy to use and the Pi has enough PWM lines to control two of them without much in the way of extras.

A basic servo has just three connections, ground, a power line and a signal line. The colors used vary, but the power line is usually red, ground is usually black or brown and the signal line is white, yellow or orange.

The power wire has to be connected to a 5V supply capable of providing enough current to run the motor - anything up to 500mA or more depending on the servo. In general, you cannot power a full-size servo from the Pi's 5V pin, you need a separate power supply.

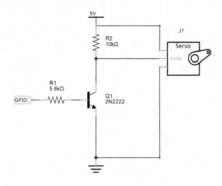

You can power some micro servos directly from the Pi's 5V, line but you need to check the specifications. The good news is that the servo signal line generally needs very little current, although it does, in theory, need to be switched between 0 and 5V using a PWM signal.

This is the correct way to drive a servo, but in nearly all cases you can connect the servo to a 5V supply and the pulse line directly to the 3.3V GPIO line. In other words, in most cases you don't need a transistor driver and the circuit shown below will work:

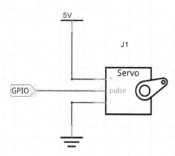

Now all we have to do is set the PWM line to produce 20ms pulses with pulse widths ranging from 0.5ms to 2.5ms or a duty cycle of 2.5% to 12.5%, but this varies quite a lot according to the servo.

The simplest servo program you can write is something like:

```
int main(int argc, char **argv)
{
    pwmAction(OpenChan, 0, 0);
    int t = 20 * 1000000;
    pwmAction(SetFreq, 0, t);
    int d1 = t * 2.5 / 100;
    int d2 = t * 12 / 100;
    pwmAction(EnableChan, 0, 0);
    for (;;)
    {
        pwmAction(SetDuty, 0, d1);
        sleep(1);
        pwmAction(SetDuty, 0, d2);
        sleep(1);
    }
}
```

This moves the servo to two extreme positions, pausing between them. This works with the direct drive servo circuit, but not with the transistor drive circuit. The reason is that the transistor voltage driver is an inverter. When the PWM line is high the transistor is fully on and the servo's pulse line is effectively grounded. When the PWM line is low the transistor is fully off and the servo's pulse line is pulled high by the resistor.

The standard solution in this case is to use two transistors to generate a non-inverted pulse. The simplest solution of all is to ignore the problem in hardware and solve the problem in software. This is generally a good approach - before you consider modifying the hardware always see if there is an easier software fix. Instead of generating 20ms pulses with pulse widths 0.5ms to 2.5ms, you can generate an inverted pulse with 20ms pulses with widths in the range 17.5ms to 19.5ms. The principle is that, if the servo needs a 10% duty cycle, we supply it with a 90% duty cycle, which the transistor inverter converts back to a 10% duty cycle. The range of duty cycles we need goes from 17.5ms to 19.5ms, which in percentages is 87.5% to 97.5%.

Fortunately we have a simpler solution than having to manually invert the duty cycles. Each PWM channel has a polarity file, which if you write inversed results in the PWM signal polarity being flipped. Writing normal returns it to active high rather than active low. We can add another case to our pwmAction function to set the polarity:

```
case InvertChan:
    va_start(params, chan);
    param = va_arg(params, int);

    snprintf(buf, 150, "%s%s%s",
            "/sys/class/pwm/pwmchip0/pwm", schan, "/polarity");
    fd = open(buf, O_WRONLY);
    if (param == 0)
    {
        L = snprintf(buf, 150, "%s", "normal");
        write(fd, buf, L);
    }
    if (param == 1)
    {
        L = snprintf(buf, 150, "%s", "inversed");
        write(fd, buf, L);
    }
    close(fd);
    break;
}
```

We also need to modify the enumeration to read:

```
enum pwm
{
    OpenChan,
    SetFreq,
    SetDuty,
    EnableChan,
    DisableChan,
    CloseChan,
    InvertChan
};
```

The final parameter is 0 for normal and 1 for inverted.

To drive the servo with a transistor buffer you can use:

```
int main(int argc, char **argv)
{
    pwmAction(OpenChan, 0);

    struct timespec delay = {0, 6667 * 2};

    int t = 20 * 1000000;
    pwmAction(SetFreq, 0, t);
    int d1 = t * 2.5 / 100;
    int d2 = t * 12 / 100;
    pwmAction(InvertChan,0,1);
    pwmAction(EnableChan, 0);

    for (;;)
    {
        pwmAction(SetDuty, 0, d1);
        sleep(1);
        pwmAction(SetDuty, 0, d2);
        sleep(1);
    }
}
```

These methods may work, but in either case the servo might not reach its limits of movement. Servos differ in how they respond to the input signal and you might need to calibrate the pulse widths. Many robot implementations, for example, calibrate the servos to find their maximum movement using either mechanical switches to detect when the servo is at the end of its range or a vision sensor. Hence you will often see a robot apparently doing a "warm up" before moving. What is happening is that each servo is being moved until it activates the limit switch giving the duty cycle needed to move it to that position. Low-cost servos are particularly hard to pin down in terms of specification and variations in behavior generally have to be taken account of in software.

What Else Can You Use PWM For?

PWM lines are incredibly versatile and it is always worth asking the question "could I use PWM?" when you are considering almost any problem. The LED example shows how you can use PWM as a power controller. You can extend this idea to a computer-controlled switch-mode power supply. All you need is a capacitor to smooth out the voltage and perhaps a transformer to change the voltage. You can also use PWM to control the speed of a DC motor and if you add a simple bridge circuit you can control its direction and speed.

The amount of power delivered to a device by a pulse train is proportional to the duty cycle. A pulse train that has a 50% duty cycle is delivering current to the load only 50% of the time and this is irrespective of the pulse repetition rate. So the duty cycle controls the power, but the period still matters in many situations because you want to avoid any flashing or other effects. A higher frequency smooths out the power flow at any duty cycle.

With a sufficiently fast period you can also use PWM as a digital to analog converter. Simply add a low-pass filter to remove the pulsing and you have a steady voltage proportional to the duty cycle. This can be used to create an audio signal if the clock is fast enough.

Finally, you can use a PWM signal as a modulated carrier for data communications. For example, most infrared controllers make use of a 38kHz carrier, which is roughly a 26μs pulse. This is switched on and off for 1ms and this is well within the range that the PWM can manage. So all you have to do is replace the red LED in the previous circuit with an infrared LED and you have the start of a remote control, or data transmission, link.

Complete PWM Program

This version of the program allows a variable number of parameters:

```c
#define _DEFAULT_SOURCE
#include <stdio.h>
#include <stdlib.h>
#include <errno.h>
#include <unistd.h>
#include <fcntl.h>
#include <string.h>
#include <stdarg.h>

// #define Pi5

FILE *doCommand(char *cmd)
{
    FILE *fp = popen(cmd, "r");
    if (fp == NULL)
    {
        printf("Failed to run command %s \n\r", cmd);
        exit(1);
    }
    return fp;
}
void checkPWM()
{
    FILE *fd = doCommand("sudo  dtparam -l");
    char output[1024];
    int txfound = 0;

    char indicator[] = "pwm-2chan";
    char command[] = "sudo dtoverlay pwm-2chan pin=12
                                    func=4 pin2=13 func2=4";
    while (fgets(output, sizeof(output), fd) != NULL)
    {
        printf("%s\n\r", output);
        fflush(stdout);
        if (strstr(output, indicator) != NULL)
        {
            txfound = 1;
        }
    }
    if (txfound == 0)
    {
        pclose(fd);
        fd = doCommand(command);
    }

    pclose(fd);
}
```

155

```c
enum pwm
{
    OpenChan,
    SetFreq,
    SetDuty,
    EnableChan,
    DisableChan,
    CloseChan,
    InvertChan
};

int pwmAction(enum pwm action, int chan, ...)
{
    static int fdf[2];
    static int fdd[2];

    int fd;
    char buf[150];
    char schan[6];
    va_list params;
    int param;

    if (chan != 0 && chan != 1)
        return -1;

#if defined(Pi5)
    char path[] = "/sys/class/pwm/pwmchip2/";
#else
    char path[] = "/sys/class/pwm/pwmchip0/";
#endif
    char chanNum[2];
    snprintf(schan, 6, "%s%d", "pwm", chan);
    snprintf(chanNum, 2, "%d", chan);

    int L;

    switch (action)
    {
    case OpenChan:
        checkPWM();
        snprintf(buf, 150, "%s%s", path, "export");
        fd = open(buf, O_WRONLY);
        write(fd, chanNum, 1);
        close(fd);
        sleep(2);
        snprintf(buf, 150, "%s%s%s", path, schan, "/period");
        fdf[chan] = open(buf, O_WRONLY);
        snprintf(buf, 150, "%s%s%s", path, schan, "/duty_cycle");
        fdd[chan] = open(buf, O_WRONLY);
        break;
```

```c
        case SetFreq:
            va_start(params, chan);
            param = va_arg(params, int);
            L = snprintf(buf, 150, "%d", param);
            write(fdf[chan], buf, L);
            break;
        case SetDuty:
            va_start(params, chan);
            param = va_arg(params, int);
            L = snprintf(buf, 150, "%d", param);
            write(fdd[chan], buf, L);
            break;
        case EnableChan:
            snprintf(buf, 150, "%s%s%s", path, schan, "/enable");
            fd = open(buf, O_WRONLY);
            write(fd, "1", 1);
            close(fd);
            break;
        case DisableChan:
            snprintf(buf, 150, "%s%s%s", path, schan, "/enable");
            fd = open(buf, O_WRONLY);
            write(fd, "0", 1);
            close(fd);
            break;
        case CloseChan:
            close(fdf[chan]);
            close(fdd[chan]);
            snprintf(buf, 150, "%s%s%s", path, "/unexport");
            printf("%s\n", buf);
            fd = open(buf, O_WRONLY);
            write(fd, chanNum, 1);
            close(fd);
            break;
        case InvertChan:
            va_start(params, chan);
            param = va_arg(params, int);
            snprintf(buf, 150, "%s%s%s", path, schan, "/polarity");
            fd = open(buf, O_WRONLY);
            if (param == 0){
                L = snprintf(buf, 150, "%s", "normal");
                write(fd, buf, L);
            }
            if (param == 1){
                L = snprintf(buf, 150, "%s", "inversed");
                write(fd, buf, L);
            }
            close(fd);
            break;
    }

    return 0;
}
```

```c
int main(int argc, char **argv)
{
    pwmAction(OpenChan, 0);

    struct timespec delay = {0, 6667 * 2};

    int t = 20 * 1000000;
    pwmAction(SetFreq, 0, t);
    int d1 = t * 2.5 / 100;
    int d2 = t * 12 / 100;
    pwmAction(InvertChan, 0, 1);
    pwmAction(EnableChan, 0);

    for (;;)
    {
        pwmAction(SetDuty, 0, d1);
        sleep(1);
        pwmAction(SetDuty, 0, d2);
        sleep(1);
    }
}
```

Summary

- PWM, Pulse Width Modulation, has a fixed repetition rate but a variable duty cycle, i.e. the amount of time the signal is high or low changes.

- PWM can be generated by software simply by changing the state of a GPIO line correctly, but it can also be generated in hardware, so relieving the processor of some work.

- Hardware PWM can generate high speed pulses, but how quickly you can change the duty cycle is still software-limited.

- All versions of the Pi have two hardware PWM channels which can be used and configured using Linux drivers.

- The Pi 5 has two additional channels which cannot be easily used via the driver. The PWM chip has also changed from `pwmchip0` to `pwmchip2`.

- The PWM drivers do not provide control over the PWM clock frequency which determines how accurately you can set the duty cycle.

- A typical use of PWM is to control a servo and this only requires a PWM frequency of 50Hz. The position of the servo depends on the duty cycle.

- You can easily invert the sense of the PWM signal, which is useful when the device is being driven by a single transistor.

- As well as being a way of signaling, PWM can also be used to vary the amount of power or voltage transferred. The higher the duty cycle, the more power/voltage.

- In the same way, by varying the duty cycle, you can dim an LED. As the brightness of an LED is not linear with applied voltage, you have to modify the output using a cubic law to get linear changes in brightness.

Chapter 10
SPI Devices

The Pi offers two standard ways of connecting more sophisticated devices in hardware – the Serial Peripheral Interface or SPI bus and the I2C or I-squared-C bus. In addition there is a Linux driver which supports the non-standard 1-Wire bus in software. The following chapters focus on these buses rather than specific devices. The advantage of a bus is that, once you know how to use it, connecting compatible devices is more or less the same task, irrespective of device.

There are drivers for some specific SPI devices and if such a driver exists you should use it. More information on how to do this is given later. However, if a driver doesn't exist it isn't difficult to interface to an SPI device at a lower level via the Linux SPI driver. First, however, we need to know something about how SPI works. If you just want to use a device driver skip this section until you need it.

SPI Bus Basics

In the hardware configuration most used for the Pi, there is a single master and, at most, two slaves.

The signal lines are:

- MOSI (Master Output Slave Input), i.e. data to the slave
- MISO (Master Input Slave Output), i.e. data to the master
- SCLK (Serial Clock), which is always generated by the master

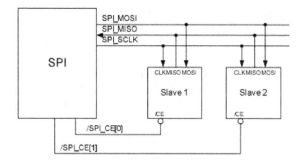

161

In general, there can also be any number of SS (Slave Select), CE (Chip Enable) or CS (Chip Select) lines, which are usually set low to select which slave is being addressed. Notice that unlike other buses, I2C for example, there are no SPI standard commands or addresses, only bytes of data. However, slave devices do interpret some of the data as commands to do something or send some particular data.

Pi SPI Interfaces

The number of SPI buses a Raspberry Pi has depends on its model. The Pi 3 and Pi Zero/W/2W have three SPI devices, but only SP0 and SP1 are available on the GPIO connector:

SPI0		
Function	Pin	
MOSI	19	GPIO10
MISO	21	GPIO09
SCLK	23	GPIO11
CE0	24	GPIO08
CE1	26	GPIO07

SPI1		
Function	Pin	
MOSI	38	GPIO20
MISO	35	GPIO19
SCLK	40	GPIO21
CE0	12	GPIO18
CE1	11	GPIO17
CE2	36	GPIO16

The Pi 4 has four full SPI interfaces, in addition to the previously mentioned SPI0 and SPI1. As in the case of other models, SPI2 exists, but isn't available for external use. SPI0 and SPI1 use the same GPIO pins as the other Pis.

The Pi 5 has nine SPI controllers, but only six are available via the external GPIO lines.

SPI0 is the same on all Pi models and is the one you should use as your first choice. You can use the other SPI interfaces on the Pi 4 and Pi 5, but notice that some of them use the same GPIO pins, SPI5 and SPI1 for example, and hence cannot be used at the same time. In the first part of this chapter we will use SPI0 because it is available on every Pi.

SPI Protocol

The data transfer on the SPI bus is slightly odd. What happens is that the master pulls one of the chip selects low, which activates a slave. Then the master toggles the clock SCLK and both the master and the slave send a single bit on their respective data lines. After eight clock pulses a byte has been transferred from the master to the slave and from the slave to the master. You can think of this as being implemented as a circular buffer, although it doesn't have to be.

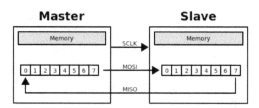

This full-duplex data transfer is often hidden by the software and the protocol used. For example, there is a read function that reads data from the slave and sends zeros or data that is ignored by the slave. Similarly, there is a write function that sends valid data, but ignores whatever the slave sends. The transfer is typically in groups of eight bits, usually most significant bit first, but this isn't always the case. In general, as long as the master supplies clock pulses, data is transferred.

Notice this circular buffer arrangement allows for slaves to be daisy-chained with the output of one going to the input of the next. This makes the entire chain one big circular shift register. This can make it possible to have multiple devices with only a single chip select, but it also means any commands sent to the slaves are received by each one in turn. For example, you could send a convert command to each A to D converter in turn and receive back results from each one.

The final odd thing about the SPI bus is that there are four modes which define the relationship between the data timing and the clock pulse. The clock can be either active high or low, which is referred to as clock polarity (CPOL), and data can be sampled on the rising or falling edge of the clock, which is clock phase (CPHA).

All combinations of these two possibilities gives the four modes:

SPI Mode*	Clock Polarity CPOL	Clock Phase CPHA	Characteristics
0	0	0	Clock active high data output on falling edge and sampled on rising
1	0	1	Clock active high data output on rising edge and sampled on falling
2	1	0	Clock active low data output on falling edge and sampled on rising
3	1	1	Clock active low data output on rising edge and sampled on falling

*The way that the SPI modes are labeled is common but not universal.

There is often a problem trying to work out what mode a slave device uses. The clock polarity is usually easy and the clock phase can sometimes be worked out from the data transfer timing diagrams by noting that:

◆ First clock transition in the middle of a data bit means CPHA=0

◆ First clock transition at the start of a data bit means CPHA=1

So to configure the SPI bus to work with a particular slave device:

1) Select the clock frequency - anything from 125MHz to 3.8kHz

2) Set the CS polarity - active high or low

3) Set the clock mode – to one of mode0 to mode3

SPI Driver

Before you can use the SPI bus you have to load its driver. You can do this by adding:

```
dtparam=spi=on
```

to the /boot/config.txt file. This loads a driver for SPI0 using two chip select lines. To find out how to activate other SPI channels see later. For the rest of this section we will be using SPI0.

Alternatively you can activate the driver dynamically:

```
FILE *doCommand(char *cmd)
{
    FILE *fp = popen(cmd, "r");
    if (fp == NULL)
    {
        printf("Failed to run command %s \n\r", cmd);
        exit(1);
    }
    return fp;
}
```

```
void checkSPI0()
{
    FILE *fd = doCommand("sudo  dtparam -l");
    char output[1024];
    int txfound = 0;

    char indicator[] = "spi=on";
    char command[] = "sudo dtparam spi=on";
    while (fgets(output, sizeof(output), fd) != NULL)
    {
        printf("%s\n\r", output);
        fflush(stdout);
        if (strstr(output, indicator) != NULL)
        {
            txfound = 1;
        }
    }
    if (txfound == 0)
    {
        fd = doCommand(command);
        sleep(2);
    }

    pclose(fd);
}
```

This works by first using the `dtparam -l` command to list the loaded overlays. If the `spi` overlay is already loaded nothing is done. If it isn't then it runs the command:

`dtparam spi=on`

SPIDev

The interface to the SPI driver is generally referred to as SPIdev and there is an `spidev.h` header file which provides all of the definitions you need to make use of it. When you load the SPI driver to install SPI Channel *n* a number of character devices are created in `/dev` of the general form `spidevn.m` where *n* is the channel number and *m* is the chip select line used to control the device.

For example, the basic SPI driver uses channel 0, i.e. SPI0 with two chip select lines, and thus you will find `spidev0.0` and `spidev0.1` which control the SPI device connected to SPI0 on chip select 0 and 1 respectively. By default, `spidev0.0` uses GPIO8 pin 26 and `spidev0.1` uses GPIO7 pin 28 for chip selects.

To work with an SPI device all you have to do is use ioctl to send requests to the relevant file. If you want to know more about ioctl see Chapter 4.

There are a range of configuration requests:

- `SPI_IOC_WR_MODE`   sets mode
- `SPI_IOC_WR_LSB_FIRST`   sets LSB first or last
- `SPI_IOC_WR_BITS_PER_WORD`   sets number of bits per word
- `SPI_IOC_WR_MAX_SPEED_HZ`   sets SPI clock if possible

Note: `SPI_IOC_WR_LSB_FIRST` isn't supported on Pi OS.

There are also requests with `WR` replaced by `RD` which read, rather than write, the configuration.

Once you have the SPI interface set up, you can send and receive data using the `SPI_IOC_MESSAGE` request. This is slightly different from other requests in that a macro is used to construct a request that also specifies the number of operations needed. Each operation is defined by a struct:

```
struct spi_ioc_transfer {
        __u64        tx_buf;
        __u64        rx_buf;

        __u32        len;
        __u32        speed_hz;

        __u16        delay_usecs;
        __u8         bits_per_word;
        __u8         cs_change;
}
```

The fields are fairly obvious. The `tx_buf` and `rx_buf` are byte arrays used for the transmitted and received data – they can be the same array. The `len` field specifies the number of bytes in each array. The `speed_hz` field modifies the SPI clock. The `delay_usecs` field sets a delay before the chip select is deselected after the transfer. The `cs_change` field is true if you want the chip select to be deselected between each transfer. The best way to find out how this all works is to write the simplest possible example.

A Loopback Example

Because of the way that data is transferred on the SPI bus, it is very easy to test that everything is working without having to add any components. All you have to do is connect MOSI to MISO so that anything sent is also received in a loopback mode. There is an official example program to implement a loopback, but it is complicated for a first example and has a bug. Our version will be the simplest possible and, hopefully, without bugs.

First connect pin 19 to pin 21 using a jumper wire and start a new project. The program is very simple. First we check that the SPI bus is loaded:

```
checkSPI0();
```

and next we open spdev0.0:

```
int fd = open("/dev/spidev0.0", O_RDWR);
```

As this is a loopback test we really don't need to configure the bus as all that matters is that the transmit and receive channels have the same configuration. However, we do need some data to send:

```
uint8_t tx[] = {0xAA};
uint8_t rx[] = {0};
```

The hex value AA is useful in testing because it generates the bit sequence 10101010, which is easy to see on a logic analyzer.

To send the data we need an spi_ioc_transfer struct:

```
struct spi_ioc_transfer tr =
    {
        .tx_buf = (unsigned long)tx,
        .rx_buf = (unsigned long)rx,
        .len = 1,
        .delay_usecs = 0,
        .speed_hz = 500000,
        .bits_per_word = 8,
    };
```

We can now use the ioctl call to send and receive the data:

```
int status = ioctl(fd, SPI_IOC_MESSAGE(1), &tr);
if (status < 0)
        printf("can't send data");
```

Finally we can check that the send and received data match and close the file.

Putting all of this together gives us the complete program:

```
#define _DEFAULT_SOURCE
#include <stdio.h>
#include <stdlib.h>
#include <string.h>
#include <fcntl.h>
#include <unistd.h>
#include <sys/ioctl.h>
#include <linux/spi/spidev.h>
#include <stdint.h>
```

```
int main(int argc, char **argv)
{
    checkSPI0();

    uint8_t tx[] = {0xAA};
    uint8_t rx[] = {0};

    struct spi_ioc_transfer tr =
        {
            .tx_buf = (unsigned long)tx,
            .rx_buf = (unsigned long)rx,
            .len = 1,
            .delay_usecs = 0,
            .speed_hz = 500000,
            .bits_per_word = 8,
        };

    int fd = open("/dev/spidev0.0", O_RDWR);
    int status = ioctl(fd, SPI_IOC_MESSAGE(1), &tr);
    if (status < 0)
        printf("can't send data");
    printf("%X,%X", tx[0],rx[0]);
    close(fd);
}
```

Note: The checkSPI0 function needs to be added to this listing.

If you run the program and don't get any data, or receive the wrong data, then the most likely reason is that you have connected the wrong two pins, or not connected them at all. If you connect a logic analyzer to the four pins involved – 19, 21, 23 and 24 you will see the data transfer:

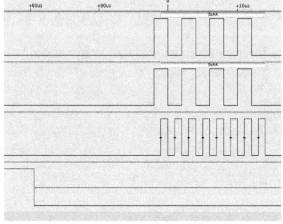

If you look carefully you will see the CS0 line go low before the master places the first data bit on the MOSI, and hence on the MISO line. Notice that the clock rises in the middle of each data bit, making this a mode 0 transfer.

If you need to configure the SPI interface you can use the ioctl calls. For example:

```
static uint8_t mode = 1;
int ret = ioctl(fd, SPI_IOC_WR_MODE, &mode);
if (ret == -1)
    printf("can't set spi mode");
static uint8_t bits = 8;
ret = ioctl(fd, SPI_IOC_WR_BITS_PER_WORD, &bits);
if (ret == -1)
    printf("can't set bits per word");
static uint32_t speed = 500000;
ret = ioctl(fd, SPI_IOC_WR_MAX_SPEED_HZ, &speed);
if (ret == -1)
    printf("can't set max speed hz");
```

After this you should see mode 1 selected and the clock going high at the start of each bit.

More Pi SPI Interfaces

So far we have used the default SPI0 bus. While this is often sufficient, it is time to find out about the other possibilities.

The number of SPI buses a Raspberry Pi has depends on its model. The Pi 3 and Pi Zero have two SPI devices:

SPI0

Function	Pin	GPIO
MOSI	19	GPIO10
MISO	21	GPIO09
SCLK	23	GPIO11
CE0	24	GPIO08
CE1	26	GPIO07

SPI1

Function	Pin	GPIO
MOSI	38	GPIO20
MISO	35	GPIO19
SCLK	40	GPIO21
CE0	12	GPIO18
CE1	11	GPIO17
CE2	36	GPIO16

The Pi 4 has five SPI interfaces - SPI0, SPI3, SPI4, SPI5 and SPI6 - and two mini-SPI interfaces - SPI1 and SPI 2.

169

The SP0 and SP1 are the same as already listed. The additional SPI interfaces that are available on the connector are:

SPI3

Function	Pin	GPIO
MOSI	3	GPIO2
MISO	28	GPIO1
SCLK	5	GPIO3
CE0	27	GPIO0
CE1	18	GPIO4

SPI4

Function	Pin	GPIO
MOSI	31	GPIO6
MISO	29	GPIO5
SCLK	26	GPIO7
CE0	7	GPIO4
CE1	22	GPIO25

SPI5

Function	Pin	GPIO
MOSI	8	GPIO14
MISO	33	GPIO13
SCLK	10	GPIO15
CE0	32	GPIO12
CE1	37	GPIO26

SPI6

Function	Pin	GPIO
MOSI	38	GPIO20
MISO	35	GPIO19
SCLK	40	GPIO21
CE0	12	GPIO18
CE1	13	GPIO27

The Pi 5 has nine SPI interfaces and SPI0 and SPI1 are the same as other Pis. Only three other SPI interfaces are available and these use different pins to the Pi 4:

SPI3

Function	Pin	GPIO
MOSI	31	GPIO6
MISO	29	GPIO5
SCLK	5	GPIO7
CE0	26	GPIO4

SPI4

Function	Pin	GPIO
MOSI	19	GPIO10
MISO	21	GPIO9
SCLK	23	GPIO11
CE0	24	GPIO8

SPI5

Function	Pin	GPIO
MOSI	8	GPIO14
MISO	33	GPIO13
SCLK	10	GPIO15
CE0	32	GPIO12

All of the SPI interfaces all have a set of drivers that follow a standard pattern, where n is the port number:

- `spin-1cs, cs0_pin=pin`   Uses a single chip select
- `spin-2cs, cs0_pin=pin1,cs1_pin=pin2` Uses two chip selects

If you don't specify a pin to be used for the chip select then the default used is the pin shown in the tables above.

SPI1 also has the possibility of using three chip selects:

- `spi1-3cs, cs0_pin=pin1,cs1_pin=pin2,cs2_pin=pin3`

It is also worth knowing that the drivers do not use the SPI hardware's chip select implementation. Instead they use a general GPIO line and set it high and low under software control. This means you can use any GPIO line as a chip select, not just the ones supported by the hardware.

You can also use the `csm_spidev` parameter to prevent the creation of an SPIdev node for the mth chip select.

171

SPI0 is the same on all models of Pi and this is the one you should use as first choice. You can use the other SPI interfaces on the Pi 4, but notice that some of them use the same GPIO pins, SPI5 and SPI1 for example, and hence cannot be used at the same time.

The MCP3008

The SPI bus can be difficult to make work at first, but once you know what to look for about how the slave claims to work it gets easier. To demonstrate how its done, let's add eight channels of 12-bit A to D using the MCP3008. There is a full driver for the MCP3008, but working with it directly via SPIdev is also very easy.

The MCP3008 is available in a number of different packages, but the standard 16-pin PDIP is the easiest to work with using a prototyping board. You can buy it from the usual sources including Amazon. Its pinouts are fairly self-explanatory:

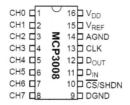

You can see that the analog inputs are on the left and the power and SPI bus connections are on the right. The conversion accuracy is claimed to be 10 bits, but how many of these bits correspond to reality and how many are noise depends on how you design the layout of the circuit.

You need to take great care if you need high accuracy. For example, you will notice that there are two voltage inputs V_{DD} and V_{REF}. V_{DD} is the supply voltage that runs the chip and V_{REF} is the reference voltage that is used to compare the input voltage. Obviously, if you want highest accuracy, V_{REF} which has to be lower than or equal to V_{DD}, should be set by an accurate low-noise voltage source. However, in most applications V_{REF} and V_{DD} are simply connected together and the usual, low- quality, supply voltage is used as the reference. If this isn't good enough then you can use anything from a Zener diode to a precision voltage reference chip such as the TL431. At the very least, however, you should add a $1\mu F$ capacitor to ground connected to the V_{DD} pin and the V_{REF} pin.

The MC3000 family is a type of A-to-D converter (ADC) called a successive approximation converter. You don't need to know how it works to use it, but it isn't difficult to understand. The idea is that first a voltage equal to $V_{REF}/2$ is generated and the input voltage is compared to this. If it is lower then the most significant bit is a 0 and if it is greater than or equal then it is a 1. At the next step the voltage generated is $V_{REF}/2+V_{REF}/4$ and the comparison is repeated to generate the next bit.

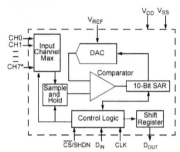

You can see that successive approximation fits in well with a serial bus as each bit can be obtained in the time needed to transmit the previous bit. However, the conversion is relatively slow and a sample-and-hold circuit has to be used to keep the input to the converter stage fixed. The sample-and-hold takes the form of a 20pF capacitor and a switch. The only reason you need to know about this is that the conversion has to be completed in a time that is short compared to the discharge time of the capacitor. So, for accuracy, there is a minimum SPI clock rate as well as a maximum.

Also, to charge the capacitor quickly enough for it to follow a changing voltage, it needs to be connected to a low-impedance source. In most cases this isn't a problem, but if it is you need to include an op amp.

If you are using an op amp buffer then you might as well implement an anti-aliasing filter to remove frequencies from the signal that are too fast for the A-to-D to respond to. How all this works takes us into the realm of analog electronics and signal processing and well beyond the core subject matter of this book.

You can also use the A-to-D channels in pairs, i.e. in differential mode, to measure the voltage difference between them. For example, in differential mode you measure the difference between CH0 and CH1, i.e. what you measure is CH1-CH0. In most cases you want to use all eight channels in single-ended mode. In principle, you can take 200k samples per second, but only at the upper limit of the supply voltage, i.e. $V_{DD}=5V$, falling to 75k samples per second at its lower limit of $V_{DD}=2.7V$.

The SPI clock limits are a maximum of 3.6MHz at 5V and 1.35MHz at 2.7V. The clock can go slower, but because of the problem with the sample-and-hold mentioned earlier it shouldn't go below 10kHz. How fast we can take samples is discussed later.

Connecting To The Pi

The connection from the MCP3008 to the Pis SPI bus is very simple and can be seen in the diagram below.

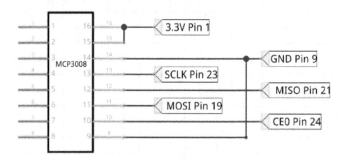

The only additional component that is recommended is a $1\mu F$ capacitor connected between pins 15 and 16 to ground, which is mounted as close to the chip as possible. As discussed in the previous section, you might want a separate voltage reference for pin 15, rather than just using the 3.3V supply.

Basic Configuration

From the datasheet, the chip select has to be active low and, by default, data is sent most significant bit first for both the master and the slave. The only puzzle is what mode to use? This is listed in the datasheet as mode 0 0 with clock active high or mode 1 1 with clock active low. For simplicity, we will use mode 0 0, which is mode0 in SPIdev.

We now have enough information to initialize the SPI bus:

```
int fd = open("/dev/spidev0.0", O_RDWR);
printf("%d\n\r", fd);

static uint8_t mode = 0;
int status = ioctl(fd, SPI_IOC_WR_MODE, &mode);
if (status == -1)
    printf("can't set spi mode");

static uint8_t bits = 8;
status = ioctl(fd, SPI_IOC_WR_BITS_PER_WORD, &bits);
if (status == -1)
    printf("can't set bits per word");

static uint32_t speed = 100000;
status = ioctl(fd, SPI_IOC_WR_MAX_SPEED_HZ, &speed);
if (status == -1)
    printf("can't set max speed hz");
```

The Protocol

Now we have the SPI initialized and ready to transfer data, but what data do we transfer? The SPI bus doesn't have any standard commands or addressing structure. Each device responds to data sent in different ways and sends data back in different ways. You simply have to read the datasheet to find out what the commands and responses are.

Reading the datasheet might be initially confusing because it says that what you have to do is send five bits to the slave - a start bit, a bit that selects its operating mode single or differential, and a 3-bit channel number. The operating mode is 1 for single-ended and 0 for differential.

So to read Channel 3, i.e. 011, in single-ended mode you would send the slave:

        11011xxx

where an x can take either value. The response from the slave is that it holds its output in a high impedance state until the sixth clock pulse, then sends a zero bit on the seventh followed by bit 9 of the data on the eighth clock pulse.

That is, the slave sends back:

        xxxxxx0b9

where x means indeterminate. The remaining nine bits are sent back in response to the next nine clock pulses. This means you have to transfer three bytes to get all ten bits of data. This all makes reading the data in 8-bit chunks confusing.

The datasheet suggests a different way of doing the job that delivers the data more neatly packed into three bytes. What it suggests to send a single byte is:

        00000001

At the same time, the slave transfers random data, which is ignored. The final 1 is treated as the start bit. If you now transfer a second byte with the most significant bit indicating single or differential mode, then a 3-bit channel address and the remaining bits set to 0, the slave will respond with the null and the top two bits of the conversion. Now all you have to do to get the final eight bits of data is to read a third byte:

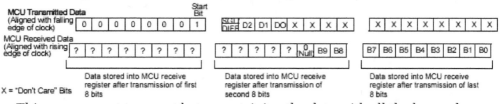

This way you get two neat bytes containing the data with all the low-order bits in their correct positions.

Using this information we can now write some instructions that read a given channel. For example, to read Channel 0 we first send a byte set to 0x01 as the start bit and ignore the byte the slave transfers. Next we send 0x80 to select single-ended and Channel 0 and keep the byte the slave sends back as the two high-order bits.

Finally, we send a zero byte (0x00) so that we get the low-order bits from the slave i.e.

```
uint8_t tx[] = {0x01,0x80,0x00};
uint8_t rx[3] ;

struct spi_ioc_transfer tr =
    {
        .tx_buf = (unsigned long)tx,
        .rx_buf = (unsigned long)rx,
        .len = 3,
        .delay_usecs = 0,
        .speed_hz = 0,
        .bits_per_word = 0,
    };
int status = ioctl(fd, SPI_IOC_MESSAGE(1), &tr);
printf("%d\n\r", status);
if (status < 0)
    printf("can't send data");
```

Notice you cannot send the three bytes one at a time using transfer because that results in the CS line being deactivated between the transfer of each byte.

To get the data out of rx we need to do some bit manipulation:

```
int data = ((int) rx[1] & 0x03) << 8 | (int) rx[2];
```

The first part of the expression extracts the low three bits from the first byte the slave sent and, as these are the most significant bits, they are shifted up eight places. The rest of the bits are then ORed with them to give the full 10-bit result. To convert to volts we use:

```
float volts = (float) data * 3.3f / 1023.0f;
```

assuming that VREF is 3.3V.

In a real application you would also need to convert the voltage to some other quantity, like temperature or light level.

If you connect a logic analyzer to the SPI bus you will see something like:

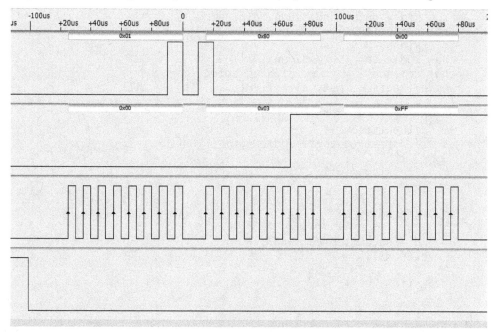

You can see the commands and the response, in this case a reading of 3.3V.
The complete program is:

```c
#define _DEFAULT_SOURCE
#include <stdio.h>
#include <stdlib.h>
#include <string.h>
#include <fcntl.h>
#include <unistd.h>
#include <sys/ioctl.h>
#include <linux/spi/spidev.h>
#include <stdint.h>

FILE *doCommand(char *cmd)
{
    FILE *fp = popen(cmd, "r");
    if (fp == NULL)
    {
        printf("Failed to run command %s \n\r", cmd);
        exit(1);
    }
    return fp;
}
```

```c
void checkSPI0()
{
    FILE *fd = doCommand("sudo  dtparam -l");
    char output[1024];
    int txfound = 0;
    char indicator[] = "spi=on";
    char command[] = "sudo dtparam spi=on";
    while (fgets(output, sizeof(output), fd) != NULL)
    {
        printf("%s\n\r", output);
        fflush(stdout);
        if (strstr(output, indicator) != NULL)
        {
            txfound = 1;
        }
    }
    if (txfound == 0)
    {
        fd = doCommand(command);
        sleep(2);
    }
    pclose(fd);
}

int main(int argc, char **argv)
{
    checkSPI0();

    uint8_t tx[] = {0x01, 0x80, 0x00};
    uint8_t rx[3];

    struct spi_ioc_transfer tr =
        {
            .tx_buf = (unsigned long)tx,
            .rx_buf = (unsigned long)rx,
            .len = 3,
            .delay_usecs = 0,
            .speed_hz = 0,
            .bits_per_word = 0,
        };

    int fd = open("/dev/spidev0.0", O_RDWR);

    static uint8_t mode = 0;
    int status = ioctl(fd, SPI_IOC_WR_MODE, &mode);
    if (status == -1)
        printf("can't set spi mode");

    static uint8_t bits = 8;
    status = ioctl(fd, SPI_IOC_WR_BITS_PER_WORD, &bits);
    if (status == -1)
        printf("can't set bits per word");
```

```
    static uint32_t speed = 100000;
    status = ioctl(fd, SPI_IOC_WR_MAX_SPEED_HZ, &speed);
    if (status == -1)
        printf("can't set max speed hz");

    status = ioctl(fd, SPI_IOC_MESSAGE(1), &tr);
    if (status < 0)
        printf("can't send data");

    int data = ((int)rx[1] & 0x03) << 8 | (int)rx[2];
    float volts = (((float)data) * 3.3f) / 1023.0f;
    printf("%f V\n\r", volts);

    close(fd);
}
```

How Fast

Once you have the basic facilities working, the next question is always how fast does something work. In this case we need to know what sort of data rates we can achieve using this A-to-D converter. The simplest way of finding this out is to use the fastest read loop for Channel 0:

```
for (;;)
{
    status = ioctl(fd, SPI_IOC_MESSAGE(1), &tr);
    if (status < 0)
        printf("can't send data");
}
```

With the clock set at 100K, the sampling rate is measured to be 2.64kHz. This is perfectly reasonable as it takes at least 24 clock pulses to read the data. Most of the time in the loop is due to the 24 clock pulses, so there is little to be gained from optimization.

Increasing the clock rate to the maximum of 1MHz increases the sampling rate to 7kHz, which isn't as much as you might expect. The reason is that the chip select line isn't changed as fast as it could be. It is held low for about 40μs after the transfer is complete.

179

The MCP3008 Driver

Although there are some advantages in dealing with the MCP2008 ADC using `spidev`, you can also use a driver that works directly with it and avoid dealing with SPI and the device commands altogether.

To do this you need to add:

```
dtparam=spi=on
dtoverlay=mcp3008:spi0-0-present,spi0-0-speed=1000000
```

to the `/boot/config.txt` file. At the time of writing you can't enable the driver dynamically. You have to specify the SPIdev node that the device is on, `spi0.0` in this case, and the speed of the clock, 1MHz in this case. If you want to use another SPI interface, you have to load a driver for it and change the SPIdev node specified.

Once you have the driver loaded, reboot after editing `/boot/config.txt`, you will discover that there are some new folders and files in `/sys/bus/`. The reason that they are in this different location is that the driver is an IIO (Industrial I/O) driver. These are described in detail in Chapter 14, but all that really matters is that the pseudo files relating to the device are in a different location. All IIO devices live in the `/sys/bus/iio/devices/` directory and a folder of the form `iio:devicex` is created for each device. In our case there is only one IIO device and so the folder we are interested in is `/sys/bus/iio/devices/iio:device0`.

If you list this folder you will find files with names that indicate their function:

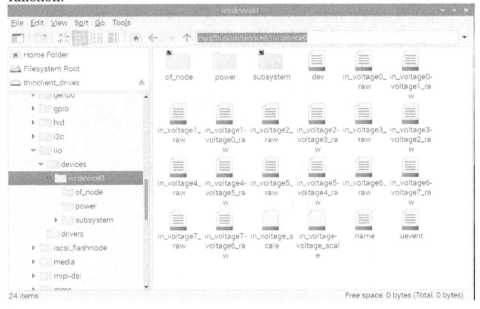

For example in_voltage0_raw is the raw reading from channel 0 of the device. Similarly in_voltage0-voltage1_raw is the differential voltage using input 0 and input 1 as a differential input.

A program to read channel 0, given that the drivers are loaded, is very simple:

```
int main(int argc, char **argv)
{
    char buf[100];
    int fd =open("/sys/bus/iio/devices/iio:device0/
                             in_voltage0_raw",O_RDONLY);

    int n = read(fd, buf, 100);

    int data;
    sscanf(buf, "%d", &data);

    printf("%d\n\r", data);
    float volts = (((float)data) * 3.3f) / 1023.0f;
    printf("%f V\n\r", volts);
}
```

The act of opening the file starts the conversion.

To read the device a second time you either have to close the file and reopen it or reposition it to the start:

```
    for (;;)
    {
        int n = read(fd, buf, 100);
        int data;
        sscanf(buf, "%d", &data);
        printf("%d\n\r", data);
        float volts = (((float)data) * 3.3f) / 1023.0f;
        printf("%f V\n\r", volts);
        lseek(fd, SEEK_SET, 0);
    }
```

Without any processing of the data, you can read data at around 9kHz.

Problems

The SPI bus is often a real headache because of the lack of a definitive standard, but in most cases you can make it work. The first problem is in discovering the characteristics of the slave device you want to work with. In general, this is solved by a careful reading of the datasheet or perhaps some trial and error, see the next chapter for an example.

If you are working with a single slave then generally things work once you have the SPI bus configuration set correctly. Things are more difficult when there are multiple devices on the same bus. The Raspberry Pi can only directly support two devices, but this is enough to make the task more difficult. Typically you will find SPI devices that don't switch off properly when they are not being addressed. In principle, all SPI devices should present high impedance outputs (i.e. tristate buffers) when not being addressed, but some don't. If you encounter a problem you need to check that the selected slave is able to control the MISO line properly.

Another problem, which is particularly bad for the Pi, is noise. If you are using a USB, or some other power supply that isn't able to supply sufficient instantaneous current draw to the Pi, you will see noise on any or all of the data lines - the CS0/1 lines seem to be particularly sensitive. The solution is to get a better power supply.

If there is a full driver for the device then it is a good idea to give it a try, but many SPI device drivers are poorly supported and documentation is usually non-existent. If you can get a direct driver to work then it will usually be faster and easier, but it might not be as stable as hand-coding your own user-side interaction with the device with the help of SPIdev.

Summary

- All versions of the Raspberry Pi have two usable hardware Serial Peripheral Interface (SPI) buses. The Pi 4 has four additional ones.

- Making SPI work with any particular device has four steps:

  1. Discover how to connect the device to the SPI pins. This is a matter of identifying pinouts and what chip selects are supported.

  2. Find out how to configure the Pi's SPI bus to work with the device. This is mostly a matter of clock speed and mode.

  3. Identify the commands that you need to send to the device to get it to do something and what data it sends back as a response.

  4. Find, or work out, the relationship between the raw reading, the voltage, and the quantity the voltage represents.

- The Linux SPI driver can be used to interface to any SPI device as long as you know what commands to send and what the data sent back means.

- The SPI driver is supported by the SPIdev header which provides the basic tools to work with the ioctl interface.

- The SPI driver uses general GPIO lines as chip select lines and not the built-in hardware.

- Using the other SPI interfaces on the Pi 4 is just a matter of selecting the appropriate driver.

- The MCP3000 range of A-to-D converters is very easy to use via SPI. It can be used directly from the SPI bus by sending commands and reading the data generated.

- There is also a specific MCP3008 driver which allows you to work with the device without having to know anything about SPI or the commands that have to be sent to read the data.

- The MCP3008 driver is an example of an IIO device.

Chapter 11
I2C Basics

The I2C, standing for Inter-Integrated Circuit and pronounced I-Squared-C, bus, is one of the most useful ways of connecting moderately sophisticated sensors and peripherals to any processor. The only problem is that it can seem like a nightmarish confusion of hardware, low-level interaction and high-level software. There are few general introductions to the subject because at first sight every I2C device is different, but there are shared principles that can help you work out how to connect and talk to a new device.

The I2C bus is a serial bus that can be used to connect multiple devices to a controller. It is a simple bus that uses two active wires: one for data and one for a clock. Despite there being lots of problems in using the I2C bus, because it isn't well standardized and devices can conflict and generally do things in their own way, it is still commonly used and is too useful to ignore.

The big problem in getting started with the I2C bus is that you will find it described at many different levels of detail, from the physical bus characteristics and protocol to the details of individual devices. It can be difficult to tie all of this together and produce a working project. In fact, you only need to know the general workings of the I2C bus, some general features of the protocol, and know the addresses and commands used by any particular device.

To explain and illustrate these ideas, we really do have to work with a particular device to make things concrete. However, the basic stages of getting things to work, the steps, the testing and verification, are more or less the same irrespective of the device.

I2C Hardware Basics

The I2C bus is very simple from the hardware point of view. It has just two signal lines, SDA and SCL, the data and clock lines respectively. Each of these lines is pulled up by a suitable resistor to the supply line at whatever voltage the devices are working - 3.3V and 5V are common choices. The size of the pull-up resistors isn't critical, but 4.7K is typical as shown in the circuit diagram:

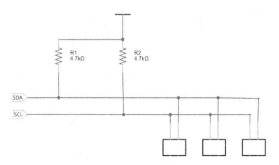

You simply connect the SDA and SCL pins of each of the devices to the pull-up resistors. Of course, if any of the devices have built-in pull-up resistors you can omit the external resistors. More of a problem is if multiple devices each have pull-ups. In this case you need to disable all but one.

The I2C bus is an open collector bus. This means that it is actively pulled down by a transistor set to on. When the transistor is off, however, the bus returns to the high voltage state via the pull-up resistor. The advantage of this approach is that multiple devices can pull the bus low at the same time. That is, an open collector bus is low when one or more devices pulls it low and high when none of the devices is active.

The SCL line provides a clock which is used to set the speed of data transfer, one data bit is presented on the SDA line for each pulse on the SCL line. In all cases, the master drives the clock line to control how fast bits are transferred. The slave can, however, hold the clock line low if it needs to slow down the data transfer. In most cases the I2C bus has a single master device, the Pi in our case, which drives the clock and invites the slaves to receive or transmit data. Multiple masters are possible, but this is advanced and usually not necessary.

At this point we could go into the details of how all of this works in terms of bits. All you really need to know is that all communication occurs in 8-bit packets. The master sends a packet, an address frame, which contains the address of the slave it wants to interact with. Every slave has to have a unique address, which is usually 7 bits, but it can be 11 bits, and the Pi does support this.

One of the problems in using the I2C bus is that manufacturers often use the same address, or same set of selectable addresses, and this can make using particular combinations of devices on the same bus difficult or impossible.

The 7-bit address is set as the high-order 7 bits in the byte and this can be confusing as an address that is stated as 0x40 in the datasheet results in 0x80 being sent to the device. The low-order bit of the address signals a write or a read operation depending on whether it is a 0 or a 1 respectively. After sending an address frame, it then sends or receives data frames back from the slave. There are also special signals used to mark the start and end of an exchange of packets, but the library functions take care of these.

This is really all you need to know about I2C in general to get started, but it is worth finding out more of the details as you need them. You almost certainly will need them as you debug I2C programs using a logic analyzer.

The clock SCL and data SDA lines rest high. The master signals a Start bit by pulling the SDA line down – S in the diagram below. The clock is then pulled low by the master, during which time the SDA line can change state. The state of the bit is read in the middle of the following high period of the clock pulse B1, B2 and so on in the diagram. This continues until the last bit has been sent, when the data line is allowed to rise while the clock is high, so sending a stoP bit – P in the diagram. Notice that when data is being transmitted the data line doesn't change while the clock is high. Any change in the data line when the clock is high sends a start or a stop bit, i.e. clock high and falling data line is a start bit and clock high and rising data line is a stop bit:

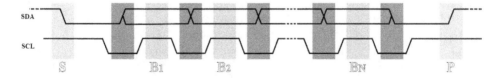

The clock speed was originally set at 100kHz, standard mode, but then increased to 400kHz in fast mode. In practice, devices usually specify a maximum clock speed that they will work with.

Data Transfer

Now that we know the low-level details of how the I2C bus works it is time to look at the detailed interaction between the master and the slave. To make use of I2C you often don't need this deeper knowledge, but as soon as something goes wrong you most definitely do.

In most cases the clock line is controlled by the master – the exception to this rule is during clock stretching, see later. Whichever entity is transmitting data, i.e. controlling the data line, the last bit is set by the other entity to signal a success – ACK, data line low, or failure – NAK, data line high.

Let's start by examining what happens when the master writes data to the slave. In all cases, first an address frame, a byte containing the address of the device you specified, is transmitted. Notice that the 7-bit address has to be shifted into the topmost bits and the first bit has to be zeroed for a write operation. So when you write to a device with an address of 0x40 you will see 0x80 on a logic analyzer, i.e. 0x40<<1.

Having sent the address frame, the master can send as many bytes as it wants to. The slave responds with an ACK or a NAK bit after each byte.

That is, the usual block write transaction sending n bytes is:

```
START|ADDR|ACK|DATA0|ACK|
          DATA1|ACK|
              ....
          DATAn|ACK|STOP
```

Notice that it is the slave that sends the ACK bit and if the data is not received correctly it can send NAK instead and a write error will be reported.

A multibyte transfer is quite different from sending n single bytes one at a time.

```
START|  ADDR  |ACK|DATA0|ACK|STOP
START|  ADDR  |ACK|DATA1|ACK|STOP
    . . .
START|  ADDR  |ACK|DATAn|ACK|STOP
```

Notice that there are now multiple ADDR frames sent as well as multiple START and STOP bits. What this means in practice is that you have to look at a device's datasheet and send however many bytes it needs as a single operation. You cannot send the same number of bytes broken into chunks. The Linux driver naturally provides a block write.

Reading works in much the same way - the master sends an address frame and then reads as many bytes from the slave as specified. As in the case of write, the address supplied is shifted up one bit and the lower order bit set to 1 to indicate a read operation. So if the current slave is at address 0x40, the read address is 0x41 and the master sends a read address of 0x81.

The read transaction is:

```
START|ADDR|ACK|DATA0|ACK|
            |DATA1|ACK|
       . . .
            |DATAn|NAK|STOP
```

The master sends the address frame and the slave sends the ACK after the address to acknowledge that it has been received and it is ready to send data. Then the slave sends bytes one at a time and the master sends ACK in response to each byte. Finally the master sends a NAK to indicate that the last byte has been read and then a STOP bit. That is, the master controls how many bytes are transferred.

As in the case of the write functions, a block transfer of n bytes is different from transferring n bytes one at a time because of the additional stop bits.

Using A Register

A very standard interaction between master and slave is writing or reading data to and from a register. This isn't anything special and, as far as the I2C bus is concerned, you are simply writing raw data. However, datasheets and users tend to think in terms of reading and writing internal storage locations, i.e. registers in the device. In fact, many devices have lots of internal storage. Indeed, some I2C devices, for example I2C EPROMS, are nothing but internal storage. In this case a standard transaction to write to a register is:

1) Send address frame

2) Send a data frame with the command to select the register

3) Send a data frame containing the byte or word to be written to the register

Notice the command that has to be sent depends on the device and you have to look it up in its datasheet. Also notice that there is a single START and STOP bit at the beginning and end of the transaction. Sometimes just the register address is sufficient, i.e. no following data. In this case you can think of the register address as a command if you like.

Reading from a register is a very standard operation, but it is slightly more complicated in that you need a combined write and read operation. That is, to read a register you need a write operation to send the address of the register to the device and then a read operation to get the data that the device sends as the contents of the register. This write/read combination is so common that I2C libraries often provide a single function to do the job.

In theory, and mostly in practice, a register read of this sort can work with a stop-start separating the write and read operations, which is what you get if you use separate write and read function calls:

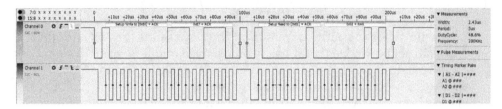

That is, the transfer sequence is:

```
START|ADDR|ACK|REGADDR|ACK|STOP|
START|ADDR|ACK|DATA1|ACK|
            |DATA2|ACK|
               . . .
            |DATAn|NAK|STOP
```

If you look at the end of the write and the start of the read you will see that there is both a STOP and a START bit between them. For some devices this is a problem. A STOP bit is a signal that another transaction can start and this might allow another master to take over the bus. To avoid this, some devices demand a repeated START bit between the write and the read and no STOP bit. This is referred to as a repeated start bit transaction. That is, the sequence for a repeated start bit register read is:

```
START|ADDR|ACK|REGADDR|ACK|
START|ADDR|ACK|DATA0|ACK|
            |DATA1|ACK|
     . . .
            |DATAn|NAK|STOP
```

Notice that there is only one STOP bit and it does mark the true end of the data transfer.

In theory, either form of transaction should work but in practice you will find that some slave devices state that they need a repeated start bit and no stop bits in continued transactions. In this case you need to be careful how you send and receive data.

Slow Read – Clock Stretching v Polling

The I2C clock is mostly controlled by the master and this raises the question of how we cope with the speed that a slave can or cannot respond to a request for data. There are two broad approaches to waiting for data on the I2C bus. The first is simply to request the data and then perform reads in a polling loop. If the device isn't ready with the data, then it sends a data frame with a NAK bit set. So all we have to do is test for an NAK response. Of course, the polling loop doesn't have to be "tight". The response time is often long enough to do other things and you can use the I2C bus to work with other slave devices while the one you activated gets on with trying to get the data you requested. All you have to do is to remember to read its data at some later time.

The second way is to allow the slave to hold the clock line low after the master has released it – so called clock stretching. In most cases the master will simply wait before moving on to the next frame while the clock line is held low. This is very simple and it means you don't have to implement a polling loop, but also notice that your program is frozen until the slave releases the clock line. The Raspberry Pi's implementation of I2C clock stretching has a flaw in that it fails if the clock stretching is very short, and as a result polling is the preferred option.

Basic Pi I2C Hardware

So far we have been considering I2C in general, but before we move on to look at an example we need to have some idea of what the Raspberry Pi offers by way of I2C interfaces. All versions of the Pi have two externally usable I2C masters, referred to in documentation as BSC (Broadcom Serial Controller) interfaces. These are essentially an implementation of the I2C bus and in general you don't have to worry about incompatibilities. There are additional I2C bus masters available on the Pi 4 and how to use them is described in Chapter 13, but initially we will concentrate on the two ports that are available for use on all Pis, BSC0 and BSC1. Their pin and GPIO assignments are:

BSC0

Function	Pin	GPIO
SDA	27	GPIO0
SCL	28	GPIO1

BSC1

Function	Pin	GPIO
SDA	3	GPIO2
SCL	5	GPIO3

BSC0 is also allocated to expansion EPROM use as part of HAT configuration and is best avoided if possible. However, if you are not using any HATs then it is available. This makes BSC1 the first choice if you want to work with I2C.

You also need to know that there are 1.8K pull-up resistors on BSC1 which sometimes makes it easier to use for I2C but if the device you are connecting already has pull-up resistors then you need to disable them. The resistors on the Pi cannot be disabled in software and removing them from the board can be tricky.

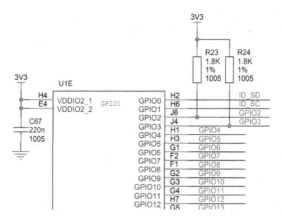

The Pi 5 uses a different implementation of I2C which provides four hardware implemented channels.

I2C0=BSC0

Function	Pin	GPIO
SDA	27 or 24	GPIO0 or 8
SCL	28 or 21	GPIO1 or 9

I2C1 =BSC1

Function	Pin	GPIO
SDA	3 or 19	GPIO2 or 10
SCL	5 or 23	GPIO3 or 11

I2C2

Function	Pin	GPIO
SDA	3 or 32	GPIO4 or 12
SCL	5 or 33	GPIO5 or 13

I2C3

Function	Pin	GPIO
SDA	3 or 8	GPIO6 or 14
SCL	5 or 10	GPIO7 or 15

You can see that the first two I2C channels are the same as found on other Pis and can be used in the same way.

Summary

- The I2C bus is a very popular serial bus that makes use of two wires to connect devices.

- Each I2C device has a built-in address or set of addresses that it can respond to. Address clashes are a particular problem if you want to mix devices on a single I2C bus.

- There are a few subtle variations on the data protocol that modify how multiple blocks of data are sent. Getting this exactly right is another common I2C problem.

- Slow devices are accommodated by either polling for the device to be ready or allowing the device to hold down the clock line, clock stretching, until it is ready.

- There is one easy-to-use I2C bus, BSC1, available on pins 3 and 5, complete with 1.8K pull-up resistors.

- There is an additional externally usable bus BSC0 I2C bus on pins 27 and 28, but it is allocated to expansion EPROM use and best avoided if possible. There are no pull-up resistors fitted.

- The Pi 5 has four I2C bus controllers the first two are the same as found in other Pis

Chapter 12

The I2C Linux Driver

There are many specific device drivers which make use of the I2C bus and, as in the case of the SPI bus, there is usually a choice of hand-coding the interaction using the I2C driver or using the specific device driver. In this chapter we will look at the basics of making use of the driver for BSC1 which works on all versions of the Pi.

Enabling The Driver

To make use of the Linux I2C driver you have to enable it by adding dtparam=i2c_arm=on to the /boot/config.txt file. Alternatively you can load it dynamically:

```
FILE * doCommand(char *cmd) {
    FILE *fp = popen(cmd, "r");
    if (fp == NULL) {
        printf("Failed to run command %s \n\r", cmd);
        exit(1);
    }
    return fp;
}

void checkI2CBus() {
    FILE *fd = doCommand("sudo dtparam -l");
    char output[1024];
    int txfound = 0;
    while (fgets(output, sizeof (output), fd) != NULL) {
        printf("%s\n\r", output);
        fflush(stdout);
        if (strstr(output, "i2c_arm=on") != NULL) {
            txfound = 1;
        }
        if (strstr(output, "i2c_arm=off") != NULL) {
            txfound = 0;
        }
    }
    pclose(fd);
    if (txfound == 0) {
        fd = doCommand("sudo dtparam i2c_arm=on");
        pclose(fd);
    }
}
```

This is slightly different to the earlier driver loading functions. The first part of the function uses `dtparam -1` to get a list of loaded overlays. If it finds `ic2_arm=on` as the last `ic2_arm` overlay then it does nothing. If it doesn't find it then it activates the overlay. As you can also use `ic2_arm=off` and it is the last overlay that controls the state of the system we need to find the last occurrence of `ic2_arm` and make sure it is "=on".

Both actions enable BSC1 and create a device file:

```
/dev/i2c-1
```

You can check that the driver has been installed using:

```
ls /dev/i2c*
```

which will return a list of I2C devices.

Using The I2C Driver From C

As is the case for all Linux devices, the I2C device /dev/i2c-x, where x is the I2C bus number, looks like a file. You can do a block read by simply opening the file for reading and reading an array of bytes:

```
int i2cfd = open("/dev/i2c-1", O_RDWR);
read(i2cfd,buf,n);
```

This reads a maximum of *n* bytes of data and returns it as an array of bytes. The only problem is how do you specify the address of the device? Opening the file only opens the I2C channel and there might be multiple devices connected to it. As in the case of other /dev character devices we need to use the standard Linux ioctl function to send a command to it.

In the case of the I2C driver the most important ioctl command is:

```
I2C_SLAVE
```

This is used to set the address of the slave that subsequent read and writes apply to. So to set the address of the device you want to read from to 0x40 you would use:

```
#include <linux/i2c-dev.h>

ioctl(i2cfd, I2C_SLAVE, 0x40);
```

Finally to reset the hardware and return all GPIO lines to their default modes you have to close the file:

```
close(i2cfd);
```

Putting all of the together a block read/write is:

```
#define _DEFAULT_SOURCE
#include <stdio.h>
#include <stdlib.h>
#include <sys/ioctl.h>
#include <unistd.h>
#include<fcntl.h>
#include <linux/i2c-dev.h>

void checkI2CBus();
FILE * doCommand(char *cmd);

int main(int argc, char** argv) {
    checkI2CBus();
    int i2cfd = open("/dev/i2c-1", O_RDWR);
    ioctl(i2cfd, I2C_SLAVE, 0x40);
    char buf[4] = {0xE7};
    write(i2cfd,buf,1);
    read(i2cfd,buf,1);
    close(i2cfd
    return (EXIT_SUCCESS);
}
```

By default stop bits are not sent between each byte read, a stop bit is only sent at the end of the block of data that is written.

If you try these programs out you will discover that the I2C clock frequency is the default 100KHz. You can't change the clock frequency dynamically but you can add:

```
dtparam=i2c_arm=on,i2c_arm_baudrate=10000
```

to the /boot/config.txt file and after a reboot the I2C clock will be set to the frequency specified as the baudrate. The baud rate is simply the clock speed in Hz. Notice that the I2C clock speed depends on the core clock rate and this can be slower than the maximum possible when the device is idling or under heat pressure. To run at the fastest clock speed, even when idling, use the command:

```
sudo sh -c "echo performance >
/sys/devices/system/cpu/cpu0/cpufreq/scaling_governor"
```

A Real Device - HTU21D

Using an I2C device has two problems - the physical connection between master and slave and figuring out what the software has to do to make it work. Here we'll work with the SparkFun HTU21D/Si7021 and the information in its datasheet to make a working temperature and humidity sensor using the I2C functions we've just met.

First the hardware. The HTU21D Humidity and Temperature sensor is one of the easiest of I2C devices to use. Its only problem is that it is only available in a surface-mount package. To overcome this you could solder some wires onto the pads or buy a general breakout board. However, it is much simpler to buy the SparkFun HTU21D breakout board because this has easy connections and built-in pull-up resistors. The HTU21D has been replaced by the Si7021, which is more robust than the original and works in the same way although the HTU21D is still available from many sources. If you decide to work with some other I2C device you can still follow the steps given, modifying what you do to suit it. In particular, if you select a device that only works at 5V you might need a level converter.

It is worth noting that there is a specific Linux driver for the HTU21D. This is described in Chapter 14 and in most cases is the preferred way to use the device. To provide a generalizable example, here we look at exactly how the device works on the I2C bus and a program that interfaces with it at a low level is described.

Wiring The HTU21D

Given that the HTU21D has pull-up resistors, we really should disable them for use on the Pi's internal I2C bus which already has pull-ups. In practice, the additional pull-ups don't seem to make much difference to the waveforms and you can leave them in place while testing. You can use a prototype board to make the connections and this makes it easier to connect other instruments such as a logic analyzer.

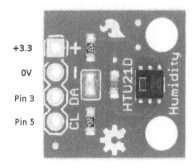

A First Program

After wiring up any i2C device the first question that needs to be answered is, does it work? Unfortunately for most complex devices finding out if it works is a multi-step process. Our first program aims to read some data back from the HTU21D - any data will do.

If you look at the datasheet you will find that the device address is 0x40 and its supports the following commands/registers:

Command	Code	Comment
Trigger Temperature Measurement	0xE3	Hold master
Trigger Humidity Measurement	0xE5	Hold master
Trigger Temperature Measurement	0xF3	No Hold master
Trigger Humidity Measurement	0xF5	No Hold master
Write user register	0xE6	
Read user register	0xE7	
Soft Reset	0xFE	

The easiest of these to get started with is the Read user register command, which gives the current setup of the device and can be used to set the resolution of the measurement.

Notice that the codes that you send to the device can often be considered addresses or commands. In this case you can think of sending 0xE7 as a command to read the register or the read address of the register, it makes no difference. In most cases the term command is used when sending the code makes the device do something, and the term address is used when it simply makes the device read or write specific data.

To read the user register we have to write a byte containing 0xE7 and then read the byte the device sends back. This involves sending an address frame, a data frame, and then another address frame and reading a data frame. The device seems to be happy if you send a stop bit between each transaction or just a new start bit.

A program to read the user register is fairly easy to put together. The address of the device is 0x40 so its write address is 0x80 and its read address is 0x81. As the I2C functions adjust the address as needed, we simply use 0x40 as the device's address, but it does affect what you see if you sample the data being exchanged:

```
#define _DEFAULT_SOURCE
#include <stdio.h>
#include <stdlib.h>
#include <string.h>
#include <sys/ioctl.h>
#include <unistd.h>
#include <fcntl.h>
#include <linux/i2c-dev.h>

void checkI2CBus();
FILE * doCommand(char *cmd);


int main(int argc, char** argv) {

    checkI2CBus();

    int i2cfd = open("/dev/i2c-1", O_RDWR);
    ioctl(i2cfd, I2C_SLAVE, 0x40);
    char buf[4] = {0xE7};
    write(i2cfd,buf,1);
    read(i2cfd,buf,1);
    printf("%x\n\r",buf[0]);
    close(i2cfd);
    return (EXIT_SUCCESS);
}
```

This sends the address frame 0x80 and then the data byte 0xE7 to select the user register. Next it sends an address frame 0x81 to read the data.

If you run the program you will see "2".

This is the default value of the register and it corresponds to a resolution of 12 and 14 bits for the humidity and temperature respectively and a supply voltage greater than 2.25V.

I2C Protocol In Action

If you have a logic analyzer that can interpret the I2C protocol connected what you will see is:

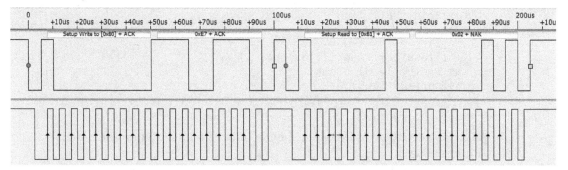

You can see that the `write_byte` function sends an address packet set to the device's 7-bit address `0x40` as the high order bits with the low order bit set to zero to indicate a write, i.e `0x80`. After this you get a data packet sent containing `0xE7`, the address of the register. After a few microseconds it sends the address frame again, only this time with the low order bit set to 1 to indicate a read, i.e. it sends `0x81`. It then receives back a single byte of data from the device, `0x02`. This demonstrates that the external device is working properly and we can move on to getting some data of interest.

Reading Raw Temperature Data

Now we come to reading one of the two quantities that the device measures – temperature. If you look back at the command table you will see that there are two possible commands for reading the temperature:

Command	Code	Comment
Trigger Temperature Measurement	0xE3	Hold master
Trigger Temperature Measurement	0xF3	No Hold master

What is the difference between Hold master and No Hold master? This was discussed earlier in a general context. The device cannot read the temperature instantaneously and the master can either opt to be held waiting for the data, i.e. hold master, or released to do something else and poll for the data until it is ready. The simplest thing to do is poll for the data. How to use clock stretching is described in the next chapter.

201

In this case we send F3 and then wait for there to be something to read. If the slave isn't ready it simply replies with a NAK and this causes the read to return -1. When the slave returns an ACK then three bytes are read and result is 3, bringing the loop to an end:

```
char buf[3] = {0xF3};
write(i2cfd, buf, 1);

while (1) {
    int result = read(i2cfd, buf, 3);
    if (result > 0) break;
    usleep(100*1000);

}
```

This polls repeatedly until the slave device returns an ACK, when the data is loaded into the data.

Putting this into a complete program gives:

```
int main(int argc, char** argv) {
    checkI2CBus();

    int i2cfd = open("/dev/i2c-1", O_RDWR);
    ioctl(i2cfd, I2C_SLAVE, 0x40);
    char buf[3] = {0xF3};
    write(i2cfd, buf, 1);

    while (1) {
        int result = read(i2cfd, buf, 3);
        if (result > 0) break;
        usleep(10*1000);

    }
    uint8_t msb = buf[0];
    uint8_t lsb = buf[1];
    uint8_t check = buf[2];
    printf("msb %d \n\rlsb %d \n\rchecksum %d \n\r",
                                        msb, lsb, check);

    close(i2cfd);
    return (EXIT_SUCCESS);
}
```

Where the checkI2CBus has been omitted as it was given earlier.

If you try this out you should find that it works and it prints something like:

```
msb 97
lsb 232
checksum 217
```

with the temperature in the 20C range.

If you look at what is happening using a logic analyzer then you will see the initial interaction:

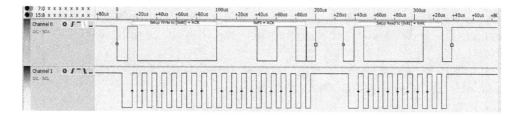

followed by repeated attempts to read the data:

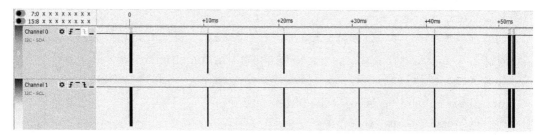

When the device is ready it responds with an ACK and the three data bytes are read:

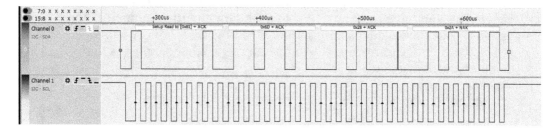

You can also see that only one start and stop bit is used.

Processing The Data

Our next task isn't really directly related to the problem of using the I2C bus, but it is a very typical next step. The device returns the data in three bytes, but the way that this data relates to the temperature isn't simple.

If you read the datasheet you will discover that the temperature data is the 14-bit value that results from putting together the most and least significant byte and zeroing the bottom two bits. The bottom two bits are used as status bits, bit zero currently isn't used and bit one is 1 if the data is a humidity measurement and 0 if it is a temperature measurement.

To put the two bytes together we use:

```
unsigned int data16=((unsigned int) msb << 8) |
                              (unsigned int) (lsb & 0xFC);
```

This zeros the bottom two bits, shifts the `msb` up eight bits and ORs the two together. The result is a 16-bit temperature value with the bottom two bits zeroed.

Now we have raw temperature value but we still have to convert it to standard units. The datasheet gives the formula:

```
Temp in C = -46.85 + 175.72 * data16 / 216
```

The only problem in implementing this is working out 2^{16}. You can work out 2^x with the expression `1<<x`, i.e. shift `1` x places to the left.

This gives:

```
float temp = (float)(-46.85 +(175.72 * data16 /(float)(1<<16)));
```

As 2^{16} is a constant that works out to 65536 it is more efficient to write:

```
float temp = (float)(-46.85 +(175.72 * data16 /(float)65536));
```

Now all we have to do is print the temperature:

```
printf("Temperature %f C \n\r", temp);
```

Reading The Humidity

The nice thing about I2C and using a particular I2C device is that it gets easier. Once you have seen how to do it with one device, the skill generalizes and once you know how to deal with a particular device other aspects of the device are usually similar. Reading the humidity using polling is exactly the same as reading the temperature - all that changes is the command code we send:

```
  buf[0] = 0xF5;
    write(i2cfd, buf, 1);

    while (1) {
        int result = read(i2cfd, buf, 3);
        if (result > 0) break;
        usleep(10 * 1000);

    }
    msb = buf[0];
    lsb = buf[1];
    check = buf[2];
```

Once we have the data the formula to convert the 16-bit value to percentage humidity is:

```
RH= -6 + 125 * data16 / 2¹⁶
```

and the Temperature in C is:

```
data16 = ((unsigned int) msb << 8) | (unsigned int) (lsb & 0xFC);
float hum = -6 + (125.0 * (float) data16) / 65536;
printf("Humidity %f %% \n\r", hum);
```

Checksum Calculation

Although computing a checksum isn't specific to I2C, it is another common task. The datasheet explains that the polynomial used is:

$$X8 + X5 + X4 + 1$$

Once you have this information you can work out the divisor by writing a binary number with a one in each location corresponding to a power of X in the polynomial. In this case the 8th, 5th, 4th and 1st bit. Hence the divisor is:

```
0x0131
```

What you do next is roughly the same for all CRCs. First you put the data that was used to compute the checksum together with the checksum value as the low order bits:

```
uint32_t data32 = ((uint32_t) msb << 16) | ((uint32_t) lsb << 8) |
                                            (uint32_t) check;
```

Now you have three bytes, i.e 24 bits in a 32-bit value. Next you adjust the divisor so that its most significant non-zero bit aligns with the most significant bit of the three bytes. As this divisor has a **1** at bit eight it needs to be shifted 15 places to the right to move it to be the 24th bit:

```
uint32_t divisor = 0x988000;
```

Now that you have both the data and the divisor aligned, you step through the top-most 16 bits, i.e. you don't process the low order eight bits which is the received checksum. For each bit you check to see if it is a **1** - if it is you replace the data with the data XOR divisor. In either case you shift the divisor one place to the right:

```
for (int i = 0; i < 16; i++) {
    if (data32 & (uint32_t) 1 << (23 - i)) data32 ^= divisor;
    divisor >>= 1;
};
```

When the loop ends, if there was no error, the `data32` should be zeroed and the received checksum is correct and as computed on the data received.

A complete function to compute the checksum is:

```c
uint8_t crcCheck(uint8_t msb, uint8_t lsb, uint8_t check) {
    uint32_t data32 = ((uint32_t) msb << 16) |
                      ((uint32_t) lsb << 8) | (uint32_t) check;
    uint32_t divisor = 0x988000;
    for (int i = 0; i < 16; i++) {
        if (data32 & (uint32_t) 1 << (23 - i)) data32 ^= divisor;
        divisor >>= 1;
    };
    return (uint8_t) data32;
}
```

It is rare to get a CRC error on an I2C bus unless it is overloaded or subject to a lot of noise.

The Complete Program

```c
#define _DEFAULT_SOURCE
#include <stdio.h>
#include <stdlib.h>
#include <stdint.h>
#include <string.h>
#include <sys/ioctl.h>
#include <unistd.h>
#include <fcntl.h>
#include <linux/i2c-dev.h>

void checkI2CBus();
FILE * doCommand(char *cmd);
uint8_t crcCheck(uint8_t msb, uint8_t lsb, uint8_t check);

int main(int argc, char** argv) {

    checkI2CBus();

    int i2cfd = open("/dev/i2c-1", O_RDWR);
    ioctl(i2cfd, I2C_SLAVE, 0x40);
    char buf[3] = {0xF3};
    write(i2cfd, buf, 1);

    while (1) {
        int result = read(i2cfd, buf, 3);
        if (result > 0) break;
        usleep(10 * 1000);

    }
    uint8_t msb = buf[0];
    uint8_t lsb = buf[1];
    uint8_t check = buf[2];
    printf("msb %d \n\rlsb %d \n\rchecksum %d \n\r", msb, lsb,
                                                     check);
```

```c
    unsigned int data16 = ( (unsigned int) msb << 8) |
                                (unsigned int) (lsb & 0xFC);
    float temp = (float) (-46.85 + (175.72 * data16 /
                                    (float) 65536));
    printf("Temperature %f C \n\r", temp);
    printf("crc = %d\n\r", crcCheck(msb, lsb, check));
    buf[0] = 0xF5;
    write(i2cfd, buf, 1);

    while (1) {
        int result = read(i2cfd, buf, 3);
        if (result > 0) break;
        usleep(10 * 1000);
    }
    msb = buf[0];
    lsb = buf[1];
    check = buf[2];
    printf("crc = %d\n\r", crcCheck(msb, lsb, check));
    data16 = ((unsigned int) msb << 8) |
                                (unsigned int) (lsb & 0xFC);
    float hum = -6 + (125.0 * (float) data16) / 65536;
    printf("Humidity %f %% \n\r", hum);
    close(i2cfd);
    return (EXIT_SUCCESS);
}

uint8_t crcCheck(uint8_t msb, uint8_t lsb, uint8_t check) {
    uint32_t data32 = ((uint32_t) msb << 16) |
                        ((uint32_t) lsb << 8) | (uint32_t) check;
    uint32_t divisor = 0x988000;
    for (int i = 0; i < 16; i++) {
        if (data32 & (uint32_t) 1 << (23 - i)) data32 ^= divisor;
        divisor >>= 1;
    };
    return (uint8_t) data32;
}

void checkI2CBus() {
    FILE *fd = doCommand("sudo dtparam -l");
    char output[1024];
    int txfound = 0;
    while (fgets(output, sizeof (output), fd) != NULL) {
        printf("%s\n\r", output);
        fflush(stdout);
        if (strstr(output, "i2c_arm=on") != NULL) {
            txfound = 1;
        }
        if (strstr(output, "i2c_arm=off") != NULL) {
            txfound = 0;
        }
    }
    pclose(fd);
```

```
    if (txfound == 0) {
        fd = doCommand("sudo dtparam i2c_arm=on");
        pclose(fd);
    }
}

FILE * doCommand(char *cmd) {
    FILE *fp = popen(cmd, "r");
    if (fp == NULL) {
        printf("Failed to run command %s \n\r", cmd);
        exit(1);
    }
    return fp;
}
```

I2C Tools

There is a package of tools designed to make I2C devices usable from the command line. This might be useful if you need to experiment or test something out and they can also be used within scripts. The main use case for these tools seems to be reading I2C memory devices and this means that the main objective is to provide simple bulk transfer. There are many I2C features that cannot be controlled. In most cases it is better to ignore them and work with C and the Linux driver.

The tools should already be installed but if not use:

```
apt-get update
apt-get install i2c-tools
```

Let's deal with each tool in turn.

i2cdetect

This scans the I2C bus and tries each possible address and displays a map of what it has found:

```
pi@raspberrypi:~ $ i2cdetect 1
WARNING! This program can confuse your I2C bus, cause
I will probe file /dev/i2c-1.
I will probe address range 0x03-0x77.
Continue? [Y/n] y
     0  1  2  3  4  5  6  7  8  9  a  b  c  d  e  f
00:          -- -- -- -- -- -- -- -- -- -- -- -- --
10: -- -- -- -- -- -- -- -- -- -- -- -- -- -- -- --
20: -- -- -- -- -- -- -- -- -- -- -- -- -- -- -- --
30: -- -- -- -- -- -- -- -- -- -- -- -- -- -- -- --
40: 40 -- -- -- -- -- -- -- -- -- -- -- -- -- -- --
50: -- -- -- -- -- -- -- -- -- -- -- -- -- -- -- --
60: -- -- -- -- -- -- -- -- -- -- -- -- -- -- -- --
70: -- -- -- -- -- -- -- --
```

You do need to take notice of the warning if you are running any unusual devices. You can change which bus is scanned by specifying its number or name. It is also possible to disable interactive mode on all of these commands using -y.

i2cget

This will read an I2C register. For example to read the user register 0xE7
from the HTU21D at address 0x40 you would use:

```
pi@raspberrypi:~ $ i2cget 1 0x40 0xE7 b
WARNING! This program can confuse your I2C bus, cause data loss and worse!
I will read from device file /dev/i2c-1, chip address 0x40, data address
0xe7, using read byte data.
Continue? [Y/n] y
0x02
```

The general form is:

```
i2cget bus address register data
```

where *data* is one of b for byte, w for word, or c for write a byte/read a byte.

i2cdump

Use this to read a set of registers. Its general form is:

```
i2cdump bus address
```

This will transfer the values of all of the registers. You can limit the range of
registers using rfirst – last, you can use b,w and c to signify byte or word
transfer and I for I2C bus block transfer. You will also come across s for
smbus (System Management bus), but this is to be avoided as it is a specific
implementation of I2C used to control the setup of a PC.

i2cset

This works like i2cget and sets a register's value:

```
i2cset bus address register value data
```

In addition to data set to b or w you can also specify s or I for a smbus or I2C
block write. Block writes are determined by the number of values specified.

It is also possible to specify a mask which determines which bits of the
value are sent to the register. For example, to set the user register of the
HTU21D at address 0x40 you would use:

```
pi@raspberrypi:~ $ i2cset 1 0x40 0xE6 02 b
WARNING! This program can confuse your I2C bus, cause data loss and worse!
I will write to device file /dev/i2c-1, chip address 0x40, data address
0xe6, data 0x02, mode byte.
Continue? [Y/n] y
```

i2ctransfer

This command lets you perform a block transfer read or write. Its general form is:

```
i2ctransfer bus blocks
```

The blocks are made up of individual blocks which start with r or w for read or write, the length of the data in bytes and @address which is the address of the device the block is sent to. You only need to specify the address once unless it changes. Each block is single transaction with a single final stop bit. If you don't specify all of the data in the block you can use = to mean keep using the value, + to increment the value, - to decrement it and p to use random values. For example:

```
i2ctransfer 1 w1@0x40  0xE7 r1
```

will send 0xE7, read user register, to the device HTU21D at address 0x40 and then read a single byte back:

```
pi@raspberrypi:~ $ i2ctransfer 1 w1@0x40  0xE7 r1
WARNING! This program can confuse your I2C bus, cause data loss and worse!
I will send the following messages to device file /dev/i2c-1:
msg 0: addr 0x40, write, len 1, buf 0xe7
msg 1: addr 0x40, read, len 1
Continue? [y/N] y
0x02
```

To perform a register write of the HTU21D at address 0x40 and return three bytes you would use:

```
i2ctransfer 1 w1@0x40  0xF3 r3
```

```
pi@raspberrypi:~ $ i2ctransfer 1 w1@0x40  0xE3 r3
WARNING! This program can confuse your I2C bus, cause data loss and worse!
I will send the following messages to device file /dev/i2c-1:
msg 0: addr 0x40, write, len 1, buf 0xe3
msg 1: addr 0x40, read, len 3
Continue? [y/N] y
0x70 0xa4 0x03
```

This might seem very effective, but it doesn't work using a no-hold read as the command doesn't poll for the device to be ready. It does work with a clock-stretching-hold read, but only if the I2C time out has been set to be long enough for it to wait for the clock to go high and this is something that cannot be done from the command line.

Summary

- The I2C driver can be loaded dynamically and it provides the basic facilities to interface with any I2C device.

- The I2C driver creates a number of new folder and it also accepts ioctl commands.

- As an example of using the driver, the HTU21D is easy to set up and read. It also has a dedicated Linux driver which is discussed in Chapter 14.

- Without clock stretching support, all we can do is to poll for data to be ready to read.

- Computing a CRC is something every IoT programmer needs to know how to do in the general case.

- There are a number of command line tools that let you work with I2C, but they need to be used with caution.

Once you have seen how basic I2C works, it is time to look at some of its extensions and variations. This chapter looks at how to use the other I2C interfaces that are available on the Pi 4, and how to deal with clock stretching with a lower-level driver interface.

Other I2C Interfaces

The Broadcom Serial Controller, essentially an implementation of the I2C bus, was introduced at the end of Chapter 12 and in that chapter we used the driver for BSC1, which works on all versions of the Pi. While the Pi Zero and the Pi 3 each have three BSC controllers, BSC0, BSC1 and BSC2, the Pi 4 has eight in total, though BSC2 and BSC7 are dedicated to working with the HDMI interface, and therefore aren't available for use.

The pin and GPIO assignments of BSC0 and BSC1 were give in Chapter 11 and those of the extra, usable, controllers are:

BSC0

Function	Pin	GPIO
SDA	27	GPIO0
SCL	28	GPIO1

BSC1

Function	Pin	GPIO
SDA	3	GPIO2
SCL	5	GPIO3

BSC3

Function	Pin	GPIO
SDA	3,7	GPIO2,4
SCL	5,29	GPIO3,5

BSC4

Function	Pin	GPIO
SDA	31,24	GPIO6,8
SCL	26,21	GPIO7,9

BSC5

Function	Pin	GPIO
SDA	32,19	GPIO12,10
SCL	33,23	GPIO13,11

BSC6

Function	Pin	GPIO
SDA	27,15	GPIO0,22
SCL	28,16	GPIO1,23

Notice that these new BSC devices each have two possible pin configurations.

As already mentioned, the Pi 5 uses a different implementation of I2C and provides four hardware implemented channels.

I2C0=BSC0

Function	Pin	??Line
SDA	27 or 24	GPIO0 or 8
SCL	28 or 21	GPIO1 or 9

I2C1 =BSC1

Function	Pin	
SDA	3 or 19	GPIO2 or 10
SCL	5 or 23	GPIO3 or 11

I2C2

Function	Pin	
SDA	3 or 32	GPIO4 or 12
SCL	5 or 33	GPIO5 or 13

I2C3

Function	Pin	
SDA	3 or 8	GPIO6 or 14
SCL	5 or 10	GPIO7 or 15

You can see that the first two I2C channels are the same as found on other Pis and can be used in the same way.

There are also some additional I2C drivers that you can enable by simply using the appropriate overlay. To enable I2C bus *n*, where *n* goes from 3 to 6 you use:

dtoverlay=i2c*n*,<param>

where the parameters are:

- pins_x_y   Use pins x and y
- baudrate   Set the baud rate for the interface (default "100000")

For example, to enable i2c4 on GPIO 6 as SDA and GPIO 7 as SCL, with a clock of 50Khz you would use:

dtoverlay=i2c4 pins_6_7 baudrate=50000

You can enable the I2C bus dynamically. To enable bus *n*, and pins pin1 and pin2 use:

```
void enableI2C(int n, int pin1, int pin2) {
    char cmd[100];
    snprintf(cmd, 100, "i2c%d  pins_%d_%d=true", n, pin1, pin2);
    FILE *fp = popen("sudo dtparam -l", "r");
    if (fp == NULL) {
        printf("Failed to run command\n\r");
        exit(1);
    }
    char output[1024];
    int txfound = 0;
    while (fgets(output, sizeof (output), fp) != NULL) {
        fflush(stdout);
        if (strstr(output, cmd) != NULL) {
            txfound = 1;
        }
    }
    pclose(fp);
    printf("%d",txfound);
    if (txfound == 0) {
        snprintf(cmd, 100, "sudo dtoverlay i2c%d  pins_%d_%d=true",
                                                n, pin1, pin2);
        fp = popen(cmd, "r");
        if (fp == NULL) {
            printf("Failed to run command\n\r");
            exit(1);
        }
        pclose(fp);
    }
}
```

Notice that you have to make sure that the GPIO lines you are using aren't already in use by something else – for example, i2c4 clashes with SPI as spi0 uses GPIO-07 and hence SPI has to be disabled. Also notice that the GPIO lines don't have external pull-up resistors.

Using any of these additional i2C interfaces is just a matter of changing the filename from i2c-1 to i2c-*n* where *n* is the number of the interface. So, you could use the HTU21D with i2c6 by connecting pin 15, GPIO22, to SDA and 16, GPIO23 to SCL and changing the start of the program to:

```
enableI2C(6, 22, 23);
int i2cfd = open("/dev/i2c-6", O_RDWR);
```

Software I2C

If you can use a hardware implementation of the I2C bus then it will provide much better performance. However, there are times when you need additional I2C interfaces and there is no free I2C hardware. One solution is to use a software emulation of I2C. This has the advantage of working on any pair of GPIO lines that aren't being used for anything else.

To enable software emulation use:

```
dtoverlay=i2c-bus=n, gpio,i2c_gpio_sda=pin1, i2c_gpio_scl=pin2,
                                         i2c_gpio_delay_us=t
```

where n is the bus number you want to use, pin1 and pin2 are the GPIO lines and delay is the width of the clock pulse in μs.

For example:

```
dtoverlay=i2c-gpio,bus=8,i2c_gpio_sda=22,  i2c_gpio_scl=23
```

creates /dev/i2c-8 using GPIO22 and GPIO23 with a default clock rate of 100KHz.

You can enable a software I2C bus dynamically:

```
void enableGPIOI2C(int n, int pin1, int pin2, int clock) {
    char cmd[100];
    snprintf(cmd, 100,
                    "i2c-gpio  bus=%d
                     i2c_gpio_sda=%d
                       i2c_gpio_scl=%d
                         i2c_gpio_delay_us=%d",
                         n, pin1, pin2, clock);

    FILE *fp = popen("sudo dtparam -l", "r");
    if (fp == NULL) {
        printf("Failed to run command\n\r");
        exit(1);
    }
```

```
    char output[1024];
    int txfound = 0;
    while (fgets(output, sizeof (output), fp) != NULL) {

        fflush(stdout);
        if (strstr(output, cmd) != NULL) {
            txfound = 1;
        }
    }
    pclose(fp);
    printf("%s", cmd);
    if (txfound == 0) {
        snprintf(cmd, 100, "sudo dtoverlay i2c-gpio  bus=%d
                                    i2c_gpio_sda=%d
                                    i2c_gpio_scl=%d
                                    i2c_gpio_delay_us=%d",
                                    n, pin1, pin2, clock);
        fp = popen(cmd, "r");
        if (fp == NULL) {
            printf("Failed to run command\n\r");
            exit(1);
        }
        pclose(fp);
    }
}
```

You can only enable a particular bus number once and a second attempt will fail even if the parameters are different. As always removing a dynamic overlay isn't recommended

With this in place you could use the HTU21D with i2c8 by, working at 40KHz, by connecting pin 15, GPIO22, to SDA and 16, GPIO23 to SCL and changing the start of the program to:

```
    enableGPIOI2C(8, 22, 23, 10);
    int i2cfd = open("/dev/i2c-8", O_RDWR);
```

Clock Stretching

If a device is too slow to respond at once to a request for data, the I2C controller has to either poll for the data or it can attempt to get the slave to stretch the clock until it is ready. This used to be a very serious problem with early implementations of the Pi I2C driver but now it has largely been fixed.

The simplest program that will read data from the HTU21D is:

```c
#define _DEFAULT_SOURCE
#include <stdio.h>
#include <stdlib.h>
#include <sys/ioctl.h>
#include <unistd.h>
#include <fcntl.h>
#include <stdint.h>
#include <linux/i2c-dev.h>
#include <linux/i2c.h>


void checkI2CBus();

int main(int argc, char **argv)
{
    int i2cfd = open("/dev/i2c-1", O_RDWR);
    ioctl(i2cfd, I2C_SLAVE, 0x40);
    char buf[3] = {0xE3};
    write(i2cfd, buf, 1);
    int result = read(i2cfd, buf, 3);
    uint8_t msb = buf[0];
    uint8_t lsb = buf[1];
    uint8_t check = buf[2];
    printf("msb %d \n\rlsb %d \n\rchecksum %d \n\r", msb, lsb,
check);
}
```

If you try this on a Pi running either Bookworm or Bullseye it should work.

The logic analyzer reveals what is happening. First we send the usual address frame and write the 0xE3. Then, after a short pause, the read address frame is sent and the clock line is held low by the device (lower trace):

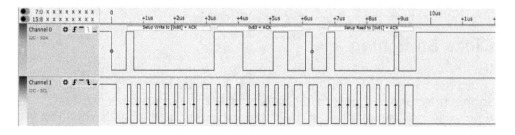

The clock line is held low by the device for over 42ms while it gets the data ready.

It is released and the three data frames are sent:

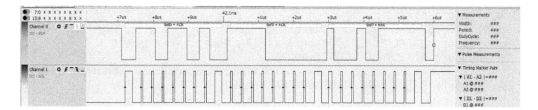

This response is a long way down the logic analyzer trace so keep scrolling until you find it.

A Lower-Level I2C

The Linux I2C device driver supports a lower-level interface that works via the ioctl function. Using this you can gain control over many different aspects of data transfer, in particular you can use it to implement a register read that removes the stop bit between the write of the register address and the read of the data. Using the file interface a write followed by a read is always separated by a stop bit. The ioctl commands currently supported are:

I2C_RETRIES	Number of times a device address should be polled when not acknowledging
I2C_TIMEOUT	Set timeout in units of 10 ms
I2C_SLAVE	Use this slave address in all read/write operations
I2C_SLAVE_FORCE	Use this slave address, even if it is already in use by a driver
I2C_TENBIT	0 for 7-bit addresses, !=0 for 10-bit addresses
I2C_FUNCS	Get the adapter functionality mask
I2C_RDWR	Combined R/W transfer (one stop bit)
I2C_PEC	!= 0 to use PEC (Packet Error Check) with SMBus

All of these are defined in i2c.h. We have already used I2C_SLAVE to specify the slave address. The timeout and retry are useful if you have to work with a slow device or one that transfers a lot of data, but notice that these do not control the clock stretch timeout. It is also worth knowing that 10-bit addressing isn't supported.

The I2C_FUNCS call, which takes a pointer to an unsigned long, returns a bit status which defines what the I2C interface is capable of. The following bit masks are available:
I2C_FUNC_I2C
I2C_FUNC_10BIT_ADDR
I2C_FUNC_PROTOCOL_MANGLING
I2C_FUNC_NOSTART
I2C_FUNC_SLAVE

219

If you try it out on any Raspberry Pi:

```
int i2cfd = open("/dev/i2c-1", O_RDWR);
uint32_t support;
ioctl(i2cfd, I2C_FUNCS, &support);
if(support & I2C_FUNC_I2C) printf("I2C Support\n\r");
if(support & I2C_FUNC_10BIT_ADDR)
                            printf("10 bit address Support\n\r");
if(support & I2C_FUNC_PROTOCOL_MANGLING)
                            printf("I2C Mangling Support\n\r");
if(support & I2C_FUNC_NOSTART) printf("I2C Nostart Support\n\r");
if(support & I2C_FUNC_SLAVE) printf("I2C Slave Support\n\r");
```

you will discover that the only feature supported is I2C. This is disappointing, but it might change in the future. The Pi 5 also supports 10 bit addressing.

The most important of the new ioctl functions is I2C_RDWR, which allows you to send and receive any amount of data as a single transaction using just one stop bit. The way that you use it is via two structs defined in i2c.h. The first is used for the data you want to send or receive:

```
struct i2c_msg {
__u16 addr; /* slave address */
__u16 flags; /*control transfer */
__u16 len; /* msg length */
__u8 *buf; /* pointer to msg data */
};
```

The following flags control what happens:

I2C_M_RD	Read data, default is write
I2C_M_TEN	Use 10-bit chip address
I2C_M_RECV_LEN	Length will be first received byte
I2C_M_NO_RD_ACK	Don't use read acknowledgment
I2C_M_M_IGNORE_NAK	Treat NAK as it is was ACK
I2C_M_REV_DIR_ADDR	Swap read and write
I2C_M_NOSTART	Send only one start bit per transaction
I2C_M_STOP	Send a stop bit after the message

You can only use the flags that are supported by the I2C interface in question, which for the Raspberry Pi is only I2C_M_RD, but this is enough to write a combined transfer function.

The second struct provides the driver with information about how many message blocks there are:

```
struct i2c_rdwr_ioctl_data {
      struct i2c_msg *msgs;        /* pointers to i2c_msgs */
      __u32 nmsgs;                 /* number of i2c_msgs */
};
```

Each message block is sent with a start bit, but a stop bit is only sent after all the message blocks have been processed. For example, to create a read register function all you need to do is send a write block followed by a read block:

```
int i2cReadRegister(int i2cfd, uint8_t slaveaddr, uint8_t reg,
                                        uint8_t *buf,int len) {

    struct i2c_msg msgs[2];
    struct i2c_rdwr_ioctl_data msgset[1];

    msgs[0].addr = slaveaddr;
    msgs[0].flags = 0;
    msgs[0].len = 1;
    msgs[0].buf = &reg;

    msgs[1].addr = slaveaddr;
    msgs[1].flags = I2C_M_RD;
    msgs[1].len = len;
    msgs[1].buf = buf;

    msgset[0].msgs = msgs;
    msgset[0].nmsgs = 2;

    if (ioctl(i2cfd, I2C_RDWR, &msgset) < 0) {
        return -1;
    }
    return 0;
}
```

The first block just sends the register number to the slave and the second block reads however many bytes the slave sends back. If you look back at the first HTU21D program, it performed a register read using separate write and read file operations:

```
int i2cfd = open("/dev/i2c-1", O_RDWR);
ioctl(i2cfd, I2C_SLAVE, 0x40);
char buf[4] = {0xE7};
write(i2cfd,buf,1);
read(i2cfd,buf,1);
printf("%x\n\r",buf[0]);
close(i2cfd)
```

This works, but it is strictly incorrect as it puts a stop bit after the write:

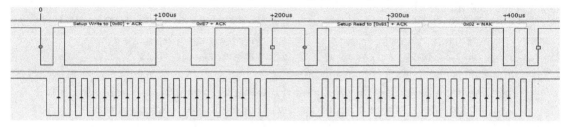

If you use the i2cReadRegister function:

```
#define _DEFAULT_SOURCE
#include <stdio.h>
#include <stdlib.h>
#include <sys/ioctl.h>
#include <unistd.h>
#include <fcntl.h>
#include <stdint.h>
#include <linux/i2c-dev.h>
#include <linux/i2c.h>

void checkI2CBus();
int i2cReadRegister(int i2cfd, uint8_t slaveaddr, uint8_t reg,
uint8_t *buf,int len);

int main(int argc, char** argv) {
    checkI2CBus();
    int i2cfd = open("/dev/i2c-1", O_RDWR);
    char buf2[1]={0};
    i2cReadRegister(i2cfd, 0x40, 0xE7,buf2,1);
    printf("%d \n\r",buf2[0]);
    return (EXIT_SUCCESS);
}
```

it works, but now sends no stop bit between the write and the read:

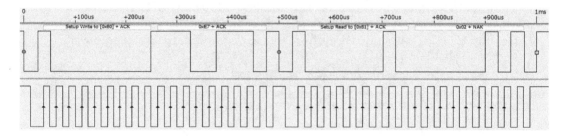

It is easy to create functions to read and write single blocks or any complex mix of read or writes as a single transaction with a single final stop bit.

Summary

- Using the additional I2C interfaces that the Pi 4 supplies is just a matter of configuring the Linux driver and using appropriate pins.

- Additional software I2C interfaces can be used on any Pi by installing the software I2C driver.

- You can make use of clock stretching on all recent Pis running the latest OS.

- The I2C driver supports a lower-level, ioctl-based, interface which provides additional control.

- At the time of writing only a few ioctl operations are supported, but they can be used to write a register address and read the result with the correct stop bits.

Chapter 14
Sensor Drivers - Linux IIO & Hwmon

As well as supporting the I2C bus in a general way, there are also a number of I2C device drivers. These allow you to use I2C devices without worrying about the exact nature of the protocol in use. Some of these device drivers conform to either one or other of a broader, protocol-independent way of implementing drivers – hwmon, relating to the hardware monitoring system and IIO, for interfacing Linux Industrial I/O devices. These form a framework for creating, publishing and using drivers for devices irrespective of the protocol used to control them. At the time of writing the following devices are supported, the majority being I2C devices:

bme680	I2C or SPI	IIO	Bosch Sensortronic BME680 Temperature, Humidity and Pressure Sensor
bmp085	I2C or SPI	IIO	Bosch Sensortronic BMP085 superseded by the BMP180
bmp180	I2C	IIO	Bosch Sensortronic BMP180 Barometric Pressure Sensor
bme280	I2C	IIO	Bosch Sensortronic BME280 Temperature, Humidity and Pressure Sensor
ds1621	I2C	hwmon	Dallas Semiconductors Temperature Sensor range inc DS1621, DS1625, DS1631, DS1721, DS1731
hdc100x	I2C	IIO	Texas Instruments HDC100x Temperature Sensor range -only HDC1010 and HDC1080 are current
htu21	SPI	IIO	HTU21 Temperature and Humidity Sensor
lm75	I2C	hwmon	Maxim LM75 Temperature Sensor and compatible devices.
max17040	I2C	hwmon	Maxim Integrated MAX17040 Battery Monitor
sht3x	I2C	hwmon	Sensiron SHT3x Temperature and Humidity Sensor
Si7020	I2C	hwmon	Silicon Labs Si7013/20/21 Humidity/Temperature Sensor
sps30	I2C	IIO	Sensirion SPS30 Particulate Matter Sensor
tmp102	I2C	hwmon	Texas Instruments TMP102 Temperature Sensor
tsl4531	I2C	IIO	AMS TSL4531 Digital Ambient Light Sensor
veml6070	I2C	IIO	Vishay VEML6070 Ultraviolet Light Sensor

There are many more devices available as drivers that you have to build and install for yourself, but these are usually provided by the manufacturer of the device and you will find instructions on the relevant websites.

The majority of these devices are available at reasonable cost in either prototype-friendly DIL packages or as breakout boards. Of course, there are many sensors that are not supported by a Linux driver, but making a choice from this list can save you a lot of time and trouble.

Some of the above device drivers are part of the Industrial I/O (IIO) subsystem project and some are part of the older hwmon subsystem. The hwmon subsystem is intended to be a way of reading and configuring sensors and devices that are built into the system. For example, you can read the CPU temperature or the supply voltage of the Pi using the built-in sensors that are part of hwmon. However, you can also add drivers to the hwmon subsystem that aren't built in. This use of hwmon as a "home" for sensors is what led to the decision to create IIO as a better and more appropriate place for sensors.

There are some big differences between hwmon and IIO. In particular IIO only deals with input devices and, in principle, it can do so in much more sophisticated ways than hwmon. Hwmon has the advantage of dealing with input and output devices, but it is much simpler. Let's start with hwmon and see the general principles in action.

hwmon

Drivers that install into the hwmon system work in the same way as most Linux drivers by pretending to be folders and files. You will find all hwmon devices in:

`/sys/class/hwmon/`

and each device creates a `deviceX` folder where X is an integer. Within each folder you will find the files you need to work with the device. In particular you will find a name file which gives the usual name of the device and often an `update_interval` file which gets and sets the update interval for the device. If you look at the Pi's `/sys/class/hwmon` folder you will see that there are already two device folders:

The first corresponds to the built-in temperature sensor and the second to the A-to-D converter that monitors CPU voltage. As an example let's read the CPU temperature. Inside the hwmon0 folder are a number of files and folders:

The ones that matter most are name, which gives the name of the sensor and temp1_input, the data file. The uevent file is present in all driver folders and it is used by the system to implement dynamic changes to the hardware, see udev in Chapter 16.

Reading the CPU temperature is just a matter of opening the file and reading:

```
#define _DEFAULT_SOURCE
#include <stdio.h>
#include <stdlib.h>
#include <string.h>
#include <unistd.h>
#include <fcntl.h>

int main(int argc, char** argv) {
    int fd = open("/sys/class/hwmon/hwmon0/temp1_input", O_RDONLY);
    char buf[100] = {0};
    read(fd, buf, 100);
    printf("%s\n\r", buf);
    float temp;
    sscanf(buf, "%f", &temp);
    temp = temp / 1000;
    printf("%f\n\r", temp);
}
```

Notice that the string returned from the file is terminated by /n and not by a zero, hence the need to initialize the buffer to all zeros.

You can use the same approach to read the CPU voltage, only the filename changes.

Installing An hwmon Device

Installing an hwmon device is very straightforward, with no surprises if you have been following how things work. As an example, let's install an LM75 temperature device. This is a low-cost I2C temperature sensor with an accuracy of around 2 degrees Celsius and a resolution of 11 bits. You can buy a suitable LM75 module, complete with prototype board, from many sources. It has three pins that can be used to set the low three bits of the address, which means you can support up to eight devices on the same bus:

You can see the standard I2C pins plus power and ground. The final pin, OS, is a thermal shutdown output which goes high when the temperature is above a set value.

To use the device you generally have to solder either pins or wires to the connections. You also have to connect the address pads on the back of the device. This can be done with a solder bridge – a blob of solder connecting the pads together. You don't need pull-up resistors as they are in place on the other side of the board. Be careful not to create a solder blob so large that it shorts out the ground and power pads.

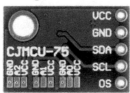

For this example, connect all of the address lines to ground, giving an address of 0x48. By connecting them differently you can use addresses from 0x48 to 0x4f. The chip has registers that can be read to discover the temperature and that can be written to set the critical temperature and the hysteresis. The over-temperature alarm is triggered when the temperature exceeds the critical temperature and it is untriggered when the temperature is lower than that set by the hysteresis.

The LM75 can be used via the raw I2C interface or you can make use of its Linux driver. At the time of writing this doesn't work on the Pi 5.

The LM75 driver is implemented by a general i2c-sensor driver which can be set to work with a range of devices. In this case we need to add:

```
dtparam=i2c_arm=on
dtoverlay i2c-sensor,lm75,addr=0x48
```

to the /boot/config.txt file. If you don't specify an address parameter the default is 0x4F.

You can also load the drivers dynamically, although currently this doesn't work on the Pi 5:

```
FILE *doCommand(char *cmd)
{
    FILE *fp = popen(cmd, "r");
    if (fp == NULL)
    {
        printf("Failed to run command %s \n\r", cmd);
        exit(1);
    }
    return fp;
}
int findInd(FILE *fd, char *indicator)
{
    char output[1024];
    int txfound = 0;
    while (fgets(output, sizeof(output), fd) != NULL)
    {
        printf("%s\n\r", output);
        fflush(stdout);
        if (strstr(output, indicator) != NULL)
        {
            txfound = 1;
        }
    }
    return txfound;
}
void checkLM75()
{
    FILE *fd = doCommand("sudo  dtparam -l");
    char indicator1[] = "i2c_arm=on";
    char command1[] = "sudo dtparam i2c_arm=on";
    char indicator2[] = "lm75";
    char command2[] = "sudo dtoverlay i2c-sensor lm75 addr=0x48";

    int txfound = findInd(fd, indicator1);
    if (txfound == 0){
        pclose(fd);
        fd = doCommand(command1);
        sleep(2);
    }
    pclose(fd);
    fd = doCommand("sudo  dtparam -l");
    txfound = findInd(fd, indicator2);
    if (txfound == 0){
        pclose(fd);
        fd = doCommand(command2);
        sleep(2);
    }
    pclose(fd);
}
```

Once the drivers are loaded you will discover that there is a new directory in hwmon:

You can see that `temp1_input` is going to be the file to read to get the current temperature:

```c
int main(int argc, char **argv)
{
    checkLM75();

    int fd = open("/sys/class/hwmon/hwmon2/temp1_input",
                                          O_RDONLY);
    char buf[100] = {0};
    read(fd, buf, 100);
    printf("%s\n\r", buf);
    float temp;
    sscanf(buf, "%f", &temp);
    temp = temp / 1000;
    printf("%f\n\r", temp);
    close(fd);
}
```

The temperature is returned as a string in millidegrees Celsius.

If you want to set the critical temperature and hysteresis you can use:

```c
    fd = open("/sys/class/hwmon/hwmon2/temp1_max", O_RDWR);
    char max[] = "20000";
    write(fd, max, 5);
    close(fd);

    fd = open("/sys/class/hwmon/hwmon2/temp1_max_hyst", O_RDWR);
    char min[] = "190000";
    write(fd, max, 5);
    close(fd);
```

This sets the critical temperature to 20°C and the hysteresis to 19°C. After this, if the temperature goes above 20°C the LED on the board will come on and stay on until the temperature drops below 19°C. Notice that you need to run this program with root permissions as it is writing to files in /sys.

Industrial I/O

The hwmon system of drivers was never intended as a way of adding external sensors – this is why Industrial I/O or IIO was created in 2015. It is a very ambitious system and it was intended to become the main way that programmers would create IoT type applications. To make this possible, the idea was that IIO devices would use a ring buffer to store readings taken independently of the user-space application. This would allow the user-space application to read the data when it was ready without loss of data and hence at sampling rates higher than could be achieved directly.

The documentation says:

> *The main purpose of the Industrial I/O subsystem (IIO) is to provide support for devices that in some sense perform either analog-to-digital conversion (ADC) or digital-to-analog conversion (DAC) or both. The aim is to fill the gap between the somewhat similar hwmon and input subsystems. Hwmon is directed at low sample rate sensors used to monitor and control the system itself, like fan speed control or temperature measurement. Input is, as its name suggests, focused on human interaction input devices (keyboard, mouse, touchscreen).*

The main innovation is the use of triggers to determine when readings will be taken, independent of when the data is read.

At the time of writing, IIO drivers are generally not full-featured and many don't support the more advanced functions such as triggers or buffering. However, it is difficult to know the current state of affairs because nearly all of the documentation is aimed at driver writers rather than driver users. This said, there is no reason not to use IIO device drivers as, at the very least, they provide the same facilities as other driver types and it is still early days for the IIO system.

You can load any of the IIO drivers using the usual `dtoverlay` line in `boot.txt` or you can dynamically load any of the drivers.

Once the driver has been loaded there will be a new folder in `sys/bus/iio/devices`. The folder will be called `iio.deviceX` where X is the number of the device.

Within the new folder are files and folders that relate to the new device and allow you to read its state and data:

For a driver conforming to IIO you should find:

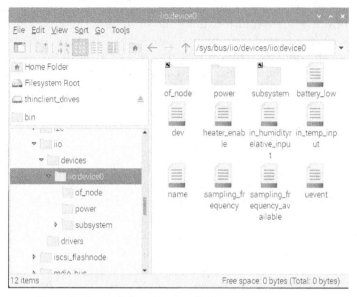

- ◆ name   Description of the physical chip
- ◆ dev   Shows the major:minor pair associated with /dev/iio:deviceX node
- ◆ sampling_frequency_available The discrete set of sampling frequency values available for the device

Consult Documentation/ABI/testing/sysfs-bus-iio in the Linux kernel to discover what each device supports, but note that it is a very incomplete list. In general you can work out what each file is for from its name. For example, in the case of the HTU21D sensor that we used earlier, you can see that:

in_temp_input is what you read to get the current temperature and in_humidityrelative_input is what you would read to get the humidity There is also a file called iio:deviceX in /dev/ which provides buffered I/O and event information.

It is important to realize that not all devices implement the same range of features and basically you have to investigate what files have been created by the driver.

As well as providing the ability to read data from the device and write configuration data, the IIO bus also lets you do more sophisticated things. For example, you can set up triggers that take readings at set intervals and you can read a ring buffer of collected data. Such facilities allow user-mode programs to gather data at rates normally only possible for system-mode programs.

An Example - The HTU21

As an example of how much easier things are using a sensor driver, let's write a program to read the data from the HTU21D Temperature and Humidity Sensor.

First we need a function to load the driver:

```
void loadHTU21() {
    FILE *fd = doCommand("sudo dtparam -l");
    char output[1024];
    int txfound = 0;
    while (fgets(output, sizeof (output), fd) != NULL) {
        printf("%s\n\r", output);
        fflush(stdout);
        if (strstr(output, "i2c-sensor  htu21=true") != NULL) {
            txfound = 1;
        }
    }
    pclose(fd);
    if (txfound == 0) {
        fd = doCommand("sudo dtoverlay i2c-sensor htu21");
        pclose(fd);
    }
}
```

As always, unloading a driver isn't a good idea.

With the driver loaded we can simply read the temperature from the appropriate file:

```
loadHTU21();
float temp;

char output[1024] = {0};
int fdtemp = open("/sys/bus/iio/devices/iio:device0/in_temp_input",
                                                    O_RDWR);
read(fdtemp, output, sizeof (output));
close(fdtemp);
printf("%s\n\r", output);
sscanf(output, "%f", &temp);
temp = temp / 1000;
fflush(stdout);
```

You can see that this is now a trivial operation. If you are wondering how the driver reads data from the device, it simply initiates the read and waits for around 50ms for the data to be read – no polling and no clock stretching.

The complete program to read both temperature and humidity is:

```c
#define _DEFAULT_SOURCE
#include <stdio.h>
#include <stdlib.h>
#include <string.h>
#include <unistd.h>
#include <fcntl.h>
#include <stdint.h>
#include <linux/i2c-dev.h>
#include <linux/i2c.h>

void loadHTU21();

int main(int argc, char** argv) {
    loadHTU21();
    float temp;
    float hum;
    {
        char output[1024] = {0};
        int fdtemp = open("/sys/bus/iio/devices/iio:device0/
                                      in_temp_input", O_RDWR);
        read(fdtemp, output, sizeof (output));
        close(fdtemp);
        printf("%s\n\r", output);
        sscanf(output, "%f", &temp);
        temp = temp / 1000;
        fflush(stdout);
    }

    {
        char output[1024] = {0};
        int fdhum = open("/sys/bus/iio/devices/iio:device0/
                          in_humidityrelative_input", O_RDWR);
        read(fdhum, output, sizeof (output));
        close(fdhum);
        printf("%s\n\r", output);
        sscanf(output, "%f", &hum);
        hum = hum / 1000;
        fflush(stdout);
    }
    printf("%f\n\r", temp);
    printf("%f\n\r", hum);

    return (EXIT_SUCCESS);
}
```

```
FILE *doCommand(char *cmd)
{
    FILE *fp = popen(cmd, "r");
    if (fp == NULL)
    {
        printf("Failed to run command %s \n\r", cmd);
        exit(1);
    }
    return fp;
}
void loadHTU21() {
    FILE *fd = doCommand("sudo dtparam -l");
    char output[1024];
    int txfound = 0;
    while (fgets(output, sizeof (output), fd) != NULL) {
        printf("%s\n\r", output);
        fflush(stdout);
        if (strstr(output, "i2c-sensor  htu21=true") != NULL) {
            txfound = 1;
        }
    }
    pclose(fd);
    if (txfound == 0) {
        fd = doCommand("sudo dtoverlay i2c-sensor htu21");
        pclose(fd);
    }
}
```

As the HTU21 driver doesn't support a buffer, you can't do buffered I/O or use a trigger to gather data. All you can do is read the temperature and humidity when you need to, but this is often enough.

If you look back to Chapter 10 you will find another example of using an IIO bus driver for the MCP3008 A-to-D converter.

The IIO Utilities

There are some utilities that can sometimes help with finding out what is
happening when you have installed an IIO device, but how useful they are is
very variable. To install the IIO utilities the simplest thing to do is search for
"iio" using the usual Pi software installer search:

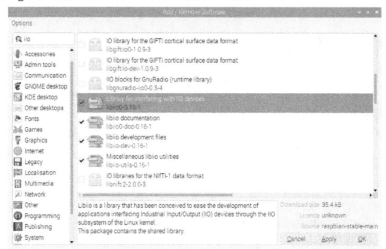

You might also want to install the Libiio library that can be used as an
alternative way to connect to IIO devices, see the next section.

iio_info and iio_attr

iio_info provides a summary of installed devices, channels and attributes.

```
Library version: 0.16 (git tag: v0.16)
Compiled with backends: local xml ip usb serial
IIO context created with local backend.
Backend version: 0.16 (git tag: v0.16)
Backend description string: Linux raspberrypi 5.4.51-v7l+ #1325 SMP Mon Jul 13 1
3:47:17 BST 2020 armv7l
IIO context has 1 attributes:
        local,kernel: 5.4.51-v7l+
IIO context has 1 devices:
        iio:device0: htu21
        2 channels found:
                humidityrelative:  (input)
                1 channel-specific attributes found:
                        attr  0: input ERROR: Remote I/O error (-121)
                temp:  (input)
                1 channel-specific attributes found:
                        attr  0: input value: 30906
        4 device-specific attributes found:
                        attr  0: battery_low value: 0
                        attr  1: heater_enable value: 0
                        attr  2: sampling_frequency value: 20
                        attr  3: sampling_frequency_available value: 20 40 70 120
```

`iio_attr` specifically lists device attributes:

```
pi@raspberrypi:~ $ iio_attr -d htu21
dev 'htu21', attr 'battery_low', value :'0'
dev 'htu21', attr 'heater_enable', value :'0'
dev 'htu21', attr 'sampling_frequency', value :'20'
dev 'htu21', attr 'sampling_frequency_available', value :'20 40 70 120'
```

It can also be used to write to an attribute by appending a value to the end of the command.

iio_readdev and iio_writedev

You can use these two to read and write to a device's buffer. The simplest form of the commands are:

```
readdev device channel   Sends data from the buffer to stdout
writedev device channel  Sends data from stdin to the device/channel
```

Notice that if the device doesn't support a buffer then these two don't work. For example, they don't work with the HTU21.

The Libiio Library

There is a "standard" library for working with IIO devices, but at the time of writing it is not well supported on the Raspberry Pi. You can download and install it, but not by the usual methods. Its documentation is also very poor and aimed at the expert, not the beginner. It provides the basic facilities of finding and using IIO devices directly, but it also has many sophisticated features, including remote access to devices running on other machines via USB or networking. In most cases, trying to use it isn't worth the effort as the actual IIO drivers don't support its more sophisticated features. If you simply want to read data at the sort of rates that the basic drivers allow, there is little to be gained from using Libiio and it is a steep learning curve. Of course, given Industrial I/O is only five or so years old things might change.

237

Summary

- The IIO and Hwmon systems are attempt to create drivers that present a standard interface, irrespective of the way that the devices are actually interfaced to the machine.

- Hwmon is the older system and was originally intended only for devices that are built into the system rather than discrete devices connected via external buses.

- The LM75 Temperature Sensor is often found built in to monitor hardware operating conditions, but it can also be connected via I2C and interfaced using the hwmon driver.

- Industrial I/O (IIO) was invented as an extension of Hwmon to create something that could support a wide range of sensors.

- IIO has many sophisticated features including triggers that can be used to make regular measurements in kernel space – most drivers don't support this.

- The HTU21 introduced in Chapter 12 has an IIO driver.

- There are a set of IIO utilities that you can install but again due to limited driver support many features don't work.

- There is also a more sophisticated library, Libiio, which makes IIO devices easier to work with, but lack of driver support makes it less attractive than working directly with devices.

Chapter 15
1-Wire Bus

The 1-Wire bus is a proprietary protocol that is very easy to use and has a lot of useful devices you can connect to it, including the iButton security devices. However, probably the most popular of all 1-Wire devices is the DS18B20 Temperature Sensor - it is small, very cheap and very easy to use. This is the device that we are going to focus on in this chapter but the techniques generalize to working with any 1-Wire device you care to use.

The Hardware

1-Wire devices are very simple and only use a single wire, hence the name, to transmit data:

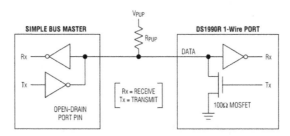

The 1-wire device can pull the bus low using its Tx line and can read the line using its Rx line. The reason for the pull-up resistor is that both the bus master and the slave can pull the bus low and it will stay low until they both release the bus.

The device can even be powered from the bus line by drawing sufficient current through the pull-up resistor - so called parasitic mode. Low-power devices work well in parasitic mode, but some devices have such a heavy current draw that the master has to provide a way to connect them to the power line - so called strong pull-up. In practice parasitic mode can be difficult to make work reliably for high power devices.

In normal-powered mode there are just three connections - V power (usually 3.3V for the Pi), Ground, and Data:

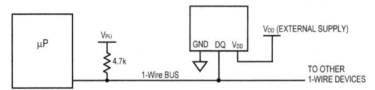

The pull-up resistor varies according to the device, but anything from 2.2K to 4.7kΩ works. The longer the bus the lower the pull-up resistor has to be to reduce "ringing". There can be multiple devices on the bus and each one has a unique 64-bit lasered ROM code, which can be used as an address to select the active devices.

The GPIO Driver

There are a number of drivers that implement the 1-Wire master, but the only one supported without extra work for the Raspberry Pi is the w1-gpio driver which implements the 1-Wire protocol on any GPIO pin that you aren't using for something else. There is also the w1-gpio-pullup variant of the driver, which is only needed if you are driving a 1-Wire device over a long wire connection.

You can enable the 1-Wire driver using:

`dtoverlay=w1-gpio,gpiopin=n`

where *n* is the GPIO line you want to use. The default is GPIO4, but you really can use any GPIO line.

You can add this dtoverlay line to the /config/boot.txt file or you can enable it dynamically using:

```
void load1w(int pin) {
    FILE *fd = doCommand("sudo dtparam -l");
    char output[1024];
    int txfound = 0;
    while (fgets(output, sizeof (output), fd) != NULL) {
     printf("%s\n\r", output);
     fflush(stdout);
     if (strstr(output, "w1-gpio") != NULL) {
       txfound = 1;
     }
    }
    pclose(fd);
    if (txfound == 0) {
     char cmd[100];
     snprintf(cmd, 100, "sudo dtoverlay w1-gpio gpiopin=%d", pin);
     fd = doCommand(cmd);
     pclose(fd);
    }
}
```

This just checks to see if there is an overlay currently active and if not it sets the pin you specify to be the 1-Wire bus.

As with all dynamic overlays, removing it isn't a good idea and in the case of the 1-Wire driver, at the time of writing, it will crash the system. Once loaded, the overlay can stay active until the next reboot.

Listing Devices

When the driver is loaded it scans the 1-Wire bus for connected devices. It repeats the scan at intervals, so keeping the system up-to-date if you add new devices. For each device it finds, it creates a directory with the same name as the serial number of the device in /sys/bus/w1/devices/. Inside the folder are, among other things, files that let you work with the sensor. In particular there is the w1_slave file that allows you to initiate a measurement and read the result.

What we have to do is read the names of the folders in /sys/bus/w1/devices/ and extract each one and use this to construct paths to each of the w1_slave files that have been created. Usually we know the class of device we are working with by the form of its serial number. Each device has a 64-bit number that is composed of a family code that tells you the type of the device and a unique serial number:

MSB	64-Bit 'Registration' ROM Number		LSB
8-Bit CRC	48-Bit Serial Number	8-Bit Family Code	
MSB LSB	MSB LSB	MSB LSB	

For example, all DS18B20 Temperature Sensors have a serial number that starts with 28-. Variations on the device have different family codes:

```
W1_THERM_DS18S20      0x10
W1_THERM_DS1822       0x22
W1_THERM_DS18B20      0x28
W1_THERM_DS1825       0x3B
W1_THERM_DS28EA00     0x42
```

All of these are supported by the Linux driver.

Working with directories in Linux isn't difficult, but you need a refresher then see *Applying C for the IoT with Linux*, ISBN: 9781871962611. The following is the usual way to find out what devices are connected, but there is arguably a better way, see later.

First we open the devices directory:

```
int getDevices(char path[][100], int *num) {
    DIR *dirp;
    char name[10][50];
    struct dirent *direntp;
    if ((dirp = opendir("/sys/bus/w1/devices/")) == NULL) {
        return -1;
    }
```

Next we scan through all of the directories that this contains, looking for names that start with 28-:

```
    *num = 0;
    while ((direntp = readdir(dirp)) != NULL) {
        if (strstr(direntp->d_name, "28-")) {
            strncpy(name[*num], direntp->d_name, 50);
            (*num)++;
        }
    }
    closedir(dirp);
```

Each one found is copied to an element of the name string array. Notice that the name array only has space for 10 devices – you could make it bigger.

Finally we construct a string array with the path to each of the w1_slave files that allow us to read each of the sensors:

```
    for (int i = 0; i < *num; i++) {
      snprintf(path[i],100, "/sys/bus/w1/devices/%s/w1_slave",
                                                        name[i]);

    }
    return 0;
}
```

Notice that when the getDevices function is called it has to be supplied with a path string array of the required dimensions.

The complete function is:

```c
int getDevices(char path[][100], int *num)
{
    DIR *dirp;
    char name[10][50];
    struct dirent *direntp;
    if ((dirp = opendir("/sys/bus/w1/devices/")) == NULL)
    {
        return -1;
    }
    *num = 0;
    while ((direntp = readdir(dirp)) != NULL)
    {
        if (strstr(direntp->d_name, "28-"))
        {
            strncpy(name[*num], direntp->d_name, 50);
            (*num)++;
        }
    }
    closedir(dirp);
    for (int i = 0; i < *num; i++)
    {
        snprintf(path[i], 100, "/sys/bus/w1/devices/%s", name[i]);
    }
    return 0;
}
```

It is also possible to arrange for an action to occur when a new device is added as outlined in the next chapter.

The DS18B20

As an example of a 1-Wire bus device the DS18B20 is a good choice as it is almost the only device anyone makes significant use of. It is low-cost, easy to use and you can use multiple devices on a single GPIO line.

The DS18B20 is available in a number of formats, but the most common makes it look just like a standard BJT (Bipolar Junction Transistor) which can sometimes be a problem when you are trying to find one. You can also get them made up into waterproof sensors complete with cable.

No matter how packaged, they will work at 3.3V or 5V.

The basic specification of the DS18B20 is:

- ◆ Measures temperatures from -55°C to +125°C (-67°F to +257°F)
- ◆ ±0.5°C accuracy from -10°C to +85°C
- ◆ Thermometer resolution is user-selectable from 9 to 12 bits
- ◆ Converts temperature to 12-bit digital word in 750ms (max)

It can also be powered from the data line, making the bus physically need only two wires - data and ground. However, this "parasitic power" mode is difficult to make work reliably and best avoided in an initial design. To supply it with enough power during a conversion, the host has to connect it directly to the data line by providing a "strong pull-up" - essentially a transistor. In normal-powered mode there are just three connections:

Ground needs to be connected to the system ground, VDD to 3.3V, and DQ to the pull-up resistor of an open collector bus.

While you can have multiple devices on the same bus, for simplicity it is better to start off with a single device until you know that everything is working.

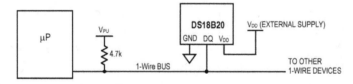

You can build the circuit in a variety of ways. You can solder the resistor to the temperature sensor and then use some longer wires with clips to connect to the Pi. You could also solder directly to the Pi, which is a good plan for the Pi Zero, or use a prototyping board.

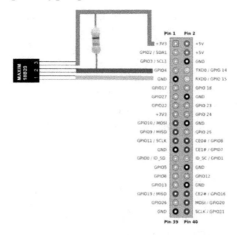

Once the driver is loaded and the device is recognized you will find a set of new folders in the w1/devices folder:

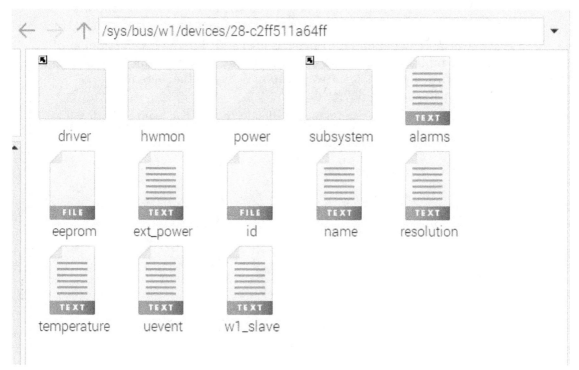

Most of the files have functions that are obvious from their names but there are some points of detail:

- **name**   Returns the name of the device which is the same as its serial number.

- **w1_slave**   uses the nine bytes that the device returns in a check sum - if the check sum is OK then the string ends with t= the temperature in millidegrees Celsius.

- **temperature**   Returns the temperature in millidegrees Celsius – the string is not null terminated.

- **resolution**   Returns the number of bits of resolution used. Writing a number to it sets the resolution if the device supports it.

- **ext_power**   Reads 0 if the device is parasitic powered and 1 if externally powered.

- **alarms**   Reads or writes the high and low temperatures, TH and TL, for the temperature alarm. The values are space separated and the lowest value is automatically used for TL.

- **eeprom**   Saves the current configuration if you write "save" to it and restores it if you write "restore". It supports a limited number of writes so should be used sparingly.

It is also worth knowing that the device is also added to the hwmon folder and that folder is replicated in the devices folder. The reason for this is to allow integration with any hwmon software you may have – there are no advantages over using the device directly.

The 1-Wire master also has some useful files in the w1_bus_master folder:

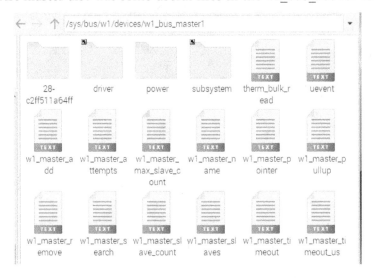

246

♦	therm_bulk_read	Takes a temperature from all devices
♦	w1_master_add	Manually registers a slave device
♦	w1_master_attempts	Number of times a search attempted
♦	w1_master_max_slave_count	Max number of slaves to search for
♦	w1_master_name	Name of the device (w1_bus_masterX)
♦	w1_master_pullup	5V strong pull-up 0 enabled/1 disabled
♦	w1_master_remove	Manually remove a slave device
♦	w1_master_search	Number of searches left to do
♦	w1_master_slave_count	Number of slaves found
♦	w1_master_slaves	Names of the slaves, one per line
♦	w1_master_timeout	Delay in seconds between searches
♦	w1_master_timeout_us	Delay in microsecs between searches

Normally a temperature conversion is triggered when you read the appropriate file but if you write trigger to the therm_bulk_read file all of the connected devices are read and the readings stored for the next time you read the device. Reading the file returns 0 if no bulk conversion is in progress, -1 if at least one device is still converting and 1 if conversion is complete but there is still data to be read from the devices.

You can set the w1_master_search to a small number if the attached devices rarely change. If your devices never change you could set it to zero and use w1_master_add to add the serial numbers.

The w1_master_timeout and w1_master_timeout_us determine the interval between searches for devices. Each time a search occurs w1_master_search is decremented and w1_master_attempts is incremented.

You can use the w1_master_slave_count and w1_master_slaves as an alternative way of discovering what devices are installed:

```
int getDevices(char path[][100], int *num)
{
    char buffer[500];
    int fd = open("/sys/bus/w1/drivers/w1_master_driver/
                    w1_bus_master1/w1_master_slaves", O_RDONLY);
    read(fd, buffer, 500);
    close(fd);
    *num = 0;
    for (char *p = strtok(buffer, "\n"); p != NULL;
                                    p = strtok(NULL, "\n"))
    {
        snprintf(path[(*num)++], 100, "/sys/bus/w1/devices/%s", p);
    }
    num--;
}
```

Notice that the names are separated by newline characters and the strtok function splits the string on "/n". You have to make sure that buffer is big enough to read all the names in one go.

A complete program that reads and displays the data of the first device connected to the 1-Wire bus is:

```c
#define _DEFAULT_SOURCE
#include <stdio.h>
#include <stdlib.h>
#include <string.h>
#include <unistd.h>
#include <sys/ioctl.h>
#include <fcntl.h>

FILE *doCommand(char *cmd)
{
    FILE *fp = popen(cmd, "r");
    if (fp == NULL)
    {
        printf("Failed to run command %s \n\r", cmd);
        exit(1);
    }
    return fp;
}

void load1w(int pin)
{
    FILE *fd = doCommand("sudo dtparam -l");
    char output[1024];
    int txfound = 0;
    while (fgets(output, sizeof(output), fd) != NULL)
    {
        printf("%s\n\r", output);
        fflush(stdout);
        if (strstr(output, "w1-gpio") != NULL)
        {
            txfound = 1;
        }
    }
    pclose(fd);
    if (txfound == 0)
    {
        char cmd[100];
        snprintf(cmd, 100, "sudo dtoverlay w1-gpio gpiopin=%d",
                                                            pin);

        fd = doCommand(cmd);
        pclose(fd);
    }
}
```

```
int getDevices(char path[][100], int *num)
{
    char buffer[500];
    int fd = open("/sys/bus/w1/drivers/w1_master_driver/
                    w1_bus_master1/w1_master_slaves", O_RDONLY);
    read(fd, buffer, 500);
    close(fd);
    *num = 0;
    for (char *p = strtok(buffer, "\n"); p != NULL;
                                    p = strtok(NULL, "\n"))
    {
        snprintf(path[(*num)++], 100, "/sys/bus/w1/devices/%s", p);
    }
    num--;
}

int getData(char path[], char name[], char data[], int n)
{
    char file[100];
    snprintf(file, 100, "%s/%s", path, name);
    int fd = open(file, O_RDONLY);
    int c = read(fd, data, n);
    close(fd);
    data[c] = 0;
    return c;
}

int main(int argc, char **argv)
{
    load1w(4);
    char path[10][100];
    int num;
    getDevices(path, &num);
    printf("%d  %s\n\r", num, path[0]);
    if (num < 1)
        exit(-1);

    char output[1024] = {0};
    char file[100];

    getData(path[0], "name", output, 100);
    printf("Name %s\n\r", output);

    getData(path[0], "resolution", output, 100);
    printf("Resolution %s\n\r", output);

    getData(path[0], "w1_slave", output, 100);
    printf("w1_slave %s\n\r", output);

    getData(path[0], "temperature", output, 100);
    printf("temperature %s\n\r", output);
    float temp;
```

```
sscanf(output, "%f", &temp);
temp = temp / 1000;
printf("temperature %f C\n\r",temp);

getData(path[0], "alarms", output, 100);
printf("alarms %s\n\r", output);
```

}

Active Pull-Up

The 1-Wire bus isn't very robust. Its use of pull-up resistors at such high
speeds means that it doesn't take much capacitance to make the pulses look
more like a capacitor charging up. Getting the wiring right for a 1-Wire bus
with multiple devices isn't easy. What is more, scanning the bus is the only
time, apart from the presence pulse, when multiple devices control the bus.
A setup that works perfectly well with a single device often has problems
when there is more than one device. In fact, a standard 1-Wire bus
debugging technique is to remove all but one device and see if what wasn't
working suddenly works.

You can get around some of the problems by lowering the value of the pull-
up resistor, but this does increase the load on the driving GPIO lines and the
slave devices. You can reduce the pull-up to 2kΩ, or even less to account for
the reduced working voltage of 3.3V. The 1-Wire bus works best at 5V when
the lines are long, but it is usually not worth the trouble to add a 3.3V to 5V
driver.

If you want to drive a very long line, or just need the highest possible
performance, there is a technique which, while it might not be worth using
in many situations, is worth knowing about. It is called by a number of
names but "controllable slew rate" is close enough. The idea is that when the
master releases the bus, we have to wait for it to be pulled up via the resistor
and this can be slow. We can make it faster by replacing resistors by active
devices.

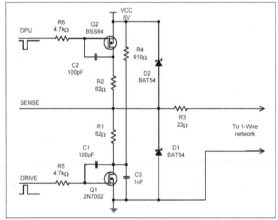

The principle used is that we can put a transistor in parallel with the pull-up resistor and use it to pull the line up faster when appropriate. For example, when the master pulls the line low for a presence pulse, it can trigger the pull-up transistor when the pulse ends to get the line back up faster than just via the resistor.

The fast pull-up transistor Q2, controlled by DPU, is switched off just before the slaves start to pull the line low. You can use the fast pull-up transistor when the master writes a 0 or reads or writes a 1. Of course, you don't need to use it when the master reads a 0 because the slave holds the line low for the whole time slot and there is no need for a fast pull-up. It is claimed that lines as long as 500m can work in this mode. Notice that you now need an additional GPIO line to drive the fast pull-up transistor. If you want to know more then refer to the Maxim design notes.

The fast pull-up is also recommended if you are planning to run a true 1-Wire device and power attached devices from the data line. A typical circuit is:

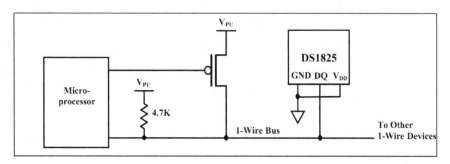

You can see that the device only needs a single wire if it can find a common ground connection. You can also see that the transistor is playing the role of a fast pull-up, but in this case the reason for it is to ensure that the device gets as much current as possible to keep it running.

The documentation says:

> The 1-Wire bus must be switched to the strong pullup within 10s (max) after a Convert T [44h] or Copy Scratchpad [48h] command is issued, and the bus must be held high by the pullup for the duration of the conversion (tconv) or data transfer (twr = 10ms). No other activity can take place on the 1-Wire bus while the pullup is enabled.

If you work with 1-Wire devices at a low level then it is up to you to drive the second pull-up GPIO line manually.

If you want to use a Linux driver then there is one that takes care of this for you:

Name: `w1-gpio-pullup`

                Configures the `w1-gpio` Onewire interface module

Load: `dtoverlay=w1-gpio-pullup,<param>=<val>`

Params: `gpiopin`   GPIO for I/O (default "4")

                `extpullup`   GPIO for external pull-up (default "5")

                `pullup`   Enabled by default (ignored)

This is used in exactly the same way as the `w1-gpio` driver but now you have to specify an additional GPIO line to drive the active pull-up, the default being GPIO5.

In practice, you have to face up to the fact that you will get errors when working with the 1-Wire bus and especially so with multiple devices and parasitic power. The problem is particularly bad if you are testing a circuit using a prototype board. Things often work better when you move to properly soldered connections and cables, but you will still get errors.

The only way to live with errors is to detect them and attempt to re-read the device.

One Wire File System (OWFS)

If you are going to use a lot of 1-Wire devices then it might be worth looking into the One Wire File System, OWFS, which you can find out about at `www.owfs.org`. It is an open source project which supports a range of 1-Wire master and slaves. The downside is that it is more involved to install and get working, the pay off is that every device now has its own directory in a mountable file system and the range of devices supported is larger than the basic Linux drivers. How to use OWFS would take us a long way from the main topic of this book but it is worth looking into if you want to use a mix of 1-Wire devices.

Summary

- The 1-Wire bus is easy to use and has good Linux support.

- The `w1-gpio` driver will use any GPIO pin to implement a 1-Wire bus in software.

- All 1-Wire devices have a unique serial number, which also codes for the type of the device.

- You can list devices using directory operations or you can use the driver to interrogate the master.

- The DS18B20 Temperature Sensor is a good example of a 1-Wire device.

- You can power a 1-Wire device over the line that is used for data. This only works if you use a strong pull-up in the form of a transistor.

- If you want to make extensive use of 1-Wire devices, it might be worth looking into OWFS – the One Wire File System.

Chapter 16

Going Further With Drivers

Given the amount of space already devoted to using drivers, it may seem odd that this chapter is about drivers, However, it is worth going deeper so that you can customize your use of drivers. You can get a long way simply using overlays and what other people have worked out for you, but occasionally you have to go it alone. In such cases you need to know a little more about how things work. You need to know how drivers are manipulated and how to write your own overlays. This is a big topic and while this chapter provides a good introduction to the ideas you need, it can't cover everything - only provide you with the tools to solve new problems.

Loadable Kernel Modules

Drivers are a special case of Loadable Kernel Modules, LKMs. An LKM is a program that can be added to the Linux kernel after it has booted. It is a way to extend the kernel without having to "fork" it in its entirety before adding your own custom code to it. Most LKMs are drivers, i.e. they allow the kernel to work with hardware and provide a connection to user space programs so that they can also work with the hardware. Although much of what follows is described in terms of drivers, an LKM doesn't have to be just a driver - it can be a file system, a random number generator or even a "hello world" demo. However, in most cases the big advantage of running in kernel space is the access it provides to the hardware.

It isn't difficult to get started writing your own LKMs, but there is a lot to learn about programming in kernel space as most of the libraries that you have grown accustomed to using aren't available. Also, if you venture into writing your own drivers, this generally isn't a matter of starting from scratch. Each type of driver, IIO, hwmon and so on, has lots of code that you can make use of as a starting point, but there is also a lot to learn about that code. In most cases, writing a driver is a matter of finding an existing driver that is similar to what you want and modifying it. Depending on how you go about it, this task can leave a lot of uncertainty about how your final driver actually achieves its intended end product.

For most of us, using drivers that other programmers have created is the simplest option, even if it means restricting the hardware to supported devices.

Finding Modules

Modules are usually files with a `.ko` (for kernel object) extension. Standard modules are to be found in `/lib/modules` in a subdirectory that is specific to the kernel release that you are using. You can discover the kernel release that you are using automatically via the command `uname -r` the output of which can be quoted into other commands. So to discover the modules appropriate to your kernel you can use:

```
ls /lib/modules/`uname -r`
```

This will show a set of folders that group the modules into types. To see the total list of modules available, use the command `lsmod`, and to discover what modules are currently loaded use `modprobe -c-` you might be surprised at how many there are. Some modules are built into the kernel and don't need to be loaded. To find out what these are you can use:

```
cat /lib/modules/$(uname -r)/modules.builtin
```

Loading Modules The Old Way

Before the device tree was introduced there were, and still are, commands that allow you to work with modules. It is worth knowing about this more fundamental way of doing things for times when it is the only way to make something work or to explore what it going on. In most cases, however, you should use the device tree and overlays to work with drivers.

There are two commands that let you insert a module into the kernel – `insmod` and `modprobe`. The `modprobe` command is far more versatile and it is the one to use in most cases. Simply, `modprobe modulename` installs the module and `modprobe -r modulename` removes it. The command automatically looks in the correct module directory for the version of Linux it is running on. It also uses configuration files to find what other modules the one being loaded depends on and makes sure that they are loaded first. You can see the configuration using the `-c` option and override it using the `-C` option.

Configurations are stored in the folder `/etc/modprobe.d` and any files ending in `.conf` are read and used to configure modules.

In addition to loading modules, you can also provide parameters in the form of key=value pairs following the module name. You can also pass parameters to modules loaded at boot time by adding:

```
modulename.parameter=value
```

to the boot loader's command line which you will find in `/boot/cmdline.txt`.

For example, you can load the 1-Wire driver using:

```
sudo modprobe w1-gpio gpiopin=4
```

Another complication is that modules can have aliases so that they can be loaded using a range of different names. Modules can also be blacklisted at boot time by creating .conf files in /etc/modprobe.d/ containing lines of the form:

```
blacklist modulename
```

You can manually load a blacklisted module at a later time and the module will be loaded anyway if it is used by a module that isn't blacklisted.

Udev

Many of the things that blacklists and other ways of autoloading drivers were designed to take care of are now dealt with by udev. This is a dynamic device directory which takes account of hotplug devices. It is what takes care of finding and loading a driver when you plug in a USB device at any time after boot. When a device is created, udev automatically reads the corresponding sys directory to find out its attributes. These attributes are processed and stored as a database of currently active devices.

All important udev files are stored in /etc/udev/. Every received device event is matched against the set of rules read from files located in /lib/udev/rules.d and /run/udev/rules.d. You can add rules of your own to /etc/udev/rules.d and all rules files end in .rules. Files are processed in name order and earlier rules have precedence – this accounts for the common practice of using numbers at the start of the name of a rule file. There are also LABEL and GOTO commands that can be included in rule files to skip to a specific file, but they are best avoided.

Each rule is simple in theory, but can quickly become quite complex in practice. A rule consists of a set of key value pairs all on one line, use the continuation symbol / if you want to split lines. Keys come in two broad types – match keys and assignment keys. Match keys determine the event that the rule is activated for and assignment keys determine what the rule actually does when an event occurs. Assignment keys include RUN which allows you to run a script or a program when the event occurs so perhaps "assignment" isn't a good description of what they can do. The full list of keys is available in the documentation and they generally aren't difficult to understand.

The main use of udev is to deal with USB devices that are hot-plugged while the machine is running. Some common uses are to give a device a more human-oriented name. For example, you can write a rule that recognizes a particular USB stick and mounts it with a relevant name.

Another common use is to set the permissions on folders and files in the /sys folder so that they can be accessed without running as root. In principle, this is easy, but it is complicated by the fact that the folders and files in /sys are dynamically created. For example, you can create a rule that allows a folder to be used by a program running with a particular group's permission, but if the program writes something that configures the device in such a way that new folders or files are generated, the entire set of folders that represent the device are regenerated with the default permissions. It is difficult to catch all changes that need a udev rule to be triggered.

Most IoT applications don't make use of hot plugging. The one big exception is the 1-Wire bus as described in the previous chapter. In particular, i-Buttons are intended to be hot plugged to provide identity based access. Although it isn't generally realized, the 1-Wire bus sends events to the kernel that udev can respond to. This is best explained by way of a simple example.

udev and The 1-Wire bus

When a device is added or removed from the 1-Wire bus it triggers a udev event that we can use to react to the change. We simply need to create a udev rule.

First we need a simple script that lets us know our rule has been used. Create a file /bin/device_added.sh and enter the lines:

```
#!/bin/bash
echo "USB device added at $(date)" >>/tmp/scripts.log
```

You also need to make the file executable:

```
sudo chmod +x /bin/device_added.sh
```

This script has nothing to do with udev – it is just a script to show that the rule has been activated by writing a message to a file.

To check that everything is working you can see what events udev is processing using the:

```
su
udevadm monitor
```

command. If you try this out and disconnect and connect a 1-Wire device you will see something like:

```
pi@raspberrypi:/sys/bus/w1/devices/28-73fa511a64ff $ su
Password:
root@raspberrypi:/sys/bus/w1/devices/28-73fa511a64ff# udevadm monitor
monitor will print the received events for:
UDEV - the event which udev sends out after rule processing
KERNEL - the kernel uevent

KERNEL[635434.766262] remove    /devices/w1_bus_master1/28-73fa511a64ff/hwmon/hwmon3 (hwmon)
UDEV  [635434.794656] remove    /devices/w1_bus_master1/28-73fa511a64ff/hwmon/hwmon3 (hwmon)
KERNEL[635496.311780] add       /devices/w1_bus_master1/28-73fa511a64ff/hwmon/hwmon3 (hwmon)
KERNEL[635496.320597] add       /devices/w1_bus_master1/28-73fa511a64ff (w1)
UDEV  [635496.335529] add       /devices/w1_bus_master1/28-73fa511a64ff/hwmon/hwmon3 (hwmon)
UDEV  [635496.345868] add       /devices/w1_bus_master1/28-73fa511a64ff (w1)
```

This confirms that the devices are being added and removed with the help of udev.

You can find out more about the device using:

```
udevadm info —path=/sys/bus/w1/devices/w1_bus_master1
                                           —attribute-walk
```

which, for the device '/devices/w1_bus_master1', produces something like:

```
looking at device '/devices/w1_bus_master1':
 KERNEL=="w1_bus_master1"
 SUBSYSTEM=="w1"
 DRIVER=="w1_master_driver"
 ATTR{w1_master_timeout}=="10"
 ATTR{w1_master_slave_count}=="2"
 ATTR{w1_master_max_slave_count}=="64"
 ATTR{w1_master_timeout_us}=="0"
 ATTR{w1_master_remove}=="write device id xx-xxxxxxxxxxxx
                                          to remove slave"
 ATTR{w1_master_name}=="w1_bus_master1"
 ATTR{w1_master_attempts}=="67834"
 ATTR{w1_master_add}=="write device id xx-xxxxxxxxxxxx
                                          to add slave"
 ATTR{w1_master_pullup}=="1"
 ATTR{w1_master_pointer}=="0x58e38d87"
 ATTR{w1_master_search}=="-1"
 ATTR{therm_bulk_read}=="0"
```

Now that we know that the SUBSYSTEM is "w1" we can write a udev rule. Create a text file /etc/udev/rules.d/100-w1.rules containing:

```
SUBSYSTEM=="w1",ACTION=="add",RUN+="/bin/device_added.sh"
```

The name of the file should ensure that it is the last loaded and so it is unlikely to be overridden. The match keys specify an add action in the w1 subsystem and when this event occurs our script is run. After you save the file you can restart udev using:

```
sudo udevadm control --reload-rules
```

This should restart the udev system, but sometimes a complete reboot is needed. Now if you add a new 1-Wire device you should see the message in the /tmp/scripts.log file. If it doesn't seem to work you need to know that removing a 1-Wire device takes a few seconds because the driver doesn't immediately remove a device that is missing on one of its regular searches to allow for temporary loss of connectivity. If you can, check that the events occur using udevadm.

Even for the 1-Wire bus, the actual usefulness of udev is limited. The time it takes to recognize a device being disconnected or connected can be too slow for many purposes and the range of things you can do usually don't fit in with controlling the device from code. Where udev does prove useful is if you have any USB devices that you want to set up the same way every time they are connected.

Finally, notice that udev is the source of the file included in most device folders called uevent. It writes the latest relevant udev event into this folder.

Customizing The Device Tree

We have already met the Device Tree, DT, in Chapter 7, but only in the context of using supplied overlays to install device drivers. There often comes a time when a driver exists but the available overlays aren't quite what you need. There are also drivers which can support additional devices if you add an overlay that specifies what you want. Knowing how to create your own overlays is therefore useful and not that difficult. What is difficult is finding out what parameters are needed in your custom overlay – again the problem is lack of documentation.

A device tree or an overlay is written using a markup language usually referred to as Device Tree Source DTS and stored in `.dts` files. The syntax of DTS is C-like and you should recognize its general form. Before a device tree or overlay is used it has to be compiled to a binary format known as a Flattened Device Tree, FDT, or a Device Tree Blob, DTB, stored in `.dtb` files. The tools you need to compile a device tree are installed as standard. DTS files that are to be included in other DTS files, using a C-like include instruction, by convention have file names ending `.dtsi`.

You can look up the syntax of the full DTS which you need to create a complete overlay, but for most of us the smaller task of creating overlays means we have to master a subset of the language and use it in a slightly different way. Few of us have to create a device tree for a completely new device, but being able to modify or add devices by way of overlays is more common.

The first thing to say is that not all drivers are device tree compatible in the sense that they might well be loaded from a device tree node, but they don't necessarily understand everything that might be included in that node. For example, which device driver should be loaded is specified using `compatible = name` where at its simplest the `name` is the actual filename of the driver. A device tree-aware driver will also recognize names that are not the file name of the driver and indicate a wider range of use. You can generally find the name of the compatible driver in the bindings documentation at `/linux/Documentation/devicetree/bindings/` in the GitHub repo, but this is not always everything you need to know.

The best way of getting started is to look at a typical overlay.

Custom LEDs

The driver for the existing LEDs, `gpio-leds`, introduced in Chapter 3, has the ability to support new LED devices on any GPIO line. To find out how this works you need to look up the documentation in: `linux/Documentation/devicetree/bindings/leds/leds-gpio.txt`

It says:

> *Each LED is represented as a sub-node of the gpio-leds device.*
>
> *Each node's name represents the name of the corresponding LED.*

What this means is that we can use an overlay to introduce a new sub-node to the `gpio-led` node. Following this, a lot of sub-node properties are listed, but as we are considering adding a simple LED on a GPIO line the one that is relevant is `gpios`, which should specify the LED's GPIO, see "gpios property" in `Documentation/devicetree/bindings/gpio/gpio.txt`. Active low LEDs should be indicated using flags in the GPIO specifier.

Clearly we can use this to add an LED on a specific GPIO but we need to know how to specify a GPIO line. The documentation says that you specify a GPIO line using something like `<controller,line offset, options>`. It then says that the options are controller-dependent, which means you now have to look elsewhere for details. However, the general documentation says:

> *The exact meaning of each specifier cell is controller specific, and must be documented in the device tree binding for the device, but it is strongly recommended to use the two-cell approach.*

Before this the "two-cell" approach is specified as using a single option for active state - a `0` for active high and `1` for active low.

Putting all this together and we can write a simple overlay:

```
/dts-v1/;
/plugin/;
/ {
    compatible = "brcm,bcm2708";
    fragment@0 {
        target = <&leds>;
        __overlay__ {
            my_led: myled {
                gpios = <&gpio 4 0>;
            };
        };
    };
};
```

The first two lines are standard comments. The `compatible` line is also standard and is defined this to be an overlay that works on all Pis. If you want to use resources that are only available on a Pi 4 then use `brcm,bcm2711`. In more general cases, `compatible =` is used to specify the driver to be used by the node.

261

The `fragment@0` starts the actual details of the overlay. You can write a number of fragments in the file, but they have to be numbered sequentially. The `target =` determines the node that the overlay will modify. In this case it is identified by a label `&leds`, which is set within the main device tree to reference the `gpio-leds` node. You can only discover this by reading the device tree or seeing it used in an example as it doesn't seem to be documented anywhere. After this the `__overlay__` block defines what is added to the node and in this case we add a single LED on GPIO4:

```
  my_led: myled {
              gpios = <&gpio 4 0>;
          };
```

Again, you have to know that `gpio` is a label for GPIO controller 0 and you can only find this out by reading the device tree or seeing it used in another example. Notice that we have also created a label for our new node. We can use `my_led` as an alternative name for the node within the overlay.

Start a new text file and enter all of the above to produce a file called `MyLed.dts`:

```
/dts-v1/;
/plugin/;

/ {
    compatible = "brcm,bcm2708";
    fragment@0 {
        target = <&leds>;
        __overlay__ {
            my_led: myled {
                gpios = <&gpio 4 0>;
            };
        };
    };
};
```

Once you have saved the file you need to compile it using:

```
dtc -@ -I dts -O dtb -o MyLed.dtbo MyLed.dts
```

You can look up the details of the options for the dtc compiler, but this is typical for compiling an overlay. After this you need to copy the compiled file into the overlay directory:

```
sudo cp MyLed.dtbo /boot/overlays/
```

In the case of other drivers you would now load the overlay dynamically, but the `gpio-leds` driver doesn't support this. As a result you need to add `dtoverlay = MyLed` to `boot/config.txt` and reboot.

When you do you will find that there is a new LED device that you can control in the usual way:

```c
#include <stdio.h>
#include <errno.h>
#include <unistd.h>
#include <fcntl.h>
int main(int argc, char **argv)
{

    int fd = open("/sys/class/leds/myled/brightness", O_WRONLY);
    while (1)
    {
        write(fd, "0",1);
        sleep(2);
        write(fd, "1",1);
        sleep(2);
    }
}
```

You can see that the custom LED is installed with the standard set of files in the appropriate folder:

If this doesn't work then add:

```
dtdebug=1
```

to the start of the /boot/config.txt file and after rebooting use:

```
sudo vclog --msg
```

to see the error messages.

You might find it interesting to see what the compiler has generated using the command:

```
fdtdump /boot/overlays/MyLed.dtbo
****fdtdump is a low-level debugging tool,not meant for general
use.
**** If you want to decompile a dtb, you probably want
**** dtc -I dtb -O dts <filename>
/dts-v1/;
// magic:            0xd00dfeed
// totalsize:        0x1b1 (433)
// off_dt_struct:    0x38
// off_dt_strings:   0x180
// off_mem_rsvmap:   0x28
// version:              17
// last_comp_version:      16
// boot_cpuid_phys: 0x0
// size_dt_strings: 0x31
// size_dt_struct:  0x148
/ {
    compatible = "brcm,bcm2708";
    fragment@0 {
        target = <0xffffffff>;
        __overlay__ {
            myled {
                gpios = <0xffffffff 0x00000004 0x00000000>;
                phandle = <0x00000001>;
            };
        };
    };
    __symbols__ {
        my_led = "/fragment@0/__overlay__/myled";
    };
    __fixups__ {
        leds = "/fragment@0:target:0";
        gpio = "/fragment@0/__overlay__/myled:gpios:0";
    };
};
```

The __fixups__ section lists the symbols that don't have values yet as they haven't been merged with the full device tree where they do have values.

You can, as the previous listing suggests, use the decompiler option to get slightly less information:

```
dtc -I dtb -O dts /boot/overlays/MyLed.dtbo
```

You can also use the decompiler to get a complete listing of the current state of the device tree:

```
$ dtc -I fs -O dts /proc/device-tree
```

If you do this you can find the node that the LED overlay adds to:

```
leds {
        compatible = "gpio-leds";
        phandle = < 0x7a >;

        act {
                gpios = < 0x0a 0x2f 0x01 >;
                label = "led0";
                phandle = < 0x2d >;
                default-state = "keep";
                linux,default-trigger = "actpwr";
        };

        myled {
                gpios = < 0x0a 0x04 0x00 >;
                phandle = < 0x7d >;
        };
};
```

You can see that it hasn't added quite as much information as for the standard act LED.

Once you have a basic overlay you can start to improve on it. For example the documentation says: !***!

```
linux,default-trigger      This parameter, if present, is a string
                           defining the trigger assigned to the
LED.   Current triggers are:
      "backlight"          LED will act as a back-light, controlled
                           by the framebuffer system
      "default-on"         LED will turn on (but for leds-gpio
                           see "default-state" property in
                           Documentation/devicetree/
                           bindings/leds/leds-gpio.txt)
      "heartbeat"          LED flashes at a load average rate
      "disk-activity"      LED indicates disk activity
      "ide-disk"           IDE disk activity (deprecated),
                           in new implementations use
                           "disk-activity"
      "timer"              LED flashes at a fixed, configurable
rate
      "pattern"            LED alters the brightness for the
                           specified duration with one software
                           timer (requires "led-pattern" property)
```

Of course, we already know that the Pi supports more than this, see Chapter 3. Another useful section is the aliases node which lists many of the labels that we use in overlays.

With this information, setting a default trigger for the new LED is easy:

```
ts-v1/;
/plugin/;
/ {
    compatible = "brcm,bcm2708";
    fragment@0 {
        target =<&leds>;
        __overlay__ {
            my_led: myled {
                gpios = <&gpio 4 0>;
                linux,default-trigger = "heartbeat";
            };
        };
    };
};
```

After a reboot you will see the standard double-flash heartbeat on GPIO4.

Parameters

We can make overlays more useful by way of parameters. In fact, we have been making use of parameters to customize overlays since our first encounter with them. In the case of the custom LED overlay, for example, it would be better to allow the user to define the default trigger and the GPIO pin to use via parameters. You can define any parameters that you might want to set in an __overrides__ node.

Parameters are defined using a standard syntax:

```
name = <&label>,"property";
```

where *name* is the name of the parameter, i.e. it is what you use in the dtparam or dtoverlay line to set the property. The label is the node that the property you want the parameter to set is in.

There are a range of different ways to specify the property according to how you want the value that is assigned to the parameter to change it. The simplest is a string property, which simply takes whatever is assigned to the parameter and sets the property equal to it. For example:

```
trigger =  <&my_led>,"linux,default-trigger";
```

sets the linux,default-trigger property within the node labeled by my_led to whatever the user specifies for the trigger parameter as part of a dtparam or dtoverlay.

A complete example is:

```
/dts-v1/;
/plugin/;
/ {
    compatible = "brcm,bcm2708";
    fragment@0 {
        target =<&leds>;
        __overlay__ {
            my_led: myled {
                gpios = <&gpio 4 0>;
                linux,default-trigger = "heartbeat";
            };
        };
    };
    __overrides__ {
    trigger =  <&my_led>,"linux,default-trigger";

    };
};
```

If you now change `config.txt` to read:

```
dtoverlay = MyLed
dtparam = trigger = none
```

the trigger will be set to none and the LED won't flash at all. You can set the trigger to be anything that is supported. You can set multiple properties using the same parameter – just write a comma-separated list of labels and properties.

Setting a simple string via a parameter is easy, but what about selecting the GPIO pin number? The problem here is that the number is embedded in a list of values:

```
gpios = <&gpio 4 0>;
```

How can you change a single value in a list of values? The answer is to make use of the offset specification. If you want to define an integer parameter then there a number of possible forms depending on the size of the integer:

```
name = <&label>,"property.offset"; // 8-bit
name = <&label>,"property;offset"; // 16-bit
name = <&label>,"property:offset"; // 32-bit
name = <&label>,"property#offset"; // 64-bit
```

This looks straightforward, but the key is the offset specification. A numeric property is treated as a set of bytes and the offset, in bytes, determines where the parameter's value will be inserted into the set.

For example:

```
gpios = <&gpio 4 0>;
```

is a set of 32-bit integers – the first four are the GPIO controller number, the next four are the GPIO pin number and the final four are the active high/low selector. To store a value in the GPIO pin number we need to store a 32-bit integer offset by four bytes. That is:

```
gpio_pin = <&my_led>,"gpios:4"
```

This creates a `gpio_pin` parameter and sets bytes 4, 5, 6 and 7 bytes of the `gpios` property to its value as a 32-bit integer.

If you now change `config.txt` to read:

```
dtoverlay=MyLed
dtparam=trigger=none
dtparam=gpio_pin=4
```

you will discover that you can customize the new LED device to use any trigger and any GPIO pin.

The complete overlay is:

```
/dts-v1/;
/plugin/;
/ {
    compatible = "brcm,bcm2708";
    fragment@0 {
        target =<&leds>;
        __overlay__ {
                my_led: myled {
                gpios = <&gpio 4 0>;
                linux,default-trigger = "heartbeat";
                };
            };
        };
    __overrides__{
        trigger =  <&my_led>,"linux,default-trigger";
        gpio_pin = <&my_led>,"gpios:4";
        };
};
```

Device Tree – Where Next?

The device tree is a relatively young idea and is still being developed. This brief introduction is enough to get you started writing overlays, but there are many topics that have been omitted. In particular, we haven't touched on the topic of specifying hardware in terms of addresses and interrupts, and we haven't looked at loading and configuring device drivers that aren't officially supported. The reason for these omissions is that they are not common requirements when creating custom overlays for existing devices. This said, we have encountered many of the basic ideas and techniques. If you want to take this further than the best advice is to read existing overlays and bindings and see how they work.

Summary

- Loadable Kernel Modules, LKMs, are a way of extending the Linux kernel after it has booted.

- LKMs are most often used for drivers, but they are completely general and can be used to implement any desired behavior.

- Writing an LKM isn't difficult, but there is a great deal to learn as you no longer have access to user space libraries, and drivers in particular tend to have their own frameworks.

- Module are usually stored in `/lib/modules` and you can load and generally work with a module using `modprobe`, although the device tree is the preferred way of doing most things relating to drivers.

- Udev is the Linux subsystem that deals with devices that can be hot-plugged -mostly USB devices.

- When a device changes its state a `udev` event is triggered and you can define actions to be taken in a `.rules` file.

- IoT devices are generally not hot-plugged, but 1-Wire bus devices can be handled using `udev` rules.

- You can write custom overlays to add to or modify the device tree. For example, you can add additional LEDs for the LED driver to control.

- Custom overlays can be made more general with the use of parameters.

Appendix I

GPIO Sysfs Interface

The GPIO sysfs interface has been deprecated since 2016 and was expected to have been removed from the kernel by now. It should not be used for new projects, but it has been so extensively used in the past that you might need some knowledge of how it works for some time to come. This appendix is a brief overview.

Note: Only GPIO sysfs was has been deprecated, the rest of sysfs is perfectly usable.

Working With Sysfs

Sysfs is a virtual file system that provides all sorts of access to hardware and the operation of the Linux kernel. You can spend a lot of time exploring sysfs, but the part we are interested in here is the `gpio` folder. Sysfs is usually mounted in the `sys` folder and the folder that corresponds to the GPIO device is usually:

`/sys/class/gpio`

To see what is in the folder, simply list it:

`ls /sys/class/gpio`

```
pi@raspberrypi:    ls /sys/class/gpio
export  gpio4  gpiochip0  unexport
pi@raspberrypi:    ▮
```

The list includes the GPIO lines that are already in use by some process or other. Notice that the gpio numbers are not external pin numbers, but internal gpio numbers. So, for example, to use the GPIO line that is on physical pin 7 on the connector you need to refer to GPIO4.

The steps in using a line are always the same:

1) Reserve or "export" the GPIO line so that no other process can use it

2) Set its direction and read or write it

3) Unreserve it or unexport it

You can do these steps from any language that supports file operations, including the shell.

You might ask why you have to "export" or reserve a GPIO line rather than just use it? The answer is that the export operation will only work if the OS, or some other process, hasn't claimed the GPIO line for its own use. You can think of the export/unexport process as making sure that you don't misuse GPIO lines and that you don't share them with other processes.

To reserve a GPIO line you have to write its number to the export folder and you can do this using the shell command. For example, assuming we want to work with GPIO 4:

```
echo 4 > /sys/class/gpio/export
```

You can of course change 4 to any valid gpio number.

You can do the same job in C:

```
#include <stdio.h>
#include <string.h>
 int main(int argc, char** argv) {
     int gpio = 4;
     FILE* fd = fopen("/sys/class/gpio/export", "w");
     fprintf(fd, "%d", gpio);
     fclose(fd);
     return 0;
}
```

The fopen function opens export for write, the fprintf string prints the number of the gpio line and then the file is closed with fclose. If you are not familiar with C file operations, see *Fundamental C: Getting Closer To The Machine,* ISBN:9781871962604 or, at a more advanced level, *Applying C For The IoT With Linux,* ISBN:9781871962611.

Once you have the pin reserved, you will see a gpio4 folder corresponding to it in /sys/class/gpio. Now you can set its direction and read or write it. To do this you have to read from or write to the appropriate subfolder of the gpio folder just created.

If you list all of the folders in gpio4 you will see:

```
pi@raspberrypi:    ls /sys/class/gpio/gpio4
active_low  device  direction  edge          subsystem  uevent  value
pi@raspberrypi:    █
```

Each of these folders controls some aspect of the GPIO line's functioning. The most important are direction, in which the line can be set to in or out, and value, which can be set to 0 or 1 for output and 0 or 1 for input. There is also active_low, which determines which way the logic operates and whether the line low corresponds to a 1 or a 0.

For example, to read GPIO 4 from the command line use:

```
echo "in" > /sys/class/gpio/gpio4/direction
cat /sys/class/gpio/gpio4/value
```

and to set it as output and to go high and then low use:

```
echo "out" > /sys/class/gpio/gpio4/direction
echo 1 > /sys/class/gpio/gpio4/value
echo 0 > /sys/class/gpio/gpio4/value
```

You can do the same using C, but it is slightly more verbose due to the need to open and close files and build the appropriate strings.

Toggling A Line

As an example, consider the following C program which sets GPIO 4 to output and then toggles it high and low as fast as possible:

```
#include <stdio.h>
#include <string.h>

int main(int argc, char** argv) {
    int gpio = 4;
    char buf[100];

    FILE* fd = fopen("/sys/class/gpio/export", "w");
    fprintf(fd, "%d", gpio);
    fclose(fd);

    sprintf(buf, "/sys/class/gpio/gpio%d/direction", gpio);
    fd = fopen(buf, "w");
    fprintf(fd, "out");
    fclose(fd);

    sprintf(buf, "/sys/class/gpio/gpio%d/value", gpio);
    fd = fopen(buf, "w");

    for (;;) {
        fd = fopen(buf, "w");
        fprintf(fd, "1");
        fclose(fd);
        fd = fopen(buf, "w");
        fprintf(fd, "0");
        fclose(fd);
    }
    return 0;
}
```

The program first exports gpio4 and then writes out to its direction folder to set the line to output. After this the value file is open for writing and 1 and 0 are written to the file repeatedly. Notice the use of sprintf to create strings

273

which incorporate the number of the gpio line you are using so that you can open the correct folder.

You might be puzzled by the loop that opens the file, writes a value and then closes it. Why not just keep the file open? The reason is that the file buffer isn't flushed unless the file is closed. This is the usual way of dealing with the problem, but it is not very fast and it is part of the reason that sysfs has a bad reputation.

If you try the program you will discover that the pulse train has a frequency of around 4kHz and a pulse width of $100\mu s$ on a Pi Zero and 18Khz and $28\mu s$ respectively on a Pi 4.

We can, however, do much better by not closing the file every time we write to it. Instead we can use fflush to flush the file buffer by changing the for loop to:

```
for (;;) {
    fprintf(fd, "1");
    fflush(fd);
    fprintf(fd, "0");
    fflush(fd);
}
```

The difference is quite amazing. Now, on a Pi Zero, the frequency is 130Khz and the pulse width is $3.6\mu s$ and, on a Pi 4, 450Khz and $1.1\mu s$. This is still about 10 times slower than using the library, but useful for some applications.

Sysfs GPIO may be obsolete, but it was simple and logical.

VS Code Files for Remote Development

Chapter 2 covers how to use VS Code to develop programs for the Raspberry Pi and recommends remote development using files created specifically for this book which you should create in the .vscode folder. They can also be found at www.iopress.info.

Notice that these tasks all work with a single file C project. If you want to develop larger programs using them, you would need to modify the build commands appropriately to use make or Cmake.

launch.json

```json
{
  "configurations": [
    {
      "name": "Remote C Debug",
      "type": "cppdbg",
      "request": "launch",
      "program": "${config:remoteDirectory}/
              ${relativeFileDirname}/${fileBasenameNoExtension}",
      "args": [],
      "stopAtEntry": false,
      "cwd": "${config:remoteDirectory}/${relativeFileDirname}",
      "environment": [],
      "externalConsole": false,
      "pipeTransport": {
          "debuggerPath": "/usr/bin/gdb",
          "pipeProgram": "C:/Windows/System32/OpenSSH/ssh",
          "pipeArgs": [
                  "${config:sshUser}@${config:sshEndpoint}"
              ],
          "pipeCwd": "${workspaceFolder}"
      },
      "MIMode": "gdb",
```

```
    "setupCommands": [
        {
            "description": "Enable pretty-printing for gdb",
            "text": "-enable-pretty-printing",
            "ignoreFailures": true
        }
    ],
    "sourceFileMap": {
            "${config:remoteDirectory}/${relativeFileDirname}":
                                        "${fileDirname}"
    },
    "preLaunchTask": "CopyBuildRemote",
    }
    ]
}
```

tasks.json

```
{
    "version": "2.0.0",
    "tasks": [
        {
            "label": "copyToRemote",
            "type": "shell",
            "command": "scp -r ${fileDirname} ${config:sshUser}@
                ${config:sshEndpoint}:${config:remoteDirectory}/",
            "problemMatcher": [],
            "presentation": {
                "showReuseMessage": false,
                "clear": true
            }
        },
        {
            "label": "copyHeader",
            "type": "shell",
            "command": "mkdir ${workspaceFolder}/headers/;
                scp -r ${config:sshUser}@${config:sshEndpoint}:
                        ${config:header} ${workspaceFolder}/headers/ ",
            "problemMatcher": [],
            "presentation": {
                "showReuseMessage": false,
                "clear": true
            }
        },
        {
            "label": "buildRemote",
            "type": "shell",
```

```json
        "command": "ssh ${config:sshUser}@${config:sshEndpoint}
            'gcc  -g -std=${config:std} ${config:remoteDirectory}/
            ${relativeFileDirname}/${fileBasename}
            ${config:libs} -o${config:remoteDirectory}/
            ${relativeFileDirname}/${fileBasenameNoExtension}'",
        "problemMatcher": [],
        "presentation": {
            "showReuseMessage": false,
            "clear": false
        }
    },
    {
        "label": "runRemote",
        "type": "shell",
        "command": "ssh ${config:sshUser}@${config:sshEndpoint}
            '${config:remoteDirectory}/${relativeFileDirname}/
            ${fileBasenameNoExtension}'",
        "problemMatcher": [
            "$gcc"
        ],
        "presentation": {
            "showReuseMessage": true,
            "clear": false
        }
    },
    {
        "label": "CopyBuildRunRemote",
        "dependsOrder": "sequence",
        "dependsOn": [
            "copyToRemote",
            "buildRemote",
            "runRemote"
        ],
        "problemMatcher": [],
        "group": {
            "kind": "build",
            "isDefault": true
        }
    },
    {
        "label": "CopyBuildRemote",
        "dependsOrder": "sequence",
        "dependsOn": [
            "copyToRemote",
            "buildRemote",
        ],
        "problemMatcher": [],
    },
```

```json
    {
        "label": "StopREmoteC",
        "type": "shell",
        "command": "ssh ${config:sshUser}@${config:sshEndpoint}
                                 'pkill ${fileBasenameNoExtension}'",
        "problemMatcher": [],
        "presentation": {
            "showReuseMessage": true,
        }
    },
    {
        "label": "copyARMheaders",
        "type": "shell",
        "command": "mkdir ${workspaceFolder}/include/;
            scp -r  ${config:sshUser}@${config:sshEndpoint}:
                        /usr/include ${workspaceFolder}/include/ ",
        "problemMatcher": [],
        "presentation": {
            "showReuseMessage": true,
            "clear": true
        }
    },
    ],
}
```

c_cpp_properties.json (for Mingw)

```json
{
    "configurations": [
        {
            "name": "Win32",
            "includePath": [
                    "${workspaceFolder}/**",
                    "C:/Program Files (x86)/mingw-w64/
                        i686-8.1.0-posix-dwarf-rt_v6-rev0/
                            mingw32/i686-w64-mingw32/include"
                    ],
            "defines": [
                    "_DEBUG",
                    "UNICODE",
                    "_UNICODE"
                    ],
            "cStandard": "c99",
            "intelliSenseMode": "gcc-arm"
        }
    ],
    "version": 4
}
```

Index

Raspberry Pi IoT in C, Third Edition
ISBN: 978-1871962840 (Paperback)
ISBN: 978-1871962154 (Hardback)

In this book you will find a practical approach to understanding electronic circuits and datasheets and translating this to code, specifically using the C programming language. The main reason for choosing C is speed, a crucial factor when you are writing programs to communicate with the outside world. If you are familiar with another programming language, C shouldn't be hard to pick up. This third edition has been brought up-to-date and includes the Pi Zero 2W and the latest OS. An entire chapter is devoted to the Pi 5 and it is covered elsewhere in the book wherever possible.

Raspberry Pi IoT in Python With Linux Drivers, Second Edition
ISBN: 9781871962864 (Paperback)
ISBN:9781871962178 (Hardback)

This is the Python version of this book and covers much of the same ground. It explains how to use Python to connect to and control external devices with the full current range of Raspberry Pis, including the Pi 5 and the Raspberry Pi Zero 2W using the standard Linux drivers.

Raspberry Pi IoT in Python With GPIO Zero, Second Edition
ISBN: 978-1871962871 (Paperback)
ISBN: 978-1871962192 (Hardback)

The GPIO Zero library is the official way to use Python with the GPIO and other devices and has recently been updated to Version 2 which supports the new Raspberry Pi 5. This second edition looks at how to use it to interface to the full current range of Raspberry Pis, including the Pi 5 and the Raspberry Pi Zero 2W and at how it works so that you can extend it to custom devices. Studying GPIO Zero is also a great way to improve your Python.

Applying C For The IoT With Linux

ISBN: 978-1871962611

If you are using C to write low-level code using small Single Board Computers (SBCs) that run Linux, or if you do any coding in C that interacts with the hardware, this book brings together low-level, hardware-oriented and often hardware-specific information.

It starts by looking at how programs work with user-mode Linux. When working with hardware, arithmetic cannot be ignored, so separate chapters are devoted to integer, fixed-point and floating-point arithmetic. It goes on to the pseudo file system, memory-mapped files and sockets as a general-purpose way of communicating over networks and similar infrastructure and continues by looking at multitasking, locking, mutex, condition variables, and scheduling. Later chapters cover managing cores and C11's atomics and memory models. It rounds out with a short look at how to mix assembler with C.

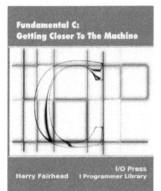

Fundamental C: Getting Closer To The Machine

ISBN: 978-1871962604

At an introductory level, this book explores C from the point of view of the low-level programmer and keeps close to the hardware. It covers addresses, pointers, and how things are represented using binary and emphasizes the important idea is that everything is a bit pattern and what it means can change.

When programming in C you need to think about the way data is represented, and this book emphasizes the idea of modifying how a bit pattern is treated using type punning and unions and tackles the topic of undefined behavior, which is ignored in many books on C. A particular feature of the book is the way C code is illustrated by the assembly language it generates. This helps you understand why C is the way it is and the way it was always intended to be written - close to the metal.

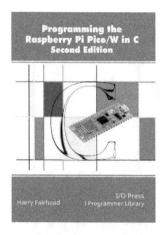

Programming The Raspberry Pi Pico/W In C, Second Edition
ISBN: 978-1871962796 (Paperback)
ISBN: 978-1871962055 (Hardback)

This book explains the many reasons for wanting to use C with the Raspberry Pi Pico and Pico W, not least of which is the fact that it is much faster. This makes it ideal for serious experimentation and delving into parts of the hardware that are otherwise inaccessible. Using C is the way to get the maximum from the Pico and this book shows you how with many near-complete projects.

Master the Raspberry Pi Pico in C: WiFi
ISBN: 978-1871962819 (Paperback)
ISBN: 978-1871962079 (Hardback)

At a more advanced level, there is far too much to the Pico to cover in a single book and this follow-on title focuses on WiFi using the lwlp and mbedtls libraries to take your Pico C programming to the next level. For the Pico W it covers TLS/HTTPS connections, access point mode, other protocols and using FreeRTOS. Chapters are devoted to advanced hardware features such as DMA, watchdog timer and saving power.

Programming the Raspberry Pi Pico/W in MicroPython, Second Edition
ISBN: 978-1871962802 (Paperback)
ISBN: 978-1871962062 (Hardback)

The Raspberry Pi Pico is a remarkable microcontroller. It has a power and sophistication that would have been unthinkable just a short time ago. Instead of struggling with the machine, you can now focus on a good implementation of your algorithms. The original version of this book, which covers getting the most from the Pico using MicroPython, predated the launch of the WiFi-enabled Pico W which is covered in this second edition.

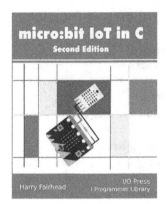

Micro:bit IoT In C, Second Edition
ISBN: 978-1871962673

The second edition of this book covers V2, the revised version of the micro:bit. The other important change is that it now uses the highly popular VS Code for offline development and lets you get started the easy way by providing downloadable templates for both V1 and V2 of the micro:bit. The micro:bit lacks WiFi connectivity but using a low-cost device we enable a connection to the Internet via its serial port which allows it to become a server. The book rounds out with a new chapter on the micro:bit's radio and the V2's sound capabilities

Programming the ESP32 in MicroPython
ISBN: 978-1871962826(Paperback)
ISBN: 978-1871962093 (Hardback)

The ESP32 is a remarkable device. It is low cost, but with many different subsystems that make it more powerful than you might think. You can use it for simple applications because it is cheap, but you can also use it for more sophisticated applications because it is capable.
The purpose of the book is to reveal what you can do with the ESP's GPIO lines together with widely used sensors, servos and motors and ADCs. After covering the GPIO, outputs and inputs, events and interrupts, it gives you hands-on experience of PWM (Pulse Width Modulation), the SPI bus, the I2C bus and the 1-Wire bus. We also cover direct access to the hardware, adding an SD Card reader, sleep states to save power, the RTC, RMT and touch sensors, not to mention how to use WiFi.